SEAGULLS
IN MY SOUP

SEAGULLS IN MY SOUP

Further Adventures of a Wayward Sailor

TRISTAN JONES

SHERIDAN HOUSE

First paperback edition
published 1996 by
Sheridan House, Inc.
145 Palisade Street
Dobbs Ferry, NY 10522

Library of Congress Cataloging-in-Publication Data

Jones, Tristan, 1924-1995
        Seagulls in my soup: further adventures of a wayward
        sailor/ by Tristan Jones
                p. cm.
Sequel to: Saga of a wayward sailor
1. Jones, Tristan, 1924-1995—Journeys.
2. Cresswell (Ketch) 3. Voyages and travels—1951-1980.
 I. Title. G490. J73 1991
910.4'5'092—dc20   91-27982
[B]   CIP

Printed in the United States of America

ISBN 1-57409-005-4

DEDICATION

To Nat and Katie Page
who helped me make 'fact' out of 'fiction'.

Contents

SEAGULLS
IN MY SOUP

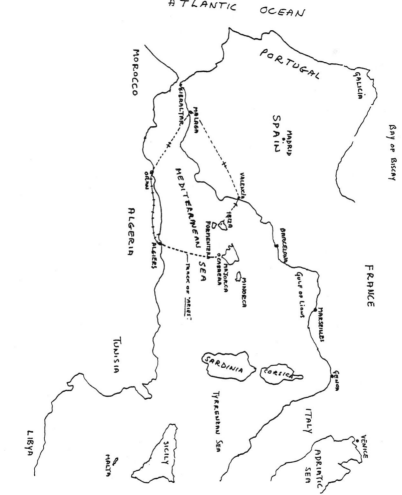

---➤➤ TRACKS OF CRESSWELL

MAJORCA

PALMA

ANDRAIXT

DRAGONERA

CABRERA

BANJO
LOST ½
HERE

IBIZA

○ TAGOMAGO

S. ANTONIO

MEDITERRANEAN
SEA

1553

IBIZA

ES VEDRA

○ ESPARDELL

ES PALMADOR

PORT

SAN FRANCISCO

FORMENTERA

630

CABO BERBERIA

PUNTA DE CALA CALADOR

Foreword

So MANY PEOPLE—most of them women—have told me how much they enjoyed *Saga of a Wayward Sailor*, that I have written of this microcosm of cruising life in the late sixties for their further enjoyment.

The "yachtie's" life was simpler then—and much harder and riskier. There were no electronic aids to navigation; it was all by dead-reckoning, sextant, tables, guess and God. Neither did miracle materials exist that now make boats so much more easily maintainable and a sailor's life so comparatively lazy. But what then did still exist among sailors was an "esprit de corps," camaraderie, great good humor, and a largess of respect, all for each other and for our kinship with the sea.

If *Saga of a Wayward Sailor* was my song of love for the women of the sea, this is my paean to the misfits who found refuge among us and perhaps some comfort in our company. The shore rejected them; we observed them (what sailor would not), accepted them, and in the end loved them. Whatever their faults—and there were many—they were free of that worst and most common fault of landsmen: *dullness*.

This book, originally written in 1979, is in the recently "discovered" and much acclaimed literary mode of *fictionalized fact*. But all human memory is that. Embroidering memories is what makes us human. God forbid the day when none of us can do that! Over the past twenty years, unrecognized by most shore-bound critics, I have done much to pioneer this mode of storytelling. Be assured: *all the main facts of these tales are true*, but the tales (as all life is a dream) are "fiction."

TRISTAN JONES
Anchor House, Rawai, Thailand   1991

I'll sing ye a song of the Blackball Line,

Chorus: *To me way, hay, ho, hi ho!*

That's the line where ye can shine.

Chorus: *Oh a long time ago!*

In the Blackball Line I served me time,
That's the Line where I wasted me prime.

It's when a Blackballer hauls out of the dock,
To see them poor 'Westers,' how on deck they do flock.

There's tinkers an' tailors, an' fakirs an' all,
They've all shipped as A.B.s aboard the Blackball.

It's 'fore-tops'l halyards' the Mate he will roar,
It's 'lay along Paddy, ye son-o-a-whore!

"A Long Time Ago" was a halyard chantey, popular on British and American ships in the 1880s and '90s. The Blackball Line plied between New York and Liverpool. The captains and mates of its ships were notorious for their hard-driving and brutality.

1

A Long Time Ago

"A I SAY . . . Tristan *dahling!* Yoo-hoo!"
I stirred under my blanket and listened for a moment to the patter of rain on *Cresswell*'s deck overhead. Autumn nights and early mornings in the western Mediterranean can be quite chilly to ordinary mortals, but Cecilia (Sissie) Saint John, the Bishop of Southchester's sister, was always awake and astir at the crack of dawn, no matter what the weather.

Again she screeched, "Skippah . . . Yoo-hoo, *dahling!*"
I stretched one trousered and seabooted leg out of my berth. Nelson bumped his tail on the cabin sole, stared up at Sissie with his one eye, and glowered. I, too, glared up at her. She was leaning her oilskin-bedecked upper torso down through the companionway hatch. Under her yellow sou'wester hat, her hair, as usual in damp weather, was the color of a dead aspidistra leaf. Her Saxon-blue eyes gleamed with that peculiar kind of benevolent madness only seen among the English.

"Wazzup now?" I growled. I glared at the ship's clock. Sissie had polished its brass casing the previous night, before retiring to her ritual of Bible and Booth's London Dry Gin in the tiny, low, kennel-like forepeak which she called home. *"Six-thirty. God."*
I didn't at all like to be disturbed, while the boat was in harbor, much before eight o'clock, especially when it was

3

raining and few chores could be done, and while the ones that could be done, Sissie did.

Sissie spread her rosy apple cheeks all over her chubby face in a wide grin. "Theah's a boat coming alongside, dahling!" she announced. "It's a, er . . . catamaran." She raised herself up above the cover of the companionway hatch and stared ahead, the rainwater streaming down her face into the soggy towel she had wrapped around her neck. Her eyes slitted almost closed against the drizzle. Then again she grinned. "Ai say," she howled, to no one in particular. "What a *marvelous* name . . . *Bellerophon of Bosham* . . . how simply *spiffing*." Nelson growled softly. "And dahling . . . Tristan *dahling* . . . she's *English!*"

"With a name like that she could hardly be bloody French," I observed petulantly. "At this time in the morning I don't give a fish's tit if she's Chinese."

Sissie looked down at me. Her face fell into apologetic sympathy. "Oh . . . you poor *dahling*," she murmured. "Half a mo', I'll make the tea . . . No, Ai'd bettah help this jolly old boat moor stern-to-the-jetty first." Turning, she scrambled over *Cresswell*'s whalebacked poop, showing a dimpled thigh under her yellow oilskin jacket and above her British Army socks and Irish ditchdigger's brogue boots. Agilely, she leaped over the five-foot gap between the rudder and the jetty wall. Nelson again bumped his tail, pounding it softly against the cabin table leg, pleased that his main competitor for my affection had once more gone ashore and left his master entirely for himself to watch and guard with his limitless canine loyalty.

I turned over again, wrapped the blanket around me, and settled to doze away another precious hour or so. I was still thawing out and catching up on sleep lost during the Arctic voyage five years ago.

There were the usual shouts and hollers as the arriving boat's crew heaved mooring lines at Sissie out in the now-pouring rain. Sissie's voice pierced through the drumming downpour on deck. "Ai say . . . welcome to Ibiza!"

A masculine English voice, almost as awf'ly English as Sissie's, but not quite (there were undertones of Surbiton) called back, "Nice boat you have there! Wonderful weather for ducks, eh?"

"Yes," replied *Cresswell's* mate, with a girlish giggle.

It's a wonder how sound carries over water and through the sides of a wooden boat. As I reflected on this, and listened to the alternating roar and purr of the catamaran's outboard motor, *Cresswell* gently jiggled, jingled, and pulsated with the myriad sounds of a sailboat's waking day. *"Oh, Christ,"* I said to myself, and, heaving myself up against the cabin table, staggered over to the galley, filled the kettle up from the freshwater hand pump, lit the gently oscillating kerosene stove, slammed the kettle down on the flame, and sat down again to rustle Nelson's head and murmur to him—a diurnal liturgy in *Cresswell*.

There was another sudden commotion outside. First the splash of a rope falling into the harbor water—filthy with black, slimy oil, dead fish, plastic bags and other impedimenta deleterious to cleanliness and pilotage—then the sound of a man's voice, again from the arriving vessel, called in fruity tones, "Oh, dash . . . what rotten luck!"

"Yes, isn't it?" I heard Sissie reply. "But hang on a jolly tick—Ai'll get a boathook."

Then there were the sounds of Sissie hefting her 170 pounds back over the gap 'twixt rudder and wall, and scrabbling for the boathook tied to the handrail below *Cresswell's* mizzenmast. All the while the boat pitched slightly up and down as it was first burdened with, then relieved of Sissie's dumpling thighs, Michelin waist, boxer's arms, heavy oilskin jacket, and ditchdigger's boots.

I quickly donned my Shetland jersey and slid my black oilskin around my shoulders. I clambered up the companionway ladder. I stared around through the misty rain to see one of the ugliest sailing vessels I ever clapped eyes on. She was a catamaran, but obviously home-made. She had slab sides to the hulls, far too high, and the cabin stuck up above the two hulls, box-like and shoddy, with great windows all around it. The whole boat was painted black, and the top paint had worn away in places, exposing the previous white paint in obscene-looking patches. The total effect was that of a greatly enlarged praying mantis with a skin complaint.

She was about thirty-two feet long and at least eighteen feet wide. Two figures, squat and heavy in their yellow oilskins and yellow seaboots, with the flaps of their jackets buttoned up around their chins, stood in the pouring rain on the catamaran's afterdeck, looking nonplused and rather forlorn as their vessel was slowly pulled away from the jetty again by the weight of their anchor line, which was streamed out forward. The rain drizzled down implacably on this cheerful scene.

I turned around to peer through the rain toward the jetty. There was Sissie, stretched out fully on her belly on the muddy, fish-scales-littered pavement of the town quay, leaning right out over the filthy harbor water, reaching with our boathook toward the fallen mooring line, now floating in the midst of a particularly noisome pool of slime and garbage. She was grasping the boathook by its blunt very-end, attempting to hook the line and failing to do it by a mere three inches or so.

I turned again to the catamaran. One of the figures stared at me for a moment in seeming puzzlement and confusion, then hailed me. "Morning, old chap," it called in a gruff, manly voice. "Nice weather, what?" It wore a rope belt, from which dangled a seaman's knife.

"Why don't you throw me a line?" I replied. "I'm much closer to you than is the jetty."

"Damned good idea," called the other figure, in far less gruff tones. He sounded like a choirboy whose voice was just about to break. He wore spectacles, and I imagined him regretting that, with this downpour, they were not fitted with windshield wipers. Even as he addressed me the spectacles were pointed some five yards away to my left.

By now the Knife had run over to the catamaran's guardrails and was grinning at me. "Pleased to meet you. Billy Rankin's the name, and this is my brother Tony."

Spectacles now spoke to a point three yards to my right. "What ho?"

"Throw me a line," I shouted. "Your boat is sliding away over your anchor rode, and if you don't get a line to me soon you'll have to restart your motor and do the whole exercise again . . . And anyway, your anchor is probably fouled up with mine in the middle of the harbor."

Tony the Specs turned and desperately peered through the pouring rain while Billy the Knife calmly and methodically bent down, grabbed a line, held the coil in his left hand, and heaved the fag-end with his right. The knot in the end hit me in the eye with a wallop so bitter I could taste it, just as a loud splash came from the direction of the jetty. Cursing as I recovered the rope's end from *Cresswell's* deck, my eye smarting with pain, I turned to see poor Sissie's yellow oilskin jacket just below the oily, slimy surface, rising to float, flailing, in the muck-bestrewn, turd-flotilla'd, dog-corpse-littered waters of Ibiza harbor. Then her head appeared, her whisky-colored hair now black and shiny with petroleum by-products and her face and body besmeared with flecks of effluent from a thousand fishermen, ten thousand black-clad, bereted peasants, four thousand well-fed tourists, and five or six impecunious yachties—two of whom were now haring along the town quay to Sissie's rescue, despite the early hour and the effects of the previous night's festivities.

Soon the yachties, one a Frenchman, as gallant as ever; the other a Finn, as hung-over as ever, had Sissie's arms in their calloused hands and were slowly dragging her, dripping like a dipped sheep, out of the murky basin, she still gripping faithfully onto our one-and-only boathook, spluttering all the while.

As soon as I saw that Sissie's rescue was assured and imminent, I turned again to securing the wayward vessel alongside *Cresswell*. The rising wind was yawing and veer-

ing both my boat and the catamaran alarmingly, and they
were in danger of colliding with each other.

Billy the Knife still held onto the bitter end of the rope
he had thrown me. I needed plenty of slack, so that I could
take the line onto the jetty and secure the stern-end of the
catamaran away from *Cresswell*, to windward.

"Give me slack!" I hollered. Quick as a knife, Billy
eased off the line. I scrambled aft as fast as I could, holding
onto the mooring line for dear life. I threw myself over the
gap onto the jetty, over the heaving backs of the Frenchman and the Finn, ran along to windward, and secured the
mooring line. Then Billy the Knife, with Tony the Specs still
peering helplessly around him in the rain, steadily and
sturdily heaved the stern of the catamaran away from
Cresswell, and soon the vessel was hauled up tight against
the wind.

I turned to clamber back aboard *Cresswell*. As I passed
Sissie, who by now was again stretched out on the pavement of the jetty, face down, streaming water and oil and
all kinds of unmentionable solids and liquids, she raised
her head. Tears were dolloping from her screwed-up eyes,
but she was still trying to grin. "Awf'ly sorry, Skippah,"
she spluttered.

"That's all right, mate." I tried not to patronize her, at
least not in front of the two foreigners. "You'd better go
onboard and get cleaned up. I've got the kettle on, and the
bucket's empty . . ."

"*Mais* . . ." The Frenchman started. "But she can come
onboard my boat." He was the skipper of some rich nob's
gin-palace down the line. "I 'ave ze bath . . ."

"That's a good idea," I said to the Frenchman.

Sissie looked even more distressed. "Oh, Ai don't
think Ai could *really*." She leaned over to me. "He's not
merried, you know," she said in a hoarse whisper. She
started toward *Cresswell*'s stern just as Billy the Knife clambered onto the jetty.

"Rotten luck, ma'am," said Billy, respectfully. "Look,
why don't you come onboard *Bellerophon*? We've got lots of

water and you can take a shower." Billy's voice was like a fog horn as he hitched up his knife lanyard like a cowboy hoisting a gunbelt.

Sissie turned momentarily. "Thank you very much indeed," she said, "but deah, dahling Tristan . . ." she puckered her lips and pointed a begrimed chin at me . . ." has simply *everything* in hend . . ."

Billy turned to me, hitched up his knife lanyard again, and said, "Well, look old chap, I'm sure you'll agree we at least owe you lunch, what?"

I looked at Billy, thinking 'a meal's a meal for all that an' all that,' and said, "Lunch? Why yes, of course . . . what time?"

"One o'clock, old bean. My brother and I always work until then, and take two hours off for lunch, you see."

"Right, you're on," said I to Billy. Then I turned to the Frenchman and the Finn, thanked them, and made my way to the little dark *bodega* Antonio at the end of the quay, there to while away the time over a tiny cup of thick, treacly, black coffee, until the Dragon of Devon, the English games–mistress, had completed her ablutions.

As I traipsed away, breakfastless, through the persistent rain along the town quay, I heard the soft, gentle patter of Nelson's three-paw steps astern of me. I didn't need to turn around to know it was he, nor did I need to look at his eye or the droop of his old head to know that his senses of virtue and modesty, instilled in him by his old master, my first sailing skipper, Tansy Lee (1866-1958), had been deeply offended by Sissie's divesting herself of her oil-filthy vestments before he'd had a chance to reach the companionway ladder. Nothing if not Victorian, was Nelson.

An hour later the rain had stopped. Through the low front door of the dim bodega I gazed over the still half-full tiny cup of coffee, over the berets of the usual assembly of a dozen or so sad-eyed fishermen, too old now to do anything much more than dream of past catches and criticize the tight pants of their offspring, and dote over the tiny offspring of the loins displayed by the very tight pants they criticized. Over their heads, which were silhouetted against the bright shafts of sunlight shining through the miasma of early-morning harbor mist, I saw Sissie's form marching along the jetty. She strode into the bodega like a Grenadier guardsman. She had, I observed, changed her British Army socks and brogue boots for a pair of calf-length black seaboots, while her torso was again resplendent in her dark blue English games-mistress gym slip, the skirts of which reached almost halfway down her dimpled thighs, which quivered as she weaved her way, smiling benignly, through the assembly of septua-, octo-, and nonagenarians—all of whom, without exception, glanced at her haunches lasciviously and held their breath until she had squeezed her way past their crowded tables.

Sissie's lips pursed until they looked like bicycle pedals. Her blue eyes gleamed with the fondness of freshly burnished bayonets. She plonked herself down opposite me. For a moment there was silence as the Ibizan fishermen recovered their collective breath.

"Coffee?" I asked her.

"Oh, *dahling* Tristan," she gushed, laying one calloused hand on my sunburned arm, "oh, golly, that *would* be supah . . . but you've not had your *brekky.*"

I pointed my thumb at a round wooden box lying on the stone floor of the bodega. It was a quarter-full of dried codfish, set out neatly, their mahogany-colored bodies overlapping each other, all looking extremely sorry for themselves. "We can have some yellow peril here." Dried cod was about the cheapest food in Spain at the time—about five cents per whole bony corpse.

"Oh, that *will* be nice," said Sissie as Antonio, the ancient proprietor, in shirtsleeves, his grubby white apron drooping all the way down to his ankles, approached our table.

I ordered our breakfast, then, and Antonio shuffled away in his incredibly tattered carpet slippers. I looked at my watch. "By the time we've finished this little lot it will be time to go to the post office. Why don't you come with me?"

Again Sissie's hand descended gently on my forearm. "Oh, *dahling*, thet *will* be supah. Oh, goody, *goody* gumdrops," she chortled. Then, after a moment's reflection, which she signified by staring into mid-space, her North Sea eyes opened as wide as she could manage, she said, "Ai say, Skippah, what *terrific* cheps they are onboard the catamaran. They told me they are to stay in Ibiza for several days . . ."

"Then why didn't you go onboard their boat for a shower and use their bloody fresh water instead of ours?" I queried.

"Oh, dahling, I simply couldn't jolly-well go onboard a boat alone with *two cheps* . . ."

"Oh, well . . . only natural, I s'pose," I grunted, thinking of the diminishing water in *Cresswell*'s tanks. Another thirty gallons would cost another thirty pesetas (about eighty cents).

As Sissie strode, Nelson limped, and I traipsed along Ibiza's waterfront, the sun again broke through the high clouds and gold-plated the cathedral and fortress atop the steep hill to our left. Across the harbor, on the east side, another heavy rainstorm reminded me of the eleventh commandment: "Thou shalt not loiter ashore too long when dirty weather is in the offing."

Sissie gazed up at the gold-lined clouds above us. "Just like a jolly old Gainsborough painting!" she gurgled, as she clomped heavily among the heaps of lobster pots, fishing nets, sacks of potatoes, and other 'heaps of bric-a-brac,' as she called the means of livelihood of a hundred hard-working souls.

"Hammerheads," I replied, glancing up at the clouds, black-bellied and menacing. "Going to be a right bloody gale later on. We'd better not hang around too much. We'll have to keep a good watch on the anchor—otherwise we're going to be bashing the rudder against the jetty again, and

I've only just finished repairing it from the hammering we got last week."

At the *correos* there were two letters for Sissie; one from her brother the bishop (*dahling* Willie) and one from *deah* Toby, the ex-*majah*, who was now assistant station-*mawstah* at Victorloo in London. For me there was one telegram.

We made for the Hotel Montesol, in the main square of Ibiza. There we sat at an outside table in the fleeting sunshine and sipped sweet coffee. I ripped open my telegram.

"GOOD DELIVERY JOB FOR YOU PLUS ONE MATE MALAGA STOP MEET ME HOTEL LA PRINCESA TEA TIME TUESDAY STOP SHINER."

"Good news, I hope, Skippah?" murmured Sissie, watching me anxiously. Always ripe for a touch of drama, was Sissie. She laid her hand on my arm.

"Yes, looks like it. Probably a boat delivery from Mál-aga. It's from my old mate Shiner Wright. He doesn't say how long it'll be, but I doubt if it will be more than a couple of days—at this time of year it's probably some nob wants his gin-palace taken to Gibraltar. So what about if you look after the boat and Nelson for me . . ." Nelson, at the sound of his name, bumped his tail against my leg under the table . . . "and I'll split the delivery proceeds twenty-five, seventy-five with you when I get back."

Sissie squeezed my arm suddenly, like a bosun's mate grabbing a marlinspike. "Oh, *dahling* Skippah, thet won't be at *all* necessary—you know I'd do it anyway."

As she said this she noticed a Spanish cavalry officer passing along the street verge in front of the hotel, only six feet away from us. The officer was leading a beautiful white horse by its bridle. Sissie screwed up her Spithead-blue eyes, pursed her lips, and smiled at the horse. The cavalry officer leered lecherously at Sissie. A blue-overcoated, white-helmeted traffic policeman on the corner of the square, a dozen yards away from us, halted the traffic. The horse halted and, as the officer still returned Sissie's smiles with *muy macho* poses, the horse relieved its bowels right in front of a group of camera-aiming, Bermuda-shorted, Hawaii-shirted American tourists, who, after the first sputtered shocks, were hurled back, bespattered, all around our table.

The traffic, the macho officer, and the horse moved off again, and the Americans shouted for "more Kleenex, goddamit!" The non-English-speaking waiters merely stood and grinned politely. I gently lifted Sissie's hand from my arm. "Come on, mate, we'd better get our shopping done before this storm works up."

By noon we had all our morning chores completed onboard *Cresswell* and by twelve-thirty we were spruced up to go onboard the catamaran for lunch. This means that I had changed from my working jeans into my only other pair of pants—corduroys, which were reasonably clean, and Sissie had exchanged her seaboots for her ditchdigger's brogues, which were once again dry after the thorough scrubbing she had given them earlier that morning.

As we approached the catamaran, Sissie sang out, "*Bellerophon* ahoy, can we come aboard?"

Two voices replied from down below—the gruff, low voice and the high, choir-boy's voice. "Yes, do come, we're almost ready. And take off your shoes, please!"

Sissie and I clambered over one of the sterns of the catamaran and entered the spacious cabin, which extended almost the full beam of the boat—about sixteen feet. This, after *Cresswell*'s cabin width of six feet, was a bit like comparing No. 10, Downing Street, with the White House.

Inside the cabin was a prospect I shall never forget. All around the windows there were chintz curtains, all flower-patterned with roses and such. On every horizontal surface, or so it seemed, there was a small vase decorated with plastic flowers, roses and such. The inside surfaces of the cabin were decorated with flowery *wallpaper*, all roses and such, while the cabin sole (or deck) was covered with a rose-patterned *carpet*. It was a bit like being in a flower-nursery greenhouse. There were roses everywhere.

As my senses recovered from the visual shock, I was now in for an aural shock. Billy, whose voice of course I immediately recognized, called up from inside the galley, which was lower than the main cabin, in one of the hulls.

"Welcome aboard, old chap," I heard him say. I turned, expecting to see a biggish, burly man of about thirty-five. Instead, to both Sissie's and my instant confusion, a most attractive woman of around twenty-eight or so, clad in a flowery dress—roses and such—tripped lightly up the small ladder, grabbed hold of Sissie (who later told me she was too astonished to move), kissed her on the cheek, and held her hand!

Billie had medium-length dark hair and beautiful blue eyes, and was very attractive indeed by any standards. Then Tony appeared. Instead of a choir-boy-like adolescent of about fifteen, which both Sissie and I expected to encounter, we were confronted by a slight, balding man of about forty-eight, wearing thick-rimmed spectacles and stooping with the weight of responsibilities which only captains know. (Either that or his sleeping berth was too short for his length, which was about six feet, two inches.)

After we had shaken hands with Tony and mouthed pleasantries, I again looked around the cabin of *Bellerophon* and saw then one of the strangest things I've ever come across in a small sailing craft. Fitted right across the forward end of the cabin was a full-scale, pedal-operated chapel organ, complete with pipes and stops, bellows and knobs, and all sorts of paraphernalia. I stared for a full two minutes at the organ, then turned to see Tony, his head bent as he stooped under the cabin roof, grinning hugely at me. "You like music, eh?" he asked.

"Well . . . a bit of classical stuff. You know, Brahms, Beethoven, stuff like that," I replied.

Quickly Tony, who I now noticed had bird-like movements, sat himself down on the stool in front of the organ and started pedaling away at the bellows, all the while grinning at me. "You'll like this one," he said. "Always start the day off with this one." He stopped pedaling for a second or two. "Guess what it is?"

I tried to look nonplused; and so I was, not at Tony's question but by the whole lunatic-seeming scene. Here was a six-foot-odd giant with a choir-boy's voice, and a sister who sounded like a regimental sergeant-major and looked like a Hollywood star, sitting at an organ onboard the ugliest sailing vessel I had ever seen. I shook myself from my reverie. "You've got me," I said. "Handel's Water Music?"

Tony again commenced to pedal madly. Then he suddenly threw his head back, thrust his hands out in front of him, fingers outstretched and quivering with intensity. Violently he drew out some stops, stretched his arms out again, like a conjuror showing he has nothing up his sleeves, and plunged into the keyboard. As the notes blared out of the organ, both he, in his piping treble, and his sister Billie, in a fine, ringing bass, accompanied the music . . . *Rule Britannia!*

Halfway through the first verse I turned to Sissie. She was still holding hands with Billie, who stood at attention as she bellowed out the words. Sissie was gazing at me in seeming adoration. Hardly able to stop myself from bursting out in hysterical laughter, I ambled over to one of the huge cabin windows, eased aside one of the chintz curtains, and stared out over the harbor of Ibiza, now rain-swept again, and wondered how the devil anyone could ever have thought that *I* was slightly crazy.

When at last the organ stopped wheezing and groaning the overture, Billie and Sissie stepped down into the galley. Together, as Tony played a selection from "The Merry Widow," they prepared a delectably tasty lunch of pâté, ham, and salad, with Spanish wine.

There was no more work done that day, either in *Bellerophon* or in *Cresswell*. All afternoon, after the dishes had been cleared up by Billie and Sissie, and as Tony the Specs huffed, pedaled, and pounded like mad on the organ, the women and I lounged in the spacious cabin of

the catamaran in between hoisting full bottles of red and
white wine out of the cool stowage in the bilge below the
stainless steel galley sink, and adding to the pile of empty
wine bottles just outside the cabin door.

During the afternoon we hailed all of our neighbors in
the boats tied up at the town jetty. Several of them came
onboard *Bellerophon*, ostensibly to listen to the organ music,
but in reality to assist in easing the weight of fifty bottles of
wine which, we all agreed, if left low in the boat would
surely impair her ability to go efficiently to windward.

It was a cosmopolitan crowd that gathered. There was
Willy the German; Rory O'Boggarty the Irish Writer, looking like a very young G.B. Shaw; two Italians, who could
barely drag their eyes away from the lovely Billie; a Turkish
doctor, who soon had Sissie oohing and aahing over the
ancient Hittite civilization and the effects of too much
freedom for women; a tall Dutch lady who had once been
the lover of Gurdjieff (so she said—and she looked it); a
short, benevolent-looking elderly gentleman, whom I later
discovered owned a steel factory in Johannesburg which
manufactured manacles for the South African government;
and an internationally renowned Danish pop singer and his
beautiful but very hard-faced wife. (There was something a
little strange about both their ''Danish'' accents. I was later
told that he was actually an ex-Nazi Hitler Youth and she
was a retired whore from Surrey Hills, Sydney, Australia!)

To relieve the weight of this company there were also
the Frenchman and the Finn who had rescued Sissie earlier
that day from a death worse than fate. But as the evening
came on, and Sissie busied herself washing fresh glasses for
wine, the events of the morning were completely forgotten
as the wind outside howled and the rain lashed down on
Bellerophon's decks about us and above our heads, and the
catamaran yawed and swerved to her anchor, and Tony the
Specs still pedaled away at the ship's organ with demonia-
cal fury.

All the while this infernal scene was being played out, I
was thinking about my forthcoming delivery job. I needed a

mate to go with me. The only men present who might need to earn money were the Frenchman and the Finn. I broached the matter to both of them, separately. Neither of them wanted to come; the Frenchman was the skipper of a large Italian motor yacht and the Finn was a poet, "too busy writing."

After an hour's thought I hied myself over to the organ and sat at Tony's side. He was still pumping and playing and piping. Over the racket I asked him, "How long have you been sailing, Tony?"

He didn't look at me—he was too busy pulling and pushing stops. It was "Clair de Lune" now. "Oh, only eight months. We left England last year, but we wintered the boat over in France and rejoined her this spring at Sète."

"Are you interested in a little sailing trip from Málaga to Gib?" I shouted over the roar and groan of the bass pipes.

He turned and questioned me with his owl-like eyes.

"I've got a delivery job. I have to go over to Málaga next week. I earn my living that way, you see . . . and I need a mate, but no one else here wants to go, and the nearest mate I have, apart from Sissie, is Pete Kelly, and he's up in Monaco . . ."

Suddenly Tony stopped playing. There was a hush in the cabin. "Say no more. You helped us out; I'll help you out. Put my name down on your bally list, old chap. The cat'll be safe here . . ."

"And Sissie can lend Billie a hand if she needs it, and Nelson is a good guard dog . . ." I interjected.

"Yes, I'm all for a little side trip, and I love Gibraltar."

"Then it's a deal? I'll split the delivery fee with you, 40 for you and 60 for me, OK?"

Tony grabbed my hand and shook it violently. "Done, old chap."

Just as suddenly he turned back to the organ and, pumping for all he was worth, started another rendition of "Rule Britannia."

I turned toward Sissie, who was strenuously fending off the by-now amorous Turk. I nodded my head and winked. She at first raised her eyebrows, then smiled broadly.

Now all the women present were beautiful, elegant, and intelligent; all the men were handsome, debonair, and witty—and only one bottle of wine remained. Soon that, too, was in the pile of empties, placed there gently and precisely by the Finnish poet, who had to be supported by Gurdjieff's ex-lover, who in turn was supported by Willie the German and Rory O'Boggarty, the savant Son of Erin.

The following Tuesday morning, Tony and I caught the rackety Iberia Dakota plane from Ibiza to Valencia, then another Dakota to the great port-city of Málaga, and made our way in the late afternoon to the Hotel La Princesa.

If either of us had had any idea, any inkling, of what lay ahead of us, we would have caught the first plane back to Ibiza. I might have been forewarned by the following Halloween episode, which occurred shortly before our departure . . .

Death, be not proud, though some have calléd thee
Mighty and dreadful, for thou art not so:
For those whom thou think'st thou dost overthrow
Die not, poor Death; nor yet canst thou kill me.
From Rest and Sleep, which but thy picture be,
Much pleasure, then from thee much more must flow;
And soonest our best men with thee must go—
Rest of their bones and soul's delivery!
Thou'rt slave to fate, chance, kings and desperate men,
And dost with poison, war and sickness dwell;
And poppy or charms can make us sleep as well
And better than thy stroke. Why swell'st thou then?
One short sleep past, we wake eternally,
And Death shall be no more: Death, thou shalt die!

"Death"—John Donne

2

A Grave Matter

THE MORNING after the party onboard *Bellerophon*, Sissie and I left Nelson to guard *Cresswell* and went ashore to do our daily rounds; she to head for the mail at the post office and I to have a beer at the *bodega* Antonio, the tiny fisherman's bar at the head of the town quay. The Alhambra, with its crowd of rogues and sly hucksters, was no place, after all, for a sailor with a hangover. The fishermen, although stern-faced and quiet, were gentle and kind, and understanding of sailors' ways. With them there would be no accusing stares, no weighing up of wealth, no reckoning of worth, no estimates of proclivities. At Antonio's I would be a sailor among sailors, and on that October morning that's all I wanted—peace and quiet and solitude, with a bottle of San Miguel beer to stiffen me up.

As I approached the tiny, low, white-washed bodega, with its usual crew of ancient mariners outside, silently scrutinizing and supervising the activities in the harbor, Sissie, bless her, silently gave me a cheery wave and a smile and, with her raffia shopping bag slung over her shoulder, steamed off along the main waterfront. As usual her wake was marked by a scattering of children and chickens and the turning heads of a few male idlers. Previous to her appearance the men had been loitering on the quay; but now, as her electric ginger hair and bare thighs flashed by, they almost sprang to attention, Sissie steering among them like the Royal Yacht sailing between lines of minor fleet-craft at a naval review.

Antonio, who always looked as if he'd never been to bed, board, or bath in his life, bobbed his head as I ducked mine to pass through the low door. "*Café, Senõr?*"

"*No, por el amor de Dios*—CERVEZA, Antonio! For the love of God, a beer," I replied as I peered around the gloomy room and felt my way to one of the tiny tables.

"Mornin' Cap'n Jones!"

The voice was flat, tinny, Irish, and sounded as if it were being transmitted over a long-distance telephone line. I knew right away it was Rory O'Boggarty, the lounging litteratus, the erudite Eriner, the impecunious imp, the poor man's Bernard Shaw. He was usually to be found at Antonio's at an early hour, the mid-day hour, and the very late hour, with a virgin-lined notebook and a bottle of beer in front of him. Rory was a martyr to the writer's occupational hazards—the need for solitude and solace, company and conversation, privacy and prey—all at the same time. His voice signaled on: " . . . and how're the barnacles and binnacles today?"

I peered at him, thinking 'how's the bloody blarney today?' He was about twenty-nine and looked like a shabby leprechaun, with his red hair and mischievous eyes set in a pudgy, pasty face—what I could see of it in the midst of a long, red beard, which reached down as far as where the top button of his yellow shirt would have been if the shirt had had a button. Rory was so small and Bohemian that if Antonio had been a dancing girl instead of a funereal, elderly bar-owner, you would have thought Rory was Toulouse-Lautrec sitting in the Moulin Rouge.

"Top o' the morn to you!" Rory was the only real Irishman I ever met who actually said this.

"Hi, Rory," I sighed. I sat down opposite him with my back to the bodega door. Behind Rory there was a grimy picture of Jesus holding a heart, dripping dollops of blood, surrounded by a halo. Christ was gazing upward and to one side. I sighed again.

Rory took a swig of his beer with a lascivious look in his blue-green button eyes.

"How the hell can you drink that stuff at this time in the morning?" I kidded him.

"Cap'n Jones," he replied irascibly, "will you stop . . . It's a clock-watcher you are. It's Barclay's Bank you should be workin' in, beJasus!"

Antonio put a beer in front of me as sadly as if it were a death-sentence.

"Yeah, I'd nick the lot and have it away on my toes so fast you'd think I'd a rocket up my jacksy . . ."

"So you would, an' all, so you would, indeed you would, even if it's myself that says it, I do believe you would!" said Rory. "I see ye've the black dog on ye this fine day, and anyway, me lad, how's your Celtic face and the Gaelic heart of ye, old son?"

"O'Boggarty," said I, sensing his sarcasm, "it's a shit-face I have this morning, and my heart's the heart of a Lord Commissioner of the Admiralty, as black as thunder and as hard as Portland granite!"

"Ach, areen," replied Rory, "so it's missing your navy days, you are old son?"

As I listened, half amused, half furious, O'Boggarty quietly and sonorously, in his flat yet lovely sounding round-voweled Western Irish voice, quoted Joyce: *"That's your glorious British navy, says the citizen, that bosses the earth. The fellows that never will be slaves, with the only hereditary chamber on the face of God's earth and their lands in the hands of a dozen gamehogs and cottonball barons. That's the great empire they boast about of drudges and whipped serfs . . ."*

"Oh, come off it, O'Boggarty," I interjected. "That's been over and done with these twenty . . . forty years past."

Rory's voice rose now, and his words—Joyce's words—rolled and reverberated from the dirty walls of the bodega. *"They believe in rod,"* he roared, as with the end of each phrase he banged a closed, pudgy fist on the table, *"the scourger almighty, creator of hell on earth and in Jacky Tar, the son of a gun, who was conceived of unholy boast, born of the fighting navy, suffered under rump and dozen, was scarified, flayed and curried . . ."* O'Boggarty's eyes gleamed now with a rascally joy as he watched me wincing . . ."*yelled like bloody hell, the third day he rose again from the bed, steered into haven, and sitteth on his beam end until further orders whence he shall come to drudge for a living and be paid."*

O'Boggarty's quote, as he well knew, was word-for-word perfectly accurate. I screwed up my forehead as I quoted back at him: *"But, says Bloom, isn't discipline the same everywhere? I mean wouldn't it be the same here if you put force against force?"*

"Ah!" O'Boggarty shouted with delight. "Ah ha!" He laid his bottle of beer down, rubbed his lips with his wrist, and went on now in a low, melodramatic tone: *"Didn't I tell you? As true as I'm drinkin' this porter if he was at his last gasp he'd try to downface you that dying was living."*

Rory, keeping a half-malicious grin on his face and his gleaming elf's eyes on me, half-turned his head away. Then, after a moment or two, his eyes left mine, his grin dissolved, and he slumped down further and stared at his almost-empty bottle, which dully returned his look as if it were bereaved by the loss of its former contents.

"How's it goin', Rory?" I murmured.

The little Irishman perked up and smiled at me hugely. "The very best, it is!" He reached in his pocket. He brought out a large, bent envelope. He scuffled it open with his white, soft, pudgy fingers. He riffled through a pile of English banknotes, an inch thick, all fivers by the look of them. Again he grinned from ear to ear. "Enough for six months' booze," he said, and winked one gnome's eye at me. "Six hundred of the best!"

"So you got your advance through?" I knew he had been waiting anxiously for a publisher's advance on a "long novel" (not a word of which had so far been written).

"Yeah, Sleazy Frank brought it back from London for me, like I asked him to. Can't trust the Spanish mails . . ." O'Boggarty replaced the money in his pocket, all the while watching me—for traces, I suppose, of envy. But of course I gave him no satisfaction, for I had none. Sissie's allowance

was due, and that would see us over until my next delivery
job, which was already arranged. Instead, I looked around
the bodega. Antonio, sad-eyed as a hanged spaniel; O'Boggarty, happy as a Hobbit, and I were the only people in the
bar.

"Not many people about today," I remarked, to break
the silence. "And those that are look like they're going to a
bloomin' palace investiture."

"Or an execution," commented O'Boggarty.

"I wonder what the score is, Rory?"

The little elf scowled at me. He was like a bearded baby
doll frowning. "You don't know what day it is today?" he
asked. I kept silent as I looked at him. I found myself, as
usual in harbor (never at sea), trying to remember the date.

"Sure, it's the day of All Saints," he continued. "It's
the day when they . . . all us good Christians, at
least . . . remember all our loved ones who've passed
away . . ." (He looked serious as a judge while he said this.)
Then his eyes took on a dreamy glaze, and I knew another
quote was coming . . . *"across the bourne from which no traveler
returns."*

"You mean who've kicked the bucket?"

Rory O'Boggarty leaned his hairy head back and closed
his eyes. "Acch!" he intoned, "God save us from the
coarseness of the Cymry, the waggishness of the Welsh,
fellow Celts though they be. Sweet *Mary* in heaven, help us
poor Irish souls!"

I grinned at his kobold head as he leaned it forward
onto his chest and sighed, closing his eyes. Then he opened
them again and stared at me, an imperious imp. "Cap'n
Jones," he announced gravely, "it's no great respect for the
dear departed that you have."

"Aah!" (I was enjoying myself now that I was getting
back at him.) "It's a load of bullshit, O'Boggarty. It's little to
do with respect for the dead. All it is, is . . . pity for the
living, that's all!"

O'Boggarty's face clouded darkly.

I went on . . . "Self-pity, mainly, that's what it is. 'Oh, poor me, look at poor little me, left all alone.'"

I cocked two fingers at Antonio, silently ordering two beers. "The best way you can respect the dead is to live your own life as best you can, and for God's sake show more respect for the *living*."

Rory's leprechaun eyes danced in fury at the challenge. I had touched a raw nerve of a man who resented having been brought up in a repressive home and had been, to compound his self-torment, educated by Jesuits.

I gave the screw another twist. "The best way that you can show respect for the dead is to do your best to share their belief in life, but in *your* life, and by putting your life ahead of their deaths. I think more of one living child or a leaping dolphin than I do of all the generations of dead who ever lived!"

"Then you're a hypocrite!" shouted O'Boggarty, his Irish up. "You told me that you could not imagine life without the works of great writers of the past—Plato and Homer and Shakespeare and Blake . . ."

"Don't forget Joyce," I taunted.

"They don't really mean a thing to you if you've no respect for the dead . . ." He took a swig of his new beer. "I've suspected it, sure, from the very first time I saw you and heard you, Cap'n Jones—it's a bloody Druid you are! A drooling Druid! An idling idolator . . ."

"Better than being a nattering necrolator!"

O'Boggarty slumped down even farther into his rickety chair. Again he closed his eyes. Slowly he wagged his head from side to side.

"It's the little things that make up life, Rory," I said.

Still with his eyes closed, O'Boggarty asked in a low voice, "Then you don't believe in a hereafter?"

"I don't know, but if there is a hereafter, it surely can't be anything like *this* life, and if it's not like this one, then where will all the gladness and delight, the pleasure and joy, be? Where will all the *life* be? If there isn't joy and delight and pleasure . . . and yes, pain and misery and suffering, too, then how the heck can it be *life*? And if there isn't any life, then how can it be an *afterlife*?"

As I spoke O'Boggarty slowly wagged his red-shocked head from side to side, wisely, as if he were a Sunday-school teacher listening to an inquisitive child asking who created God, and why, and when, and how many of *them* were there?

He was silent for a whole minute, until, suddenly, the whole tiny bodega bar-room seemed to fill with people. He opened his eyes with a start. He stared in the gloom at the intruders for a second or two, then his face lit up like a boy whose kite has been lifted for the first time by a breeze. "*Josélito!*" he roared, "*Cómo estás, amigo?*"

Rory quickly stood up, all five-and-a-bit feet of him, and thrust his strangely small, childlike hand in front of him. The Castilian language, spoken in the accent of County Limerick, is a wonder to the ears, at least to mine, but the newcomer, who was now vigorously shaking the hand of the Green Land, evidently understood him perfectly. I turned to inspect the new arrival who had interrupted my revenge on O'Boggarty. As I did so, my attention was caught by the other figures which darkened the already dark bodega and made it seem suddenly crowded.

There was a woman—small, rotund, and dressed completely in black—her hair gleaming under a black shawl. She had one arm still lingering through the door as she awkwardly turned her body and shyly smiled at O'Boggarty. The hand on the end of the lingering arm gently rocked a perambulator, on which was balanced, precariously, it seemed to me, a large raffia-work hamper. On top of the hamper sat a little girl of three or so, while from behind the hamper gazed the red and well-fed face of a fat baby, which violently shook a rattle. It was as if the fat baby knew that both O'Boggarty and I had hangovers which would have made a rainy day after Ballinasloe Horse Fair, with every sweepstake stub in Galway swirling around in the sodden wind, and every man's hand shaking for twenty miles around, look like the midnight Christmas Mass in St. Patrick's Cathedral.

I recoiled, winced, cringed, and flinched as I stared at the fat baby. Every time it shook the rattle it drooled and laughed at me. Inside the door, clinging to the dark little woman's skirts, were two little dark, well-dressed boys, both on their best behavior, looking ineffably bored. And so they should, I thought, as I studied them. It was, after all, the Day of the Dead, and on this holy day of dread not even little boys should be little boys; it might disturb the spirits of the underworld, and *then* what would become of us?

I turned to inspect the man who was shaking hands with Rory. For a moment, as I took in his black suit, black fedora, and black armband, I didn't recognize him. Then he turned to me and flashed a wide smile as he stabbed a hard, calloused hand at me and crinkled his blue eyes. With a shock I realized that this was José, one of the fishermen who, in their blue denim pants and jackets, and straw sandals, waved cheery greetings to me out on the bay, and sometimes slapped my back in the bodega and *hola'*d and *Cómo está'*d me, grinning and joking, on normal, everyday Days of the Living. José and I had something in common— we had both served in the navies of our respective lands. For that reason José's Castilian was good and understandable.

"How are you, *Senõr* Jones?" He pronounced my name "Honays."

"I see you're all dressed up," I observed stupidly. "Going to church today?"

"*Si, Todos los Santos* . . . All Saints Day." José gave O'Boggarty and me a weak, sad grin as the Irishman flashed a warning look my way.

José looked at O'Boggarty. "You're Irish," he said.

Rory nodded, his wide-open, innocent eyes dead serious.

"Catholic?" asked José.

"Yes, of course!" said O'Boggarty, as if he'd never spent an hour in his life ridiculing his Jesuit teachers in Dublin.

José turned to me. "English," he stated.

"No, Welsh," I replied. I didn't wait for The Question. "But we have our own church—it's sort of like the Catholic church, only we don't have popes, we have poets."

That went completely over José's head. O'Boggarty glowered darkly at me from under his brow and paid for José's glass of wine; wine so red it looked as if it had been collected from the drips of the bleeding-heart picture on the wall.

José beamed at me. "Good. Look, you don't have your ancestors here—your family dead—so why don't you come along with us? We will not be long in church, and then we are going to the cemetery for lunch."

He did not bother to ask *Señora* José if it was in order. Instead he reached over to the eldest of his two silent little lads, who must have been about eight, and firmly pulled the boy to his side. "We have a whole piglet. Roasted. Manuelito here killed it last night on the kitchen table." He squeezed his eldest son's shoulder proudly. "Cut its throat. It took the little whore at least a half-hour to lose its blood and die . . . and the noise, *señors*, you should have heard it! Yes, Manuelito did a good job. We're very proud of him, very proud indeed. He's going to be a big, strong man, just like his father, hey?" José turned and shot a beam at his wife, who duly fluttered her face as she gazed at her eldest.

José, glowing with pride, turned back to O'Boggarty and me. His face took on a crafty aspect. He looked as if he knew what would entice us for sure. "Wine, too—I've four whole carafes! And a chicken, and shrimp, and roasted potatoes, and fish . . . She cooks fish *muy bien*, the best in Ibiza!"

Rory O'Boggarty laughed. "Sure!" he cried in his best Limerick-Castilian, as he grasped the little pig-slaughterer's hand and shook it. "Sure, Josélito, Capitán Honays and I will be very happy to come with you!"

I nipped back to *Cresswell* and left a note for Sissie: "Gone to Hades, back at four." Then I half-ran to catch up with the rotund little fisherman, his rotund little wife, the pig-sticker boy, the innocent younger-yet boy, their silent ladylike daughter, the rattle-waving, malicious baby, and the diminutive, red-headed Irish leprechaun, as they wended their way gravely to the church.

The mass was sung by a lavishly caparisoned priest, surprisingly young-looking. His Latin was good, even though he called out the words as if he were reading off a ship's manifest. The crowd—and it was a crowd—packed the church and, unemotionally, it seemed to me, chanted the responses and made the proper motions, presumably at the proper times. During the high point of the mass, however, while the host was raised by the priest, I was distracted by a small bird which had somehow strayed into the building and was now the cynosure of the eyes of everyone in the congregation under the age of fourteen. This pleased me greatly. After the mass was over I stepped outside jauntily, thinking about the little bird. It was as if God had sent us a lighthearted reminder that He was still alive and well and thinking of us—or at least of the children.

We reached the town cemetery, half as old as time and twice as old as space, after a walk of a mile or so. Rory O'Boggarty, who had emerged from the church as if his book had just been featured on a best-seller list, was something of an authority on the history of Ibiza. "Sure, this cemetery was originally a heathen burial site—that's before the Phoenicians arrived and built a temple here, dedicated to their chief female goddess, it was. Her name was Tannit."

"Sounds like a sunburn lotion," said I, trying to keep the party as lighthearted as I'd felt watching the bird flutter around in the gloomy church.

"Acch, it's a terrible man y'are at your lessons!" said the leprechaun, hurling a glower at me, but good-naturedly.

The whole Ibizan family was smiling at him, with the exception of the fat baby, who threw its rattle at him and pouted a deep frown. I immediately made up my mind to buy the baby a real rattle, a real *man's* rattle—like the ones they whirl at international soccer matches—as soon as I could, and to put the child at the very top of my Christmas list.

At a dignified pace, with O'Boggarty holding forth on the history of every clump of grass we passed, we all proceeded up a grassy knoll, which was bestrewn with tombs. Not your everyday, Calvinistic flat slabs, which look so definite and permanent, as if whoever is below them will never get out, under any circumstances; no, these were more like small cottages, but covered with carvings of angels and cherubs (some of which looked startlingly like the fat baby—I made up my mind to buy it a trumpet instead of a rattle). Some of the family vaults looked like little palaces, as if doting parents had ordered tiny models of Versailles to be built for their spoiled royal brats. I noted that the people who were gathered gravely around these stone wedding cakes were, in the main, wealthy-looking.

Other vaults were much simpler. They had rounded roofs, and were shaped something like beehives. They were generally discolored by dampness, which had caused green moss to grow on the stone roofs. These tombs looked like so many green-painted skulls, with their jaws buried in the ground, as if they were biting the earth.

Soon we came to a small version of these beehive tombs. It was about fifteen feet in diameter at its widest, at ground level. It was almost overgrown with moss and a kind of ivy, some of which had grown over the low black iron door. The door was rounded at the top to form an arch, and reminded me of a skull's eye socket.

While *la señora* unloaded the perambulator of the lady-like child, the picnic hamper, and the now-grinning baby, all of whom and which she dumped unceremoniously on the grass, we men (including the pig-sticking eldest son), being *men*, took charge of the situation and cleared the fronds of overgrowth from the little iron door. The fronds were dry and crackled as we cleared them, like snapping sinews.

On the door was a picture frame. Behind its glass, once José had cleaned it with a handkerchief (a clean one, courtesy of Sissie, which I had passed him) we saw a dozen photographic portraits, now yellow with age and exposure. They were all, it seemed to me, of the same small, dark man and the same small, dark woman. But José proudly pointed out who was who. We found that we were, in fact, looking at his mother and father, his father's mother and father, his father's father's mother and father . . . and so on, back to about the time when Disraeli (illegally and without permission) bought the Suez Canal on behalf of the Widow of Windsor.

Respectfully, José then stood back, delved in the pockets of his black trousers, and extracted an iron key so large that it looked as if it had been the key to the Bastille. Solemnly he inserted it into the keyhole in the tiny iron door, and forced the key around. The lock grated, then sprang with a clunk. I watched O'Boggarty's face as José placed Sissie's handkerchief over the shoulder of his black jacket and, screwing up his face, heaved.

O'Boggarty stood there, his red hair looking as if it were about to stand on end, his blue-green eyes wide open, staring, gaping in silence. He looked like a small child at a magic show, expecting a white rabbit to come popping out of José's sleeve.

The iron door creaked and squealed and cursed on its hinges, with José heaving away at it in jerks, until it stood wide open. Following José, at his beckoning, we went inside, me at the fisherman's heels, almost consumed with curiosity, feeling like Howard Carter must have felt when he reached the last door before Tutankhamen; and O'Boggarty, silent except for his heavy breathing, close behind me; then the eldest son behind him.

By the light of the butane lamp which José held out in front of him, we stepped down about six feet, down stone steps which seemed to be carved out of the actual hillside. At the bottom of the steps was a room about twelve feet square, with a stone floor. The room was surrounded on each wall by faded, heavy red velvet curtains.

As we looked on in silence José reached around one of the curtains and brought out a large card table, about four feet square. This he unfolded and set up in the center of the floor. Next he reached around and brought out five folding chairs, which he set up around the table. Then, rapidly, he told the little pig-sticker, his pride and joy, to bring down the men's food. I realized that the females and the unproved son and the fat baby were to remain outside. This was a job for *men* only.

Soon the tablecloth was laid—a lovely embroidered thing, all white and green and gold—and on it was laid a feast fit for a whole hierarchy, leave alone a king. The baby pig looked succulent (so did the eldest son's face as he gazed proudly at his handiwork). The chicken was half sliced already by *la señora*, who kept up a running barrage of chatter at her husband through the tomb door from the sunlight above.

O'Boggarty, who was a bit of a trencherman, looked now as if he had completely forgotten he was in a tomb, as his eyes wandered over the roast chicken and a dish of fresh green vegetables, and the bottles of wine—dark green, long-necked, slightly crusted, and obviously of a respectable vintage.

José yelled up through the tomb door. Something came clattering down the steps. José bent and picked it up, whistling in his teeth all the while. It was a bottle opener. José opened all four bottles and slowly, carefully, poured the dark red liquid, which seemed to have a life of its own, into the *twenty-two* crystal glasses which the pig-sticker had gently laid out on the table in a row.

That done, José stood back, his blue eyes gleaming in the light of the gas lamp. There was a dead silence, even from the sunlit land of the living outside the tomb door. O'Boggarty and I, fascinated, watched José as he stood, smiling at us. The pig-sticker stuck out his chest, proud to be a man among men. Suddenly, from somewhere came a wail. O'Boggarty's face blanched. Then he realized that the fat baby had decided to cry. His tenseness eased momentarily, and he grinned wanly at José.

José, savoring the holy moment, stood for a few seconds longer; then, just as suddenly as the fat baby had cried, he turned on his heel and pulled aside the curtain behind him. Even as we stared, all three of us—the pig-sticker fascinated, me curious, and O'Boggarty in horror, José pulled aside the other curtains on the other three sides of the chamber. In a few seconds we were surrounded by glass coffins, and in each of them a desiccated body with a grinning skull and brown, leathery-looking remnants of skin and flesh hanging from the bones.

José grabbed a glass of wine and toasted loudly, "*A los muertos!* To the dead!"

I had, before I knew it, a glass in my hand, too. "To the living!" I saluted. José wouldn't understand anyway.

Just as the eldest son raised his glass there was a clatter. I stared around. O'Boggarty had fainted clean away, flat out on the floor. José flung a questioning look at me.

"He had a bit too much to drink last night," I explained.

"Oh," said José.

By the time O'Boggarty came around, José, the eldest son, and I (and presumably the unfit and females outside) had consumed as fine a cold picnic lunch as you could expect to find south of the French frontier. We, the men, the privileged-with-the-dead, down below, had quaffed between us the whole four bottles of very good wine. It had a fine bouquet and a nutty flavor (which I thought suitable for the occasion).

O'Boggarty stirred and groaned. I took him a glass of wine. He opened his eyes. He looked at me. He stared at the young pig-sticker. He gawped wildly at José. His head spun around to gaze again at the dear departed. His eyes widened, as if he were in absolute terror. Suddenly he was up. He shot off the ground. He wailed and slobbered. He tore himself away from my grasp and skittered up the steps and out into the sunlight as José, astounded, gazed after him. I wended my way, as steadily as I could, to the top of the vault steps, and squinted through the strong sunlight all around.

There was *la señora*, weeping softly, on all fours, gathering together all the pieces of the meal, which O'Boggarty had scattered in his mad flight. There was the baby, howling its fat face out. There was the small, ladylike female child, as silent as ever. There was the still-a-child boy. And there, away down the hill, haring through the graveyard, was the Irish terrier, the terror of Bloomsbury, his yellow shirt swathing a yellow streak across the green grass of the ground of the goddess of the Phoenicians. And there was José, puzzled, at my side.

"What happened?" he asked.

"He's got a touch of tummy troubles. You know, all foreigners, all the tourists, get that . . ."

"*Ah, si, estómago malo*," murmured José. "What a pity."

It was after dusk when at last, escorted by José's whole family, I staggered back to *Cresswell*, the waiting ministrations of Sissie, and the welcoming wags of Nelson's tail.

Run our David to Lluyncelyn,
Fetch our Mati to the piggie,
But our Mati told us quickly,
That the black pig it was dying.

Chorus: *Oh, our hearts are very sore,*
Oh, our hearts are very sore,
Oh, our hearts are very heavy,
As we bury the black pig.

"Mochyn Du" (The Black Pig)

"*Mochyn Du*" was a capstan and anchor-heaving chantey, very popular on Cape Horners with Welsh crews. "Burying the black pig" mostly alluded to settling a debt or getting rid of a hang-over. The translation is mine.

3

Mochyn Du

"P OSH PLACE," I commented to Tony the Specs as we trotted up the wide front steps of the La Princesa Hotel in Málaga. An immaculate doorman, through some remarkable articulation of his right elbow, managed to both salute and hold out his hand at the same time. In fact he swiveled the arm so fast and violently that one of his white gloves fell out of his epaulette; so, while he, flustered, bent to pick up the glove, Tony and I sped past him without paying any extortion.

It was still fairly warm in Málaga, and Tony was clad in a tropical suit, of which we were both proud. It was light gray, shot with black streaks of silk. He wore a pale pink shirt open at the neck, a Panama hat, tilted toward the back of his head to compensate for his stoop, and a pair of pimp's pumps—at least that's what they looked like to me. They were white calf, with a sort of straw–colored basket-weave over the instep, and were so new that they squeaked as he walked. I had my best rig on too—it's only courtesy, after all, when you're applying for a paid position. I wore my number-one corduroy pants, which had no more than three paint spots on them; my brick-colored cotton Breton fishing smock, a tee-shirt, and my best deck shoes.

"Yes," said Tony, peering around him in the hotel reception hall, all of marble and gold trim. "Yes, old chap, a bit like the Gritti Palace in Venice."

"Oh?"

Shiner Wright was one of that remarkable breed—an Australian wheeler-dealer. I had met him some months before, when I had delivered a thirty-foot sloop for him from Genoa, where she had been built, to the island of Menorca, where Shiner was involved in a real estate deal. Since then he had arranged a couple of delivery jobs for me, and, although he was an aggressive materialist, I liked and respected him. He always treated me fair and square.

Shiner had told me that before he came to the Mediterranean he had been engaged in apartment-letting in London for several years and had, by the age of thirty-six, already made his first million pounds. He was the kind of man that most people like instinctively. He was not exactly good-looking by cornflake-packet standards; he was too stocky for that, and his auburn hair and brown eyes somehow did not seem to belong together. But he had about him a self-assurance; he always looked as if he *belonged* wherever he was, and that seemed to put other people, especially young folk, immediately at their ease with him.

I do not think he derived all his self-assurance from the money he had made. He had been born of a very poor family in the slums of Sydney. I think his assurance stemmed from the fact that he believed that everything was possible, given the guts and the will.

We were very much birds of a feather, Shiner and I, even though it would revolt my Celtic soul, then, now, and always, to receive *rent*—and even more to *pay* it. Shiner was one of the most positive men I have ever met, and also one of the most *integral*. As young Americans would so delightfully put it, "he had his shit together."

It was small surprise to me, when Tony the Specs and I enquired at the reception desk, to find a message for us to go straight up to the "Royal Suite," which was a penthouse apartment, completely self-contained, with its own kitchen and bar and staff, right up on top of the hotel roof.

We were soon whisked up in the elevator by a small, dark porter, who was suitably awed at Tony the Specs (who must have looked more like a Professor of Economics than a delivery mate) and puzzled by my appearance—so much that he attempted a conspiratorial wink at me behind Tony's back as he grasped the chrome handles of the double doors to the suite. Then the doors slid apart and I saw Shiner, as well-dressed and prosperous-looking as ever.

Shiner was sitting, or rather reclining, in a deep leather sofa. He was wearing a light blue suit, and his beige tie displayed a pin with a pearl almost as big as a Yankee quarter and almost as bright as Shiner's sudden smile as the doors silently slid shut behind us. He held up his hand and stared at the banknote he grasped in it. "Yeah, Tristan, me old mate—come in, cobber," he said in his twangy Aussie drawl. "You and your oppo sit down. I won't be a tick."

As I sat down I looked again at the banknote Shiner was holding. It was a 10,000-peseta note. At that time there were fifty pesetas to the dollar, so the piece of paper Shiner was studying was worth $200. Every few seconds, in the clock-ticking silence of the Royal Suite, Shiner looked up at the person who, with the back of his head showing toward me, was sunk low in a deep armchair facing him.

"I've got five nines," said Shiner in a low voice. He lifted one eyebrow and grinned at the armchair.

"I do not believe you, Mr. Wright . . . Show me," said the well-modulated, slightly French-accented voice which rose from the armchair.

It dawned on me, after a second or two, that Shiner and his mysterious guest were playing "spoof," a variation of "liar's dice," but played with the numbers on banknotes.

Shiner's grin widened even more as he leaned over and passed the 10,000-peseta note over to his partner. A hand languidly reached from the armchair. The French voice murmured, *"Merde . . . Vous avez de la chance . . . pute alors!"* The hand let the banknote flutter onto the richly carpeted floor, where it settled on top of a pile of other 10,000-peseta notes. I leaned over slightly to look at the pile of money. There must have been at least 150 notes, all of the 10,000-peseta denomination. I made a fast mental reckoning. There was at least $30,000 scattered over the floor between the sofa and the armchair!

Shiner stood up and smoothed down his finely tailored jacket. He strode over to me and shook my hand firmly. "Nice to see you again, old son," he said, even though he was five years my junior. He greeted Tony, reckoning him up as quick as a gnat's wink. Then he took both our elbows firmly and gently guided us over to the deep leather armchair. There, still lounging deep in luxury, was one of the most classically handsome men I have ever seen.

"Pierre Reynaud," said Shiner, as the hand that had dropped a small fortune moments before languidly reached for mine.

Reynaud was about thirty-five, or so I reckoned. His hair was curly dark blond, medium length, and it seemed to caress the temples of his finely shaped head. He was slightly sunburned—the smooth, rich sunburn which comes expensively from sitting under the Cinzano sunshades on the patios and verandahs of exclusive hotels. He wore a gold Rolex. His nose was perfectly straight and completely in proportion to the rest of him. His eyes—deep gray-green, were . . . beautiful. With their dark lashes they complemented, even spiced, everything else about him. He stood up in the graceful, sinuous manner of a man who has been everywhere, done everything, and knows everyone who matters.

He was my height, about five feet, ten inches, but his litheness gave him the appearance of being slightly taller. He reminded me of a statue I had seen in some museum or other—Adonis. His mouth was sensual. His immaculate black suit, black shirt, black tie, and black shoes, and the way he padded over to Tony brought to mind a wily tomcat. My second impression was much nearer the truth. "*Sprucer*," I said to myself, as I watched the way his body moved under the black suit. That body was not merely clothed—it was *decorated*.

The only flaws in Reynaud's outer perfection, which I noticed with a slight shock as he reached out to greet me, were the two fingers missing from his right hand, and the hard, dry feel of the hand. It was like grasping the claw of some exotic bird of paradise, and, after glancing at the shocks of beauty in the feathers, wondering about the brain; finding yourself somewhat discomforted—even threatened—by the perfection before your eyes.

Then you decide to keep things simple and coo at the bird—or you ought to. At any rate that's what I, in a flash, decided to do that day in the Royal Suite of the La Princesa Hotel, surrounded by dark Spanish furniture, glancing quickly at the thousand glass pendants of the chandelier gleaming white, blue, and gold over my head, feeling the soft decadence of the Turkish carpet under my grubby deck shoes. *'A right one we've got here,'* I thought.

A flicker in Reynaud's green-grey eyes told me, in a sliver of a fraction of a millisecond, that he knew I had been studying him.

"Monsieur Reynaud has a boat . . ." said Shiner.

"Oh, call me Pierre . . . We're all friends here," Reynaud chimed in.

Shiner smiled. "Pierre has a boat which he wants delivered from Algiers to Marseilles."

This was a surprise, but not unexpected. Tony's mouth opened slightly, but he said nothing.

"A seventy-two-foot powerboat," continued Shiner. He lit a Sobranie cigarette with a gold lighter in one continuous flow of movement, as we sailors stood silently and as Reynaud studied our faces. *"Aries,"* the Australian said.

"That's her name?" I asked, stupidly.

"Right, cobber."

"Aries?"

"That's it."

"Oh." An image of a ram flashed through my consciousness. "Algiers?"

"Algiers," Reynaud said, flatly.

I turned to him. "No problems—I mean, permits and all that? There's been quite a bit of fireworks over there lately . . ."

Reynaud looked up in slight puzzlement.

Tony piped up. "Tristan means political trouble."

Reynaud smiled and shook his head. "That's all taken care of." Then he looked at Tony. "Where are your boats now, Mr. Rankin?"

Quick as a flash, Shiner broke in. "As I mentioned to you, they're in Gibraltar . . ."

Tony's face reddened very slightly.

"Ah, yes, Gibraltar, the famous Rock," commented Reynaud. "A nice, safe place . . ."

"Yes," I lied, "We've been there for a couple of weeks now, but Tony's sailing up to Lisbon . . . to winter there."

Tony nodded as he pursed his lips and reddened even more, peering down at the Turkish carpet.

Shiner said, "Good, then it's settled. What would you like, gentlemen—tea, or a stiffener?"

Tony and Reynaud both said "Tea." I asked for a stiffener.

"Scotch and soda, right?"

"Black Label, but before we do that I'd like to sort out the details of the delivery." I looked Reynaud straight in the eye. "First of all, when do we leave for Algiers?"

"Tomorrow at ten in the morning. There's a flight to Oran—only an hour or so. Then we catch a train from there to Algiers. That's a few hours, but we should be in Algiers by nine in the evening. We can stay at a hotel overnight and go on board *Aries* in the morning, to get ready to sail . . ."

"So you're coming with us?"

"Naturally."

I looked at Shiner. He grinned at me and lifted his scotch and soda, which had been swiftly served by a silent steward. "Here's to *Aries* and a safe passage," he toasted.

"I'll drink to that as soon as we've got the fee worked out," I said, quietly.

"Join me for dinner tonight, Pierre?" Shiner asked.

"I must meet with some business colleagues," said Reynaud.

"Tristan?"

"Never turn down a good scoff," said I.

"Good. Tony?"

"Pleasure," said Tony, staring at the banknotes on the floor.

Reynaud was still watching me, studying me.

"What about payment?" I asked him.

"Ah, yes. Let's see . . ." He gestured with the three-fingered hand. "Fifty pesetas to the dollar, right?"

"About that."

Reynaud thought for a moment, then said, "Fifty thousand pesetas. Is that all right?"

I kept a straight face. "Yes, I think that'll be pretty fair. OK with you, Tony?"

"Certainly," replied my stooped, bespectacled mate.

I thought to myself, 'Fifty thousand pesetas—Jesus Christ, I'd sail bloody Franco himself around the Isle of Wight for half that right now! *A thousand dollars*—that will keep us going right through the winter.'

"Good then, that's settled," said Reynaud. His clothes moved on his body as if they were dancing partners. "I'll see you . . ." (there was a tiny hesitation) " . . . gentlemen at nine in the morning." Then he took his leave, trod over the banknotes scattered on the carpet, and slid through the double doors of the Royal Suite.

There was a moment's silence after the Frenchman left, until Shiner clapped me on the shoulder. "Well, mates, what d'ye think of this pad," he said. He strode over to the wide windows, the length of the room, and swept his arm out over the view of the whole city of Málaga, laid out below like a map.

"Must have cost a bloody packet, Shiner," I observed.

"Two hundred bucks a day," he replied, "but it's worth it. If you're doing business with the Frogs or locals, then it pays to have your nest . . . *well-feathered*, my old son."

He took Tony and me by the arms, led us over the pile of banknotes on the floor, and escorted us through the doorway into the hall.

I turned to Shiner. "What about all that akkers . . . all that money on the floor?"

"Oh, these blokes in this hotel—and the sheilas, too— are as honest as the day is long. They won't touch it."

"Don't you think it's a bit . . . ostentatious?" asked Tony in a querulous tone as we strode to the elevator.

"Well, I could have put it in the desk, but if they see it there they'd think I don't trust 'em . . . and you know how the Spanish are." Shiner spoke as if to a pair of schoolboys.

Tony and I took that in silently as the elevator dropped from the Olympian of the Royal Suite down to levels of ordinary mortality.

Shiner did us proud that night. First he showed us our rooms so we could drop our seabags. Both rooms had twin beds. "If you trip over any sheilas . . ." commented Shiner, winking at us. "Only natural, anyway." Then he treated us to a slap-up nosh—tiny eels, steak, baked potatoes, and fresh whiting, all washed down with the best Amontillado. Afterward, as we sipped Napoleon brandy on the restaurant terrace overlooking the million lights of Málaga and under a hundred thousand stars, I grinned at Shiner. "That French bloke . . . what's his name . . . Pierre . . . seems to be a pretty all-right feller?"

"Oh, yes," replied Shiner. "I'm glad you followed my lead about your boats being in Gibraltar." He looked at me craftily over his brandy glass. "The less these blokes know about your assets and their whereabouts, the better, eh?"

"Yeah," I replied as Tony peered at the pair of us.

"Anyway," continued Shiner, "how do you feel about the money side, Tris?"

"Great. It looks like Tony and I, and our crews, will be set up for the whole winter."

"Well, as soon as Pierre mentioned his problem to me . . . he's an acquaintance of a friend . . . I thought about you and the way you've been scrounging around to stay afloat and make a living. So I put in a good word for you."

"Thanks, mate. I'll remember that when I see some good beach-front property for sale cheap, somewhere that's ripe for development," I offered.

Shiner grinned. "Hope to Christ it's not in Greenland!"

Tony the Specs laughed out loud at this. Then the three of us adjourned to the bar and spent an hour or two cracking yarns.

As I fell asleep that night I reminded myself to ask Reynaud for a fifty-percent advance on the delivery fee the next day, so I could send some of it to *Cresswell* and Nelson and Sissie, to cheer them up.

When Tony and I met Reynaud at the hotel in the morning he was dressed much less formally, but still all in black. He wore a black leather jacket over a black shirt and pants, and calf-length black leather boots. As we approached him he sailed up so brightly that I was afraid he might grab us and kiss us on both cheeks in the habitual French way. Instead he shook our hands and hurried us out of the hotel, onto the street, and into a taxi. In rapid, fluent Spanish he ordered the driver to head for the airport "*A toda velocidad*"—with all speed—a phrase I have never been able to forget. Ever since, whenever I have been consciously heading or foolishly following others into risk and hazard, those Spanish words always pop up in my head. *A toda velocidad*. Fools rush in . . .

At Algiers airport we quickly passed through customs, aided by a friendly police officer who greeted Reynaud as an old friend. Once out of the airport and headed for the railway station Reynaud could hardly contain an anti-Arab bigotry so virulent that it seemed to bounce off the walls and pavement around him. In fluent English, under his breath, all the way to the station and through it, to the ticket booths, along the platform, in a low monotone directed mainly toward me, he ranted and raved about "heathens" and "dirty Algerians" and "stinking whores."

As in crowded railway stations in all big cities there were beggars and seedy-looking people. Of course there were those who no one in his right mind would trust in any circumstances, but as far as I could tell, the people in the Algiers station were little different from people anywhere— a mixture of rogues and would-be angels. To hear Reynaud you would have thought you were in the Ninth Circle of Hell. But I needed his money, and so I grinned at him and took no notice.

In the train Reynaud bribed the guard to allow us into a locked, evidently ex-first-class compartment. I thought of all the good Arabs I had known—all the decent ones, many affectionate ones, even a few very loving ones, among the lights of my life, as well as all the ordinary, every-day uncitified Arabs I had encountered throughout the Middle East, but I said nothing about them and Reynaud eventually tired of ranting and railing against them in a low voice (always in English). Besides, I was too fascinated, watching the other passengers as they left the train, wondering about their lives. Then, too, I was helping Tony solve the cross-word puzzle in a copy of the overseas *Times* of London, which he had eagerly swooped on in the Málaga airport.

I was surprised to see that there was still the usual complement of beggars and little ragamuffins at practically every halt. But the little ones, despite their rags, seemed to be having a high old time, laughing and shouting and waving at the passengers. The boys avoided our compartment, though, which made me a bit sad, because even with my rusty version of Arabic it was usually great fun to exchange badinage with them, no matter where. A couple of years later, when I traveled to London mostly by train, I watched the disinterested faces of young people in England as the train passed them, thinking they probably wished they were back in front of the goggle-box; and I remembered, as I do now, the faces of these children of the Riff. They were enjoying life. They were *living* life, and they weren't yet jaded by familiarity with frenetic mediocrity.

It was about eight o'clock when, at last, the train pulled slowly into Algiers. We made our way through the bustling crowds in the mezzanine, which was crawling with armed soldiers in pairs, to the station entrance. There Reynaud anxiously gaped around, then sighed slightly with relief as a gray van pulled up right in front of us. It was driven by a chubby, middle-aged Algerian, who said absolutely nothing the whole time he was with us. The only noise he made was a grunt when Reynaud gave him some money at the end of the ride.

In complete silence we drove through the city streets, directly to the port gates, where we were stopped by a sergeant. Reynaud handed the sergeant an envelope and spoke rapidly in Maghreb Arab—far too fast for me to understand. Then the sergeant waved us through.

The van passed through the dockyard, under the brilliant pools of light under the cranes, which were all silent and still. "I thought we were going to a hotel," I said to Reynaud.

"It's better if we go straight onboard," he said quietly. "The weather's very good for leaving tonight."

Tony spoke up. "What about fuel and stores?"

Reynaud grunted. "Everything is taken care of."

"Are you sure that this is on the level?" I asked.

Reynaud grinned. "It is for me, my friend. We all might just as well get on with it. You can't leave the . . . job now. If the authorities find out you've come over here to work, without a work permit . . . *pouf!*"

Just then the van stopped and we all piled out of the back doors. I turned to Reynaud. "Well, thanks a lot. You could have told us about this in Málaga."

Reynaud took my arm. "Look, Mr. Jones," he whispered, "I've told you, everything is all right. The boat is all ready for sea. I have good friends over here. All we have to do is leave."

"And what about when we get to France, with no exit permit from Algiers?" enquired Tony anxiously. "You know how bloody sticky the French customs are."

"*Pas de problème*, Mr. Rankin," said Reynaud. "I've got plenty of friends in high places there. They'll probably give you a medal!"

"Jesus," I exclaimed in a low voice. Then I saw, out in the middle of the eastern end of the great harbor basin, under the sliver of a moon in the calm, windless night, the low profile of a whole flotilla of craft, all rafted together.

For a moment I hesitated. Then I looked at Tony. "What do you think, mate? What he says is true. If we go to the authorities for a permit to sail . . ."

Tony's face, in the wan light, was serious. By now the van had left. Below where we stood, at the edge of the jetty, a small motor launch bobbed against the pier ladder. "I just don't know, Tris . . . I'll do whatever you think best."

"Oh, shit. Well, in for a penny . . ." I picked up my seabag; " . . . in for a bloody pound!" I dropped my bag into the launch.

Soon we were alongside *Aries*, which was rafted up on the outside of a collection of about thirty pleasure boats of all shapes, sizes, and conditions. There were little eighteen-foot sloops, forty-foot yawls, ninety-foot ex-motor-gun-boats . . . It looked a bit like the Dunkirk rescue fleet.

Aries seemed huge to me. Casting my eye over her upperworks I saw that she was splendidly accoutred with radar scanner, shortwave aerials, and searchlights. All her fittings were first-class. She was moored to small buoys fore and aft, and also tied up to the next vessel, which was almost as large.

Reynaud climbed onboard first. As I waited for Tony to clamber up the boarding ladder I looked up and saw a young Algerian soldier, with a machine pistol slung over his shoulder, talking in low tones with Reynaud. Just as I reached the top of the ladder myself I saw Reynaud pass yet another envelope. The soldier grinned and saluted; then, after I had plonked down my seabag on the deck, he descended into the launch and disappeared in the direction of the main quay.

"*Vite, vite* . . . Quick! There is not a lot of time. Put your gear in the wheelhouse. Tony, you come with me . . ."

"Where're you off to?" I asked. I knew that Reynaud realized that I had seen that the soldier had not taken his machine pistol with him, even though it wasn't anywhere around. My brain was by now working away ten to the dozen, trying to figure out a way of getting Tony and me out of this pickle all in two pieces. By now it was quite obvious, from the look of Reynaud's face, that he was a very determined man indeed. A man who would stop at nothing—probably not even murder—to achieve his own ends. The only thin thread of hope for us was to go along with him, at least until we were on our own ground—way out at sea. *Then we would see.*

"We're going to check the engine—lube oil and fuel levels," replied Reynaud. "There's no point in your trying to get ashore. If you do, the sentries will know what to do . . ."

"I've no intention of doing that," I replied. "All I want to do is check the wheelhouse and the charts and then get the hell out of here."

"Good. Naturally." Reynaud, with Tony in tow, passed aft from the wheelhouse.

I quickly scanned through the navigation desk, noting that the charts for the western Mediterranean and the Gulf of Lions were lying atop a pile of other charts, and drew off a course from Algiers to Marseilles direct. The course passed very close to the island of Menorca. Then I studied a chart of Algiers harbor, which was lying on the desk, and noted that the position of *Aries'* berth had been marked. Also drawn in was the line of a barrier chain which was strung across the small-craft harbor every night to prevent entry and exit. All this was done by the dim light of a tiny torch which had been lying on the navigation table.

Soon Reynaud was back in the wheelhouse, with Tony behind him looking nonplused. "How is it?" he asked in a low voice.

"OK. The best thing we can do is unshackle the mooring cables fore and aft, push her right off from that next bloody scow, and let her go. Hopefully the engines run . . ."

Reynaud smiled. "No problem," he said.

" . . . and there's enough fuel to get us at least to Menorca."

"There's enough to take us to Paris, if need be," he replied.

"Right, let's go then. I've got the line of the barrier chain. Slip the mooring lines."

Soon we were clear of the other boats, floating free in the dead calm harbor under the pale moonlight. Reynaud came into the wheelhouse. I watched both him and the heading of the boat as he pushed the engine starter buttons. From below there was the low rumble of power restrained.

"Brace yourselves," I said. "Here goes bugger-all!"

I slipped the engine gear lever into "Ahead." As the boat started to move I rammed the speed lever to "Full." The roar from the engines was deafening. The stern dropped suddenly, the bow lifted, and we were speeding at twenty knots, straight for the barrier cable. We were about thirty yards off the barrier, which I could now dimly see, when the machine guns opened up.

There were two lofty ships from old England came,

Chorus: *Blow high, blow low, and so sailed we!*
One was Prince of Luther *and the other* Prince of Wales,

Chorus: *All a cruising down the coasts of the High Barbaree!*

Aloft there, aloft, our bully bosun cried,
Look ahead, look astern, look to weather and a-lee!

There's naught upon the stern, sir, and naught upon our lee,
But there's a lofty ship to windward and she's sailing fast and free.

O hail her, O hail her! our gallant captain cried,
Are you a man o' war or privateer? cried he.

O, no I'm not a man o' war, nor privateer, cried he,
But I'm a salt-sea pirate, all a-looking for my fee!

For broadside, for broadside, a long time we lay,
Till at last the Prince of Luther *shot the pirates' mast away.*

O quarter, O quarter! those pirates they did cry,
But the quarter that we gave 'em was to sink 'em in the sea.

"High Barbaree" is a capstan or halyard chantey. It is very old, probably dating from the early seventeenth century. High Barbaree was the old name for the Riff Coast— specifically the coast of what is now Algeria.

4

High Barbaree!

I NEVER KNEW whether *Aries* went *through* the barrier cable or *over* it. In the several minutes of chaos that followed the first splattering zing of bullets on her steel hull, everything seemed to happen all at once. One round shattered the starboard windscreen, splintering it into a thousand opaque slivers of plexiglass. By that time we were, all three of us, heads-down—Tony and Reynaud flat on the wheelhouse deck and me squatting low, holding the steering wheel steady on course. I remember that I shut my eyes, until the thought flashed to me that it would not prevent my being shot. I opened them again and stared like a madman at the wheelspokes in front of me as, with a terrifying rumbling noise, the hull slowed down. There was a seeming eternity of straining and wrenching, with the engines now screaming in protest and the propellers grinding and whizzing in a high pitch. It was as if the boat were suspended on a high-wire. Suddenly she lurched forward so violently that my head was banged against the steering wheel. This knocked into me the presence of mind to raise myself high enough to just peep over the lower edge of the windscreen. The only light on the inside of the wheelhouse was the dim pink glow of the compass.

As far as I could see, when I glanced around, we were being fired upon from every direction except the dark gap of the wide harbor mouth. I kept the compass lined up with the course and assured myself that the throttle could be rammed no farther forward. We raced toward the harbor exit and, in a matter of what must have been no more than two minutes, we shot through the exit like a bullet—although to me it seemed a funereal pace.

By now, with the spray slashing over the bow, the windscreen was completely wet, and, as I didn't know where the wiper switch was, the view was totally obscured. I was steering blindly by compass alone. As we roared past the mole-heads a machine gun on each side of us fired away. Every window on the superstructure sides was shattered, but few bullets actually penetrated the inch-gauge steel hull and upperworks. The row from ricocheting bullets inside the cabins and wheelhouse was ear-shattering, even above the screaming of the propeller shafts and the roar of the engines. It was an almost paralyzing pandemonium of nerve-jangling noise, and the only thing that kept me holding onto the helm, I think, was the realization that this *bastard* Reynaud had really set us up; that he was a maniacal psychopath, and that he would probably finish Tony and me off before we reached Marseilles—and that I was going to make damn sure he didn't get either the chance or the excuse. Besides, I couldn't leave this world without making sure *Cresswell* was all right—and Nelson.

I peered out as best I could through the spray and splintered plexiglass of the windshields. The course ahead seemed to be clear. There were patches of pale moonlight here and there as clouds moved over the thin, weak scimitar of the new moon.

When the firing grew fainter I called to Tony. "Get the hand-bearing compass—it's in the navigation table drawer. Put in on the deck below my feet."

This he did quickly, keeping his head low. When he reached me he was panting hard, both with exertion and fear. I realized that I was, too. Reynaud ran, crouching, over to the starboard wheelhouse door, where he peeped aft around the bulkhead, watching for pursuers.

"What's that for?" breathed Tony as he put the compass below me.

"In case the bastards start firing again—so I can keep my head down." I bent toward him. "This sod is dangerous," I said.

Tony turned his spectacles toward me and gave me a sad grin. "The understatement of the year, old chap."

"There's a wheel-lashing lanyard in the second drawer of the navigation desk. Get it out as quietly as you can and keep it in your pocket. As soon as he goes into any compartment, lash the bas . . . but wait 'til I give the word."

"Right, got you." Tony went straight away and pulled the length of thin line, with a noose at one end, out of the drawer, all the while glancing at Reynaud, who still had his back to us, peering aft into the dark, tracer-streaked night.

I stood up straight now. It had been several minutes since the last bullet had zinged against the hull. (Tony later told me that *Aries* must have been a good two miles offshore before the firing from the harbor moles finally stopped.)

The boat was now cutting her way through the slight, smooth swell, into the blackness, with her stern well down and her bows streaming spray aft like a firehose. The sound of the seawater now drumming on the forward bulkhead of the wheelhouse was even noisier than the scream of the engines.

Suddenly Reynaud came to me. "I think we're being followed. I saw a dark shape pass in front of the harbor entrance lights."

"Bloody great," said I, as I again tried to push the throttle lever even farther forward. Reynaud's face was serious as he sidled over again toward his look-out post at the starboard door. Shortly Tony came to the wheel and told me the same thing.

"That prick has got a machine pistol onboard," I said in a low voice.

"I know," replied Tony.

"Do you know where he put it?"

"No. Do you?"

"No."

"Oh, crikey," he muttered.

"Yes."

"What?"

"Yes, oh crikey. You know what it might mean, right?"

"You don't mean . . ."

"I do indeed."

"Oh, crikey!"

"I don't trust that toe-rag any farther than I can see him."

"What'll we do?" asked Tony in a high, plaintive voice.

"I'll put this bugger on a course for . . ." I got no further. Reynaud, his back wet with spray, strode over to my side. Tony headed back to his post by the port door. I noticed that Reynaud, unlike either Tony or me, was as steady as a rock. You would have imagined he was out for a moonlight cruise along the Seine in a *bateau-mouche*.

"All right?" he asked, almost absentmindedly.

"Are you sure we've got enough fuel?" I asked, thinking 'My God, what a time to ask *that* question.'" My hands still shook as I tried to hold the helm steady.

"The tanks are full," he replied. "I told you, everything was arranged." He peered into the compass binnacle. "Have we the right course?"

"We're on course for Marseilles—northeast by north— but I think that's a mistake. Those characters back there know where you'll head for. They'll just keep on our tail until daybreak. Then we'll be for the high jump."

"What do you suggest we do?" Reynaud asked.

"Well, we should aim away from the course to France. We should head due north. That'll bring us to . . ."

I thought for a second or two, envisioning the chart I had studied before all hell had been let loose. ". . . to Cabrera, right on the southern tip of Majorca. By daylight, if we maintain full speed, we'll be within visual range of Cabrera light. We'll know by then if we're still being chased, and if we are, we can head into Spanish territorial waters, maybe even into Palma itself. They can't follow us in there."

Reynaud looked at me with his green eyes. There was a different look in them now—something of a degree of respect. Not much, but it was definitely there. He went over to the chart table, where I'd laid out the chart for the western Mediterranean. He bent over it, using the penlight I had left on the table, and studied the chart. A minute or two later he was back again. "I see what you mean," he said, straining his voice above the noise of the engines and the drumming of the spray.

"The range of the Cabrera light—that's a small island—is twenty-five miles. That means we'll pick it up after we've made a hundred thirty miles from Algiers. Let's see . . . If we stay at twenty knots all night we should just about see the light at six in the morning. How do you think the engines will hold up?"

"They are in first-class condition. How do you say—A1 at Lloyd's?"

"I wish I were at Lloyd's right now," said I under my breath. Aloud I said, "We'll have to check the lube oil every hour."

"Of course."

"And the circulating water, too. We don't want any fuck-ups on this little run, do we?"

Reynaud nodded, his face grim.

"Why don't you and Tony check the engines every hour," I went on. "You can alternate and rest in between checks. He can make the first check at midnight."

"What about you . . . Won't you be tired?"

"Oh, I'll be all right. I'm used to long hours at the helm, and I wouldn't be able to sleep anyway."

"Well, it sounds reasonable. Will you tell Tony?"

"Yes, and you check below at one, three, and five, OK?"

"OK."

"Pierre . . . What are we going to do if they catch up with us?"

"Leave that to me," replied Reynaud darkly. "You just keep the boat on course."

"Right."

All through the windless night we roared over the slight swell, showing no lights. At about two in the middle watch the clouds uncovered the moon. I suggested to Reynaud that we heave-to for a moment, so we could reduce the engine noise and try to check if we were being chased. This he agreed to, and as *Aries* wallowed away, slowly rocking this way and that, we all three stood on the bow and searched the southern horizon, straining our ears in the semi-silent night. We saw nothing, and Reynaud seemed pleased—but I noticed that he took great care never to turn his back on either Tony or me, nor to come too close to us when we were on deck.

I passed over to the port side and gazed steadily to the southeast, where a dark mass obscured the horizon. It was a rain squall, and even then a slight breeze was rising from the direction of the clouds.

"We'd better wait for this squall to pass over," I called to Tony and Reynaud.

The Frenchman rushed over to my side, then shuffled away out of arm's reach. "Where?" he asked.

I pointed to the blacker blackness in the black.

"There," I said. Then, as my eyes adjusted completely to the darkness, I forgot the threatening evil so close to me; forgot all thoughts of overpowering Reynaud, and watched the beauty of inanimate things—water and wind—turn to life. Soon the sound of the steadily increasing wind, like a huge beast drawing greater breaths, a sound sorrowful and startling at the same time, passed over *Aries* as she wallowed in the now-deepening troughs. I found myself searching with one hand, in the dark, for something to steady myself against. The sound traveled toward us across the starless space between the rain and *Aries*, passed directly above us, then ceased for a moment, just as suddenly as it had begun. As if the sea, too, had drawn an anxious breath of apprehension, a long, slow movement lifted and let down the waters under us.

Very shortly a mini-chaos was let loose on the surface of the sea. It seemed to leap out of the darkness between water and sky onto the backs of the slowly heaving swells; then it lifted upon the crests a livid opacity of foam, as if it were driving a multitude of pale ghosts before it—and the squall was upon *Aries* in a spitting, spluttering welter of rain and spray.

Aries, for a moment, remained jolt-upright, like a duchess whose bottom has been pinched by a footman. Then she suddenly lay over, away from the hard blast of the squall. Then it was that I wished we were under sail; for a sailboat, reefed down, would have laid to that wind and scooted ahead like a jack-rabbit. But all *Aries* did was shiver and shake from aerials to keel, like a felled mastodon, a great, stupid ox, a grounded leviathan.

By this time we were all three wet through with spray and rain, but although Tony retreated to the wheelhouse, Reynaud and I stayed out on deck—awed, possibly, by the holiness of what was happening. I swallowed mouthfuls of cool water, which the wind drove at my face. Everywhere around *Aries* water streamed and swept in cataracts lashed ragged as they shot to leeward. It was as if half the sky had fallen down upon us, and half the sea were rising up to meet it.

The awesome deluge seemed to last forever. Then, just as it all became unbearable, and I started to haul myself along the handrail to the wheelhouse, it stopped. It stopped instantly. All became quiet except for the low mumble of the idling engines. In a matter of a second it was as if the squall had never been, except for a diminishing excitement—a slight agitation on the moonlit faces of the swells. In a moment the natural forces of the world had abandoned us once more to the petty details of human existence; we were again deprived of the revelation of grandeur, released from unthinking, uncaring eternal beauty, and cast down again into our own private pits of human anxiety.

For a few moments we had been, all three of us, bound together inexorably. It was as if we had become one in some ineffable, inexpressible way. It was as if the universe had judged us and found us wanting.

Halfway to the wheelhouse door I stopped in the sudden silence and stared again at the southern edge of the black blanket of the night sky. Three lights appeared on the horizon. My heart jolted and I focused intently on the lights until I discerned that they were, in fact, three low stars, leaping and falling between the crests of the waves. Then I turned again and said to Reynaud, who still stood, sodden, looking south, "I may be wrong, but I think there's something there." I thought it just as well to keep him worried.

He started, surprised, and leaned forward to stare more intently. "Are you sure? *Vous êtes sûr?*"

"No, I'm not, but I thought I saw something just now, way out over the horizon, more to the southeast. It could be that they're searching for us on the track to Marseilles . . . But look, you're wet through—why don't you go down to the engine room and dry out."

Reynaud merely grunted at this, and then said, "Let's get going."

"OK, but you really ought to get inside the wheelhouse so you don't dry out in the headwind."

I went into the wheelhouse. Tony was standing by the navigation table. I winked at him—a mere flicker of an eyelid. He gave no response. I was not certain that he had seen me in the dull glow of the pink compass light, but I imagined that I saw a slight movement of his body.

With Reynaud close behind, watching me, I returned to the helm, pushed the engine gear lever forward, and slowly opened up the throttle. The boat moved slowly at first; then, as the speed increased, her stern lowered, her bow arose, and she was leaping again into the blackness of the night like a sprung hare. Now that the squall had disturbed the sea, her bows butted and battered, rammed and thundered over and upon the crests of the wakened seas. The hull gave off a rumbling sound to accompany the screaming whine of the engines. Once in a while a great dollop of green water, with a spitting zizz of spray, sped over the bow. We were moving at speed now, and I stared through the windscreen between douses of water. The sea now looked as if it had picked up its baggage and was moving swiftly to the star-spangled edges of the world. Even the stars themselves—the ones low down on the horizon—seemed to be marching with *Aries*, trying to race her toward our goal—or our doom.

All through the night we continued at full speed, crashing and bashing our way toward Polaris through sudden patches of pale silver moonlight reflected off the surface of the liverish sea-swells.

Toward four-thirty I picked up the loom of Cabrera light. I asked Reynaud to relieve me at the wheel while I checked our position with the hand-bearing compass. I marked the position on the chart. Then, as I returned to the helm, I glanced at Tony and nodded toward the chart. He nodded back at me and strolled over to the chart table. There I had scrawled "5 a.m."

At four-fifty we could see the light itself quite clearly. Minutes later Reynaud went down to check the engines. They were in a compartment abaft and below the wheelhouse, and reached by opening up two hatches. As soon as Reynaud had gone, I shouted at Tony, *"Now!"*

He raced—almost fell—down the short ladder at the after end of the wheelhouse, and I tumbled down after him. We both grabbed the engine compartment hatches and slammed them shut. By now Tony was lying right across both hatches.

"The lanyard," I screamed at him. He fumbled in his pocket and passed it to me. "Roll over," I shouted.

I passed the lanyard again and again through the two ring handles of the hatches, securely lashing them together. "Out of the way," I shouted. "He might have the bloody gun down there!"

Tony shot forward on his belly away from the hatches. I raced to the helm and put the engines into neutral, then ran to the small workshop at the after end of the superstructure and searched for a suitable metal bar. I found a steel wire-splicing fid, about a foot long. I hared back to the lower midships passage, where Tony was standing, shaking, and where we could hear and see Reynaud pounding on the underside of the hatches, trying to force them open.

"I don't think the gun's down there, old chap," said Tony in a high treble, staring at the hatches mournfully.

"Hang on the slack there, mate—let's make sure that bugger . . ." I stood on one side of the hatch, and, with the point of the fid, lifted the ring handles and slid the fid through them, all the while hearing Reynaud's bellowing below. "Get me something heavy to knock this in with," I said.

Tony soon returned with a small grapnel, and with it I rammed the fid home so that it wedged well and true into the brass rings.

We stood back, looking stupidly at each other for a minute, until Tony grinned. "Now what?" he panted.

"Now we find that bleedin' gun, mate! Before we do anything else . . . even if we have to rip this bloody boat apart."

Even as I spoke the engines died. There was a silence for a minute, until Reynaud shouted, "If you let me out of here I will pay you *ten thousand dollars!*"

"Where's the machine-gun?" I shouted back at him.

"What are you talking about?" he replied, in French.

"You know bloody well you kept the gun the soldier gave you. You don't come out of there until you tell me where it is."

"I have it down here," he replied, "and if you do not let me out I will shoot my way out . . ."

"You're a lying bastard!"

"He'd have shot his way out by now," murmured Tony, grabbing the handrail of the ladder to steady himself as the boat pitched.

"You stay here." I handed Tony a heavy fire extinguisher which had been stowed in a bracket in the passage. "If that son-of-a-bitch starts to force the hatch open, crown him. I'm off to find that flamin' gun."

It took me all of twenty minutes to discover the machine-pistol where Reynaud had hidden it, below the mattress in the owner's cabin. By the time I found it I had turned the cabins and lockers of *Aries* into a shambles. I returned to Tony triumphant.

"How does this bugger work?" I asked him in a whisper as I handed the weapon over.

"Let's have a look—I did a weapons course in the R.A.F. when I was . . ."

"Well, figure it out," I hissed. Then, in a louder voice I said, "If Reynaud doesn't put the engines in running order, we'll shoot the sod."

I called to Reynaud through the hatch: "You should have found a better hiding place for the gun! I have it now. If you don't have those engines going within five minutes I'll come down there and put you into a hospital for the rest of your days!"

"*Merde!*" was the muffled reply.

"You've got five minutes," I said.

I sped aft again to the workshop and checked the outboard engine I had seen stowed there. It was an Evinrude twenty-five-horsepower, almost brand new. Two gasoline tanks under the bench were almost full. I was on my way back to the wheelhouse when Reynaud's muffled voice, in a croak, told us that we could start the engines again.

By the time *Aries* was about ten miles off Cabrera Island, Tony had rigged the outboard motor on the ship's launch. I hove *Aries* to and helped Tony lower the launch over the stern. We threw our seabags down into the bobbing boat.

"We can't leave him down there," said Tony. "The boat might drift onto the shore . . . onto the rocks."

"He's not staying down there. Here, see that other dinghy over on the port side?"

Tony stared toward it.

"Get a chisel and a hammer and knock a big hole in it," I said.

As Tony went around to the workshop I headed for the roof of the wheelhouse, where a self-inflating life-raft was stowed in a fiberglass container. I pulled the rip-cord. The round box opened immediately. Compressed air was automatically pumped into the life-raft. I took out my clasp knife and slashed it right through all four compartments. The air from the bottle gushed out into the early morning. I gazed around, toward Cabrera Island, which stood, stark and black, against the blue-gray background of the Majorcan mountains.

I went below again. "Reynaud!"

His muffled voice arose from below the engine hatch. "*Quoi?*"

"I'm going to open the hatch. If you come on deck before ten minutes are up you will be shot! After that you can do what you like!"

I could almost see the hatred rising up through the hatch. He did not reply.

"Did you hear me?" I insisted.

"*Oui*," came the mumble.

I shouted to Tony to start the outboard engine. He disappeared over the stern. I untied the lanyard line on the hatch handles and, aiming the machine-pistol at the hatch, I knocked out the fid. It was only then that I realized that Tony had not shown me how to operate the gun . . .

On my way through the wheelhouse I grabbed the two engine-room fire-extinguisher levers and yanked them down. There was a sudden hiss and a muted yell from down below. I did not wait for Reynaud. Clutching the machine-pistol I raced aft, handed the gun down to Tony, and jumped into the launch. Quickly, without saying a word, we cast off the launch from its bridles and headed toward Cabrera Island.

As the distance between the bouncing launch and the wallowing *Aries* increased to fifty . . . eighty . . . one hundred yards, Tony shouted, "Are you sure he can't run us down?"

"No chance," I shouted back. "It'll take at least an hour for the carbon-tetrachloride to clear the engine room; the gas sniffers won't release the starting solenoids until it's all gone."

I turned and stared at *Aries*. She was wallowing away. Reynaud was out on deck, holding the guard-rails, staring back at us. Suddenly he started for the wrecked dinghy on the port side. As I watched him, and as the launch mounted the tops of the swells, I spied a low gray shape, far away on the southern edge of the sea. It was making toward *Aries*.

We rounded the southeastern point of Cabrera Island, close inshore, so we could run in if *Aries* should start to move toward us. I saw the low gunboat—for that is what she was—heave-to close to *Aries*. I slowed down for a few minutes and watched as the gunboat lowered a launch and sent it toward *Aries*, all the while describing the scene to Tony, whose eyesight was very restricted.

"Well, whatever that gunboat is, that's that!" I said, as I increased speed and headed for the port of Palma, twenty miles or so away.

"What shall we say in Palma?" asked Tony.

"Sweet bugger-all," I said, as I threw the machine-pistol into the sea. "If anyone asks, we've been out fishing and lost our fishing gear."

We arrived in the harbor mid-afternoon and motored into the Palma Yacht Club, where we tied up the launch. Toting our seabags we strolled into the club buildings as if we had been lifelong members. We showered in the yacht club, then, on the strength of Tony's money, we had a very tasty fish lunch in the small upstairs restaurant just outside the club gates. We visited a couple of bars, and by evening we were safely onboard the steamer ferry to Ibiza, where we arrived, safe and *almost* sound, the next morning.

Soon we were on the town quay in the early-morning sunshine, and there was dear old *Cresswell*, sitting as pretty as a picture next to her ugly-duckling friend *Bellerophon*.

As we approached *Cresswell* Nelson must have heard my voice, even though Tony and I were conversing in conspiratorial tones. Nelson had hobbled up the companionway ladder and was now on the poop, wagging his old tail and barking gruffly. Then, as I grabbed the top of the rudder to clamber onboard, Sissie's frizzy hair and apple-red cheeks appeared over the hatch coaming.

"Yoo-hoo, *dahling!* Have your brekky ready in a jiffy. *Say,* you *do* look as if you've had a simply *spiffing* time!"

"I've just earned the easiest fifty dollars I've ever earned," I said, as I dumped my bag on my berth.

"How *naice!*"

Tony and I had agreed to keep quiet about the events which had ended so fortunately for us. I told Sissie the version of the story we had decided upon—that *Aries* had been sailing for Marseilles, and that it had been arranged that we would leave her in Majorca, as we didn't get on too well with the owner!

"Oh, *deah*," she said, placing a china plate of hot bacon in front of me. "Well, nevah mind; we still have those awf'ly *supah* people next door in *Bellerophon* . . . they'll be heah for a few days."

"That's another thing, Sissie," I mumbled in between chewing the bacon. "You know, in ancient Greek mythology, Bellerophon was given the seemingly impossible task, by Zeus, the head bloke, of killing the Chimera . . . "

"The *Chimera?* Ai say, how *awf'ly* exciting!" Sissie exclaimed, setting a mug of steaming tea before me. "What on earth was *thet?*"

"It was a sort of beast—-one third lion, one third goat, and one third dragon."

Sissie sat down opposite me, on the starboard berth. "Ai *say*, how *did* he manage?"

"He got the flying horse, Pegasus, to give him a hand, and between them they knocked off the old Chimera. They sort of wore the monster out. But then old Bellerophon got too big for his boots and tried to ride Pegasus to the throne of the gods on Mount Olympus. The chief bloke, Zeus, in anger, caused Pegasus to throw Bellerophon to the ground, and after that Bellerophon wandered alone, crippled, blind, and humiliated."

I lit a cigarette while Sissie looked at me in puzzlement, obviously wondering what my wild Welsh mind was getting at. "So come on, girl, after breakfast we'll get ready to sail to Formentera."

"What . . . and leave these *awf'ly* naice people behind?"

"Leave *Bellerophon* behind," I replied.

"Why, who do you think you are, Pegasus?"

"No, I'm the Chimera. One third lion—that's for the Royal Navy; one third goat—that's for me; and one third dragon—that's for Wales . . . the old *draig a goch*. D'you see? I'm the beast that Bellerophon wore out so it died. Now let's get away from *Bellerophon* so that *she* doesn't have to wander around crippled, blind, and humiliated!"

By two o'clock *Cresswell* was all set to sail, and we made our farewells to Tony the Specs and his charming sister Billie.

" 'Bye, Sissie! 'Bye, Tristan—and thanks again for the side trip," shouted Tony as we pulled away from the jetty. "I haven't enjoyed myself so much in years!"

"Yes," I called back. "We must do it again sometime!"

By evening *Cresswell* was nestled cozily in the tiny, pretty little port on the north side of the island of Formentera. I knew that *Bellerophon* was sailing for Malta in a few days, and so if any of Reynaud's friends spotted her, it wouldn't be in Ibiza or anywhere near *Cresswell*, and that made me feel more easy.

Over the course of the next few years, in places as far apart as New York and Cape Town, from people as widely different as fishermen, artists, newsmen, yachtsmen, and bartenders, I pieced together what I think were some of the events which followed the episode described in this chapter.

The gunboat which approached *Aries* was Algerian. Reynaud was arrested and the boat was seized and taken back to Algiers. What happened to Reynaud during the next two years is not quite clear; no one I met seemed to know. But in 1967 he was rumored to have been one of the men involved in the kidnaping of Moise Tshombe, the exiled Katangan leader from the Congo, when Tshombe's plane, which had left a Spanish airfield, was hijacked and diverted to Algiers.

I was also told that his real name was not Reynaud, and that he had been quite prominent in the O.A.S., the French secret anti-Algerian-independence organization, at least until I knew him. I have never figured out why he should have changed sides, which evidently he did, to have been involved in the Tshombe affair.

Tshombe was first jailed, then kept incommunicado until his death in Algeria in 1969. He was living on borrowed time in any case; he had already been sentenced to death in his own country, *in absentia*.

"What about *Aries*," asked Sissie that evening.

"Named after a ram," I replied.

"What did Aries do?"

"He got fleeced," I said, as I prepared to write a note to Shiner Wright. It was the first letter in an exchange of correspondence to and from all parts of the globe, which continues to this day.

But I, Ulysses,
Sitting on the warm steps,
Looking over the valley,
All day long, have seen,
Without pain, without labour,
Sometimes a wild-hair'd Maenad;
Sometimes a Faun with torches;
And sometimes, for a moment,
Passing through the dark stems,
Flowing rob'd—the belov'd,
The desir'd, the divine,
Belov'd Iacchus

Ah, cool night-wind, tremulous stars!
Ah, glimmering water—
Fitful earth-murmur—
Dreaming woods!
Ah, golden-hair'd, strangely smiling Goddess,
And thou, prov'd, much enduring,
Wave-toss'd Wanderer!
Who can stand still?
Ye fade, ye swim, ye waver before me.
The cup again!

Faster, faster,
O Circe, Goddess,
Let the wild, thronging train,
The bright procession
Of eddying forms,
Sweep through my soul!

"The Strayed Reveller to Ulysses"
—Matthew Arnold

5

Strayed Revellers

APART FROM a pair of tiny, open fishing boats, and the ferry which arrived from Ibiza thrice daily, *Cresswell* was the only vessel in Formentera harbor. Apart from the chores on the boat, being talked at by Sissie, writing long-overdue letters, and shopping at the dim little store in the tiny hamlet by the port, the only thing to do was sit and look at the scenery.

Formentera harbor had two rather short, low moles. Onboard the boat, gazing over the cockpit coaming, it was almost the same as being at sea in dead calm water, only the water there was so shallow and clear and clean that we could watch shoals of angelfish and mullet swimming around over the rocky bottom, and see our anchor—set out broadside to hold the boat off the wall in case of a westerly blow—plainly, even though it was under twenty feet of diaphanous, glassy seawater.

The early-morning ferry arrived at about dawn. Her rumbling, as her propellers churned up the harbor, and the excited voices of passengers, greeters, and crew woke Sissie and me, but the noises were all good-natured, and so were we. Formentera harbor was so remote and quiet that the three daily arrivals and departures of little knots of humanity were casual comforts, and we did not resent them one bit. By the time Sissie had the tea brewed, and the bacon and eggs on a hot plate, I was usually on deck to watch the black-clad peasant women with their gravely courteous

71

husbands and their broods of children, all spic-and-span; and their baskets and boxes, cartons and sacks, bundles and buckets, all to-ing and fro-ing and chatting away in their peculiar brand of the Catalan language.

The Formenterans appeared to be among the healthiest folk I have ever seen, and it's a fact that at the far southern end of the island there was a small hamlet, near Cape Berberia, where there were, out of a population of around 200, thirty-odd persons over the age of 100 years. It was not a rare thing to see one of the ancient men, small and sunburned, dressed all in black, scrambling up the 500-foot-high cliffs of the cape as sure-footed and agile as a goat—with a full-sized turtle, weighing 100 pounds or more, slung over his shoulders.

I have seen several places like this where people live long and die happy. I have often thought about the reason for this. Is it diet? Is it something in the water? Is it something inherited? After having observed these folk in places as far apart as Turkey and Bolivia, I conclude that there are a few traits these ancients have in common: They live without haste. They have just enough for their own needs, and they want no more. They are usually jealous of what they have, but they do not covet. Neither do they seem to resent growing old. In the main they accept it as part of life, but not with sorrow, because another thing the long-lived simple folk have in common the world over is a strong faith in the hereafter. I know there are atheists who live to a ripe old age, but I suspect that's because, naturally, they're scared of a void. Anyway, you should be rich to be an atheist. Demonstrative lack of real faith usually assuages a tremendous guilt for unearned blessings.

Formentera harbor, once the peasant families and the one or two bead-bedecked hippies, lugging their worry-bags over their shoulders, had cleared out of the way, and Sissie had clomped off to buy some eggs or to swim off the nearby beach, was a haven of peace. All across the northern horizon the hills and mountains of Ibiza swept from east to west, a vast panorama of altering shades above the continually changing grays and greens and blues of the sea.

The dawns broke, sending fiery red splashes over a nickel, leaden sea. Then the black smudges to the north turned to hills, golden toward the east; and as the sun revealed its splendor and rose along God's arc, the black shadows on the western slopes were rendered to the diminishing stars. By noon the colors of the hills across the horizon were stark smudges of variegated hues, from gold to purple to vermilion, as if some celestial painter were using Ibiza as a palette. As the afternoon passed, the undulating uplands changed to viridescent emerald, to cyan blue, to aquamarine, turquoise, and lapis lazuli; and as the sun sank below the diamond-colored sea in the west, the island became a line of indigo humps, decorated with twinkling necklaces of light. Fifteen miles away, at the western end of Ibiza, the starkly sharp 1000-foot-high rock of Es Vedra transformed its color from black to brown to beige to gold, until the sun had taken its leave, on its way to greet smoking cities and coral islands. Then, as suddenly as if it had disappeared behind a curtain, Es Vedra was gone, leaving behind only the stabbing beam of its lighthouse.

During the day, the whole time that *Cresswell* was in Formentera, Nelson stayed on the seawall, either hobbling to and fro, or lying on a fishing net in the shade. The only times he came onboard was when he saw Sissie going ashore. Then he limped around, sniffing, checking that she had performed her duties well and true, until she returned, when he took off again. His only other activities were when he accompanied me to the small, dark bar of the tiny hotel near the port for a beer or two with the small, dark fishermen. Whenever Sissie and I went ashore together (which was very rarely) Nelson stayed onboard to guard the boat. He was very jealous of this privilege—even more than he was jealous of Sissie.

For the first three days in Formentera I busied myself touching up the paintwork topsides and cleaning out the engine compartment for the first time in two years or so. The neglect hadn't been a matter of slackness on my part. It was simply that I had been on the move continuously since the engine had been installed; either in *Cresswell* or delivering other people's boats—or the weather had been far too hot for working in a close, confined space. Now, in November, it was fairly cool and ideal for working below. By the time I had finished putting two coats of white gloss paint in the bilge, it looked so clean that I was tempted to leave the hatches open, in case anyone came onboard, so I could show off. But the problem with cleaning and painting one compartment is that it makes the rest of the boat look shabby, so I diverted Sissie away from the beach in the afternoons to the main cabin, where I persuaded her to slap two coats of white gloss on those bilges, too. So after a week in Formentera *Cresswell*, while she could never pretend to be a showboat, looked fairly presentable. To my satisfaction and Sissie's utter disgust, the last pieces of seal blubber from the Arctic were routed out from below the galley stove and thrown to the angelfish, while Nelson looked on and wagged his tail.

To celebrate *Cresswell*'s refurbishing I invited Sissie to join me in a hike to San Francisco Javier, the main hamlet of the island, in the center of its wind-swept plateau. This suited Sissie; she loved hiking. "Simply awf'ly *delaightful!*" she crowed. So, leaving Nelson a plate of burgoo onboard, and with Sissie in her hiking gear (knee-length khaki shorts, ditchdigger's brogues, long black woolen stockings, a shabby brown raincoat with the belt left dangling, and a sort of Rhodesian infantryman's hat perched on top of her electrically frizzy hair), we set off, with Sissie singing "Keep right on to the end of the road" at the top of her voice, and me trying to lag behind her as we passed through the hamlet, hoping that the fishermen would not think she was with me.

We wended our way along the narrow winding road, over the undulating, rocky hills, for about five miles, enjoying the air and the freedom from care. We passed hundreds of tiny, stone-walled fields and a couple of dozen gray, weather-beaten stone windmills. A few stunted, wind-sculpted trees leaned drunkenly on the horizon and in the *arroyos*. It took us about two hours to reach the main hamlet; not because Sissie was a slow walker—far from it—but because she was continually stopping and chattering away about the view. "Awf'ly *naice*," and "*Supah* . . . Look, dahling, ovah *theah*." She clambered over low stone walls to scamper fifty yards into a field to sniff a flower or to pet a kid goat.

"If you get any goat shit on your boots, don't take it onboard," I admonished her as she took hold of my sailing jerkin. "We've done enough cleaning this week."

"Such *absolutely* sweet little deahs!"

"We ought to nick one on the way back and roast the bugger."

Sissie slapped my arm lightly and turned her Saxon-blue eyes on me, like a battleship's guns. "Oh, *dahling*, you wouldn't. They're so *awf'ly* charming."

"No, 'course I wouldn't, but not because of that. Only because the bloke that owns them probably has nothing else."

Finally we reached San Francisco Javier and its one small hotel-bar, the "Fonda Alonzo." Apart from the *fonda* the hamlet consisted of only about twenty small cottages, whitewashed in the Balearic style.

We strolled into the bar, Sissie shyly, I thirstily, and found Alonzo sitting behind the bar, staring into space. Had he been literate he would have been reading. As it was, he was remembering, which is probably almost as rewarding as reading, and much cheaper.

Alonzo stood up. He was a burly man of about forty-five, with the jet-black hair and eyes and the clear but ruddy complexion which are common on the islands. He wore an open black waistcoat over an off-white collarless shirt, and black, baggy pants. On his feet were straw sandals. Most of the islanders wore clothes made by local women; Alonzo's, no doubt, were made by his diminutive wife, who was one of the hardest-working, harassed individuals I have ever seen anywhere.

Alonzo was a semi-millionaire—in *dollars*—as he had sold off various lots of inherited land to foreign real-estate investors. All the land was earth-thin and rocky, fit only for olive trees and goats. There was no water on the island— only salt- and rainwater—but the beauty of the vistas had fooled the foreigners and they had eagerly plonked down their money in pounds, francs, kronor, guilders, dollars, and lire. Alonzo had it all stashed away in clay pots in the bar cellar. He couldn't speak a word of anything but the obscure and excruciating-sounding Formenteran dialect of Catalan, which very few foreigners could ever hope to learn, so no blame could be laid to Alonzo for the foolish waste of money. The smart city-boys and girls had come to this remote, beautiful island, so near to an up-and-coming tourist Mecca, and they had, they thought, taken this ignorant, stupid-looking clodhopper and paid a song for prime beachfront property. They'd been doing it for years. The land lots were still there, as arid and rocky as ever. The goats still grazed on them and the sun still beat down on them and the blue Mediterranean lapped their golden-rock shores—and Alonzo was still there in his fonda. All the money was in the cellar, and the smart people were all back in their stuffy offices in smoky cities. So who took who? I am quite sure that, at that time at least, Alonzo had no idea of what the money represented. You might just as well have swapped him a computer for his wooden plow and sandals. It would have been all the same to Alonzo. He would have stored the computer in the cellar, too.

But Alonzo had been a great friend of Deaf Henry Gillon and Closet the Aussie, the skipper and crew of the good ship *Fanny Adams*, whose rusting iron keel was now the home of a thousand angelfish on the bottom of Formentera harbor. Anyone who was a friend of that pair was my friend, too. (See *Saga of a Wayward Sailor*.)

At first Alonzo, astonished at Sissie's appearance, stared at her for a moment; then he turned to me, flashing his white teeth. His eyebrows shot up. *"Hola, Señor Tree-stan! Cómo estás?"*

Alonzo's tiny, gypsy-dark wife, barefoot, dressed all in black, with a shawl thrown over her head, ran swiftly through the bar, carrying a basket of laundry about twice her size. Alonzo, while seemingly faithful to his wife, had a sharp eye for any foreign female between the ages of fourteen and ninety. He seemed to melt before their holy presences. Before other men and the island women he was big, healthy, strapping and strong—a man to be reckoned with. Before foreign females he was a helpless mass.

"Alonzo! How's business?"

"Oh, very good. I still have two guests in the hotel . . ." Alonzo's eyes turned toward the ceiling. "They're coming down. Of course the *señora* has been here for some time. She is a book writer. But now we have a man . . . I think he's a German or something, and . . ." Alonzo stuck out his already-bulging chest, "and he's an artist, a *painter!*"

Alonzo grabbed my shoulder and gently led me toward the one rough wooden table and bench on the bare concrete floor of the bar. Then he turned to Sissie, gleamed his white teeth at her, and with a half-bow swept his hand down in front of him toward a chair—the only one—-which he was already dusting with his other hand.

Just as Sissie, almost fainting at Alonzo's genuine good manners, sat down, through the low front door of the bar walked two figures. The first, when it was in the shade, turned out to be a woman. At a wild guess I would say she was about sixty. She was slender, frail, and very short—no more than five feet. Her hair was *blue* and cut in a pageboy style, as was the rage in the twenties. She had a tiny, bird-like face, which was plastered with powder over her deep suntan. It made her look as if she'd dipped her face in a flour bag. On her cheeks were two daubs of thick pink rouge, and her thin lips were painted with scarlet lipstick in a Cupid's bow. She wore a shiny satin dress, light blue, the waist of which was about where her hips would have been if she'd had any, but with a skirt shorter than the then-popular mini-skirts. Below this her legs were clad in beige stockings, and she was shod in silver shoes, the heels of which were at least three inches high. Around her neck, which had as many folds as my mainsail, she was decorated with about a dozen strings of pearls. She looked like the oldest teenager alive.

Her movements were sudden and jerky, as if she were under electric-shock treatment, and her face, with teeth protruding from her lips as if they were out to dry, carried an expression that said she had just remembered something, but couldn't think what it was.

Alonzo, beaming, introduced Sissie and me. "Meess Pomeroy."

Her voice was just like a bird twittering, and she ran all her words one into the other. "Ohgoodnessgracious-English? Pleasedtomeetyoul'msure," she chirped. It sounded like a metal spatula being dragged quickly, under great pressure, across a frying pan.

When I had recovered from the shock of this apparition I realized that something was blocking the sunlight from the door and making the bar even darker than usual. I looked toward the obstruction, and there, seeming to fill a good quarter of the area in the room, was one of the biggest people I have ever come across. At first I thought it was a yeti, because of the shaggy long hair, but when my eyes became accustomed to the gloomy shadow that the figure cast, I discerned that it was, in fact, first of all human, and then—a man.

Alonzo ran behind the bar. The huge man—he was at least seven and a half feet tall, with shoulders about three feet wide—made for Sissie. With each footstep the whole bar vibrated. He stood to attention before the Dragon of Devon and bowed from the waist. "Madam," he said in thick English, "I am Sven Knutsen—at your service, charming lady!"

Sissie looked as if she was about to have kittens. The giant turned to me, took my proffered hand with what seemed to be a side of beef, and wrung it as if it were a dishcloth. Even Sissie winced at my pain.

Sven's hair was the blondest of blond. It was almost albino. It fell in long white strands from the top of his head all the way down to the small of his back. It covered most of his face, so that it was difficult to see his small, button nose and his bloodshot, pale blue eyes. Around his neck he wore a chain of shields, and over his shoulders was thrown an Ibizan poncho of flannel, with stripes of a hundred different shades. Below the poncho, which drooped fore and aft, his pants were so streaked with multicolored paint that it was impossible to see of what material they were made. His huge feet were bare and dirt-encrusted. Studying them during the ensuing conversation I found myself somewhat surprised, upon counting the toes, to see that he had the usual complement of five on each. Again, making a wild guess at age, I would say he was around forty.

Suddenly, after staring at me intently in silence for a full half-minute, he turned and thudded over to the bar, behind which Alonzo was still smirking at the two foreign females as if he were imagining all kinds of exotic sexual delights.

Miss Pomeroy was smiling at me, slyly, with her Cupid's bow.

"You're a writer, Miss Pomeroy?" I enquired civilly.

"Ohyesbutonlyforchildren," she giggled. I found that she giggled after almost everything she said. It seemed to me that she would have giggled after declaiming a church-yard elegy.

"Have you had anything published?" asked Sissie

Miss Pomeroy glanced nervously at Sissie. "Ohno-notyet . . . I'mhalfwaythroughmyfirstbookatthemoment." She giggled again.

"How long have you been at it?" I asked gently.

"OnlythreeyearsandIshouldhaveitfinishednextyear." Another giggle. Her accent was posh English, but with Northern undertones. Charlotte Brontë probably had the same accent.

"Really?" said I. "How did you get into that line of business?"

"OhIwasonceEnidBlyton'ssecretarybutonlyforthree weeks." Giggle.

By this time Sven had collected four bottles of the rough house-wine from Alonzo, and scrawled his name and four chalk strokes on the slate behind the bar. He turned and thudded over to our table. As he walked, he thrust one shoulder at a time ahead of him, as if he were forcing his way through thick, head-high undergrowth. His roll reminded me of a destroyer in a full gale.

Sven slammed the bottles down on the table and bent his head over until it almost collided with the bottles. Then he reached over to Sissie, gently took her hand, raised it to his lips, and gave it a great, slobbering kiss. "For you, charming English lady, nothing but the best is good enough," he murmured. His hair had fallen over his face. He looked like a giant, insane polar bear. Sissie almost turned liquid.

Alonzo set four (for once) clean glasses on the table. He reached for a wine bottle, but Sven was at it before him. With a hand like a gorilla he splashed the thick, dark-red, bitter plonk into the glasses without pausing between pouring, so that wine ran all over the table. One stream trickled onto Sissie's khaki hiking shorts and she pushed herself back quickly.

Sven thrust himself upright and reached over toward Sissie. "My dear charming English lady, do please accept my most humble apologies . . ."

"Oh, it's *quaite* all right." Sissie smiled bravely at the giant.

"But please let me . . ." A hand came from under the poncho, bearing a grubby, paint-flecked, once-white handkerchief.

"Oh, no, I *assure* you, Sven," Sissie blushed, "it's *eb*solutely all right. I assure you, I *really*, honestly *do!*"

Sven sat down, grabbed a glass of wine, and swallowed it in three gulps. He refilled his glass, then looked at me as if nothing at all untoward had ever occurred in this world or any other.

"You met Miss Pomeroy?" he asked in a flat voice.

"YesMisterJonesandIhavejustbeenhavingalittlechat," giggled Miss P.

The giant turned to the tiny woman at his side. Slowly, thickly, he said, "Shut up. I didn't ask you. In bed you talk. At the table you shut up."

"Yesdearohmy!" Giggle.

The giant refilled his glass again and drank the wine. Actually he didn't drink; he literally *poured* the stuff into his gullet.

"Hey, Englishman," he bellowed at me, "you know Copenhagen?"

"Well, I've been there a few times, years ago. To tell you the truth I can't remember much about it," I said casually.

"You don't remember Copenhagen? What are you, stupid?"

"I've told you, I don't remember it much . . ."

"You sailing?" Sven bawled, as the two women sat paralyzed.

"Yeah."

"How long you been sailing?"

"Oh, a couple of years."

"Where you been?"

"Here and there . . ."

"Here and there," he mumbled to himself. "Here and there? Here and there? Where the fuck you *been?*"

"I told you. Here and there." I took a sip of the most vinegary wine south of the Pyrenees. I was astonished at how steady my hand was, though inside I was raging and trembling at the same time.

"You never sailed into Copenhagen?"

"As I told you, I've been there a couple of times."

"It's the Paris of the North!" he bellowed at the top of his voice. "We got everything there. We make the finest pottery, we make the best furniture, the best paintings, the best of anything—the best in the world!"

"Your marine diesel engines aren't bad, either," I said, quietly, as Sven gulped down another glass of wine.

"Engines? Engines?" He poured another glass and drank it. Then he grabbed another bottle and drank a third of it from the neck. He leaned his head between his hands, with his elbows on the table. "What about the fuckin' Royal Palace?"

"I saw the town hall on the main square."

There was silence for a full minute, except for Sven gurgling down another third of the bottle. By now a small crowd of locals had gathered at the door of the bar to watch the strange foreigners. Fascinated, they inspected us as carefully as scientists would some new-found biological specimens.

Sven hammered the bottle down on the table. He looked at me. His eyes closed to mere slits behind the mop of blond hair. He saw me watching the crowd at the door. He reached over with his huge mitt, grabbed a glass and, without turning to aim, flung it at the crowd. The dozen or so people, mostly children and youths, scattered in retreat.

"Hey, Alonzo!" Sven shouted. Alonzo ran from behind the bar, trembling, but still as humble as ever. The Dane reached into his pocket, brought out a dirty fifty-peseta note, and thrust it into Alonzo's hand. "For the glass," he said in English. Alonzo nodded and smiled anxiously. He took the note with a shaking hand and put it in his pocket.

The Dane turned to me again. "Hey, Englishman," he snarled, "you know anything about painting?"

"Well," I replied quietly, "Sissie and I have just finished painting the insides of our boat." I looked at Sissie and grinned. "Haven't we?"

Sissie was too frightened to reply. She merely nodded with a weak smile.

The giant's eyes almost popped out of his head. He choked on the wine he was swallowing, crashed the bottle down, and glared at me. He wiped the back of a huge fist across his lips, belched, and scoffed. "Huggh!" He banged his fist on the table. The bottles and glasses jumped. "Engelsman, you don't know a damned thing. You don't know one fuckin' *thing*."

Both Sissie and Miss Pomeroy were holding onto their glasses and staring at the Dane, like rabbits hypnotized by a cobra. He had their full attention now, just as a crying, spoiled child would have his mother's.

Again he stared at me. "The base of religion, that's what art is. Look at them—look at the Buddhists, the Christians, the Jews, the Catholics—look at any of them!" he shouted. The crowd had gathered at the door again to see the show.

"You know when religion started to die?" Sven slammed another bottle down. "You know?"

"About the time of the Vikings, wasn't it?" I said.

"Shut up. I'm serious, Englishman." He took another gulp. "You know when the faith started to die?"

"No idea."

"Of course not. Well, I'll tell you. It was when they discovered *perspective*." He brought his fist down on the table with each syllable as he repeated in a loud roar, "PER . . .SPEC . . .TIVE!" His voice dropped, almost to a low moan. "Perspective—bullshit!" He almost spat the words out. He grabbed yet another bottle and gulped again.

"You know what we do?" he shouted. "All of us, from Giacco to Picasso, from Ma Yuan to Hokusai?"

I shook my head.

"We express . . . aspirations. That's what we do! We express the whole of human experience, the whole of philosophy!" He slugged at the bottle again, slammed it down, and shouted, "*Alonzo!*"

Alonzo ran to the table and stood trembling at attention. Sven laid a huge arm across tiny Miss Pomeroy's shoulders. It seemed as if it would compress her frail body into one of her silver shoes. "Tell this idiot to go upstairs and fetch my latest painting." He poked a massive thumb at me. "He's buying it."

Alonzo sped away to do as he was bid. Sissie started to say, "But Tristan doesn't have any . . ."

"Shut up!" the giant roared. I grinned at Sissie, who was almost in tears.

"That's all right, Sissie," I said. "We can have a look, anyway."

About three minutes later, with the mad Dane still ranting and raving and slamming the table, Alonzo returned carrying a framed canvas, about three feet long and two feet wide. Smiling now, like a pleased child, Sven took the canvas and held it in front of him for us to see.

Sissie's eyes bulged out. I looked at the canvas and could barely stop myself from laughing. There, on an otherwise completely empty canvas, were two small splashes of red paint in one corner. It was as if the giant had dipped a small paintbrush into vermilion paint, flicked the hairs of the brush at the canvas, and quit.

Sven beamed through his hair. Suddenly he flung his arms out to both sides violently, and with a crash he fell forward, his head thumping the table. He gave a great snore, like a dinosaur in pain.

I stood up. "Well, that's that," I said. "Sissie, if you want to catch the last ferry over to Ibiza we'd better start walking back to the port."

Miss Pomeroy was weeping bitterly. Sissie looked at me. Great dollops of tears fell down her rosy cheeks. "Ai'm certainly not going to leave *deah* Miss Pomeroy in the hands of thet . . . thet . . . *brute!*"

"Well, take her with you, then. She's a big girl now."

"Why don't you come to Ibiza with me, Miss Pomeroy?" Sissie said.

The tiny body shook; then, with her make-up streaked down her face and tears descending onto her baby-blue dress, La Pomeroy wept aloud to me, "ButIcan't-leavehim . . ." Her body heaved. "He'smyman . . .he'smy-man . . .he'sallI'vegotintheworld. . . ."

"You've got your writing. You shouldn't give that sod another minute of your life," I said to her.

Miss Pomeroy shook and heaved and wailed in utter despair. "Buthe'smymanandhe'ssuchababyandIlovehimsomuch ohdearohdearlordwhatshallIdo . . ." No giggle; only a sob.

I took Sissie's arm and firmly led her past the sad-faced watchers at the bar-room door. As I followed her out into the bright afternoon sunshine I turned momentarily to see Miss Pomeroy with one thin, frail arm over the senseless mountain of flesh prostrate on the table. She was still sobbing and wailing, like a soul damned to eternal hell.

We walked back in silence to the boat. I was never so pleased in my life to see Nelson's tail wagging. Sissie caught the nine o'clock ferry to Ibiza, where she was to collect mail for us both and draw a minute sum from her diminishing bank balance. I set to making supper for myself and Nelson, anticipating for once a quiet evening's repose alone under the clear, star-laden night sky, and a good night's sleep.

Sissie came back the next day on the noon ferry. I had one letter from the British Income Tax Authority, telling me that one third of my naval pension was being stopped for payment of back taxes on some money I had earned years before delivering a yacht to Jamaica.

Sissie was aglow, hopping around and humming.

"What's up now?" I asked her.

"Oh, Tristan, Ai've simply been *dying* to tell you. Oh, happy, *happy* day!"

"What . . . did you win the football pools?"

"No, silly, but almost as good. My dahling, *dahling* brothah Willie is coming to Ibiza on holiday *next week!*"

My heart sank. Willie was the Bishop of Southchester. "Where's he staying?" I asked. It's bad luck to have clergy onboard.

"In the Hotel Montesol," she said.

"Good." I immediately felt better.

"And *dahling*, I met such an *awf'ly* sweet, terribly naice gentleman. He's an art collector and owns simply *oodles* of works by famous . . ."

I didn't wait for her. "Painters. Haven't we had enough of bloody painters on this little trip?"

"But this cheppie is *supah!* I'm told he's related to the Hungarian royal *femily* . . ."

"Yeah, and I'm the Pope of Gozo."

" . . .He's *eb*solutely sweet, and simply knows everyone, and he's invited me to take Willie to tea in his villa in the Old Town, and oh *dahling* Tristan," she sighed wistfully, "it's so bally *naice* to have tea with *really* supah people and simply spiffing conversation. Ai mean theah seem to be so many simply *peasanty* sort of . . . sordid, *pimply* people about these days, aren't theah?"

"Let's hope the tea is Lipton's and not that bloody Lapsang Souchong," I muttered. "OK, then we'll sail back to Ibiza on Sunday."

"Oh, *supah!* Then you'll be able to come to tea with Willie and me next Tuesday?"

"Maybe. What's this art-collector bloke's name?"

Sissie fished in her junk-filled raffia bag and brought out a tiny address book. She peered inside. "Ah, yes, dahling, heah it is . . . Elmyr Dore-Boutin."

"Sounds more like French to me, but you never know, of course, with these bloomin' foreigners."

"He's such a simply *charming* cheppie!"

"Probably a pox-doctor," I joked, as Sissie set to making lunch.

Little did I realize that I was shortly to meet one of the strangest, most notorious, intriguing, pitiful, and funny characters that the art world of this century has known.

Oh, they calls me Hangin' Johnny,

Chorus: *Away, boys, away!*

They says I hang for money,

Chorus: *So hang, boys, hang!*

They says I hang for money,
But hangin' is so funny,

At first I hanged me daddy,
And then I hanged me mammy,

Oh yes, I hanged me mother,
Me sister and me brother,

I hanged me sister Sally,
I hanged the whole damned family,

I'd hang the mate and skipper,
I'd hang 'em by their flippers,

I'd hang a rotten liar,
I'd hang a bleedin' friar,

A rope, a beam, a ladder,
I'd hang you all together,

We'll hang and haul together,
We'll hang for better weather.

"Hangin' Johnny" is a t'gallant halyard chantey or "sweating up" chantey. There is a marked resemblance to "Shenandoah" in the tune. It is distantly related to a song of the American Civil War, sung by black Union regiments.

When the halyard had been hauled it was then swigged; that is, the last few centimeters of line were hauled in and belayed. The sing-out for this operation was: "Hang me bullies, heavy asses! Hang, you sons o' whores, hang! Hang heavy!"

6

Hanging Johnny

ON SATURDAY, having not much else to do but sit on deck, watch the changing scenery, and wonder where we would be in a year's time, we sailed for the sandy, low island of Espalmador (The Golden Palm), about two miles to the north of Formentera. There *Cresswell* anchored in a beautiful wide bay on the western, leeward side of the island. The bay was fronted by a mile-long crescent of clean, white sand, and backed by a single low white house in a grove of olive trees, and a long line of golden palm trees, which shimmered in the morning breeze.

The island was owned then by an Irishman who had fought on the side of Franco during the Spanish Civil War. The previous owner had been a Government supporter; it was rumored that he had been executed by the Falangists, and the island handed over to its present owner by way of reward. But the Irishman was never on the island at any time while I was there, and in any case I would have been delighted to anchor in such a beautiful spot, even if it had been backed by the Adlerhof at Berchtesgaden.

With *Cresswell's* shallow draft of only two feet, nine inches, we were able to anchor the boat within feet of the white sand. *Cresswell* sat among the tiny wavelets like a dowager duchess in an infants' school. The water of the bay was so clean that we could clearly see the killock anchor on the sea-bottom thirty feet astern of the rudder. Schools of tiny fishes, gleaming when they turned their squadrons beam-on to the sun, darted and darkened, like a sudden frown, in the shade under the hull.

In the afternoon Sissie and I waded into the beach and walked to the windward side of the island, past the grove of olive trees, all leaning to the west like seamen holding themselves against a high gale. I collected a few birds' eggs—just enough for breakfast the next day, and Sissie found some dainty seashells.

On the way back to the boat we paused for a moment in the shade of the lone old palm tree which had given its name to the island and marked the grave of the previous owner. His ghost, it was said, still walked the shore on moonlit nights. Younger palms, glittering green, swept in a long line right the length of the island, their leaves rolling and flashing in the intermittent breezes which suddenly, dramatically failed, leaving the line of trees hushed and the lone palm drooping, weeping over the grave. Then the wind would stir again, and a gust would stagger down the beach before an advancing wave of sunlight and shadow, tossing leaves that rippled like silk against the blue sky.

In the evening, just before dusk, when the air was full of fluttering bats, Sissie and I again walked ashore. In the gloaming the boarded-up house seemed as if its life was over. The bats swirled around it, and among the gnarled olive trees whose noduled, bunioned branches all streamed toward the west, away from the prevailing breeze, as if they were Odysseus' crew reaching for the Ocean.

We walked to the far side of the island, to a place where the sea folded over itself, over and over, onto an invisible beach. We stood there looking out into the solid black nothingness of the night as the seas rolled in and crashed onto the rocks at the edges of the beach. We had some difficulty in finding our way back to the boat, but it was a small island and we were free and unhurried, and we knew that *Cresswell* was sleeping in the phosphor-starred waters of the bay somewhere on the other side. We walked almost all the way around the island, but we found her and were back in time for a supper of fish and chips. Then we lolled topsides, first in the dark, then in starlight as the breeze gently cleared the sky, and listened to the BBC overseas program, the London Symphony Orchestra. Brahms and silence from Sissie. Nirvana.

The stars cast their shimmering magic down through the night over Espalmador. Slowly the light breeze backed to northerly. Looking north we could see Ibiza enfolded in the night, and cheering glimpses of twinkling lights high up the mountainsides. It was as if the Creator had commanded a thousand new constellations to keep Polaris company. The offshore breeze brought the scent of woodsmoke to us. All was peaceful and restful. The murmur of the sea on the rocks on the other side of the island was not something for *Cresswell* to fear. The soft strumming of the sea's bass notes kept Brahms good company.

We were both up at four a.m. Under a canopy of stars Sissie weighed both anchors while I hoisted the creaking maingaff. Up went the mainsail. I hoisted next the working jib, which backed as the light breeze caught it. Round went the hull, almost in the boat's own length; smack went the mainsail, and we were off and moving as humans were meant to move, with muted sounds, a full sail, a taut helm, and a starry sky.

Once through the mile-wide strait between Espalmador and Ibiza we found a courteous easterly breeze awaiting us. It carried *Cresswell*, dancing with anticipation of the coming fine day, on a beam reach directly toward the entrance to Ibiza harbor. Outside the entrance the sound of surf was curiously evocative and, in some strange way, comforting, although for voyagers there are often times when it is the most feared of sounds. But after three hours of the sea's limited vocabulary it was the voice of the shore that was friendly to us.

Cresswell sailed, in the breaking dawn, through the harbor entrance at the end of the high seawall. The town raised itself above the breast of the hill to the west of us. The whitewashed houses, reflecting the red dawn, seemed to be made of pink sugar icing. The narrow streets wound up toward the biscuit-colored ancient walls of the Old Town, atop which the fortress frowned and the cathedral tower admonished the scarlet-slashed sky like an upraised finger.

Approaching Ibiza from the sea was at first startling, then a little depressing; but after Ibiza had worked its spell on us we could accept the shabby, shop-spoiled lower town. It was like being in love with someone who stutters and drops things.

Cresswell rounded the *muelle abrigo*, the outer mole, and, as Sissie lowered the maingaff, I headed for the town quay. As the boat slowly, silently lost speed, everything fitted together—the light breeze, the lightening dawn sky, the young sunshine, the whitening, shining town. In a moment we had cut ourselves away from our vision of the sea. A barrier of hills and cliffs and a high seawall were now between us and the large horizons.

Soon, as we approached the quay, the slope of the town rose ahead of us, solemn and enormous, while the harbor in which we floated, now stopped, was quite calm. The boom was slung inboard, the morn-bedewed mainsail canvas was collapsed in folds over the coachroof, and Sissie, in her gym-slip, was standing on the bow, staring at me intently, waiting for my command to anchor, like an Olympic torch-bearer hovering, nerve-tensed, for the passing of the sacred flame.

So quiet was Ibiza town in the dawn that we could hear an echo of our words from the high cliffs close by. I stared around me. Everything was still. I perused the town quay and saw that all the boat-berths were occupied. A visiting squadron of six or seven powerboats—Spanish, from their looks, probably from the Barcelona Yacht Club—were lined up stern-to at the quay in a chromium-plated display of wealth. A deckhand idled on the foredeck of one of these floating mansions, watching *Cresswell*, suspecting that she was about to trespass into the realms of power and money.

"No room, Sissie," I called to my deckhand.

"Oh, Ai say, what a *pity*. Ai'm sure the people on those boats must be ebsolutely spiffing . . . "

"Yes . . . Right, well, hoist the main again. We'll go over to the north side of the bay and moor alongside one of those old hulks."

Soon Sissie, her muscles bulging like baby's bottoms, had the maingaff hoisted again and the working jib taut against the masthead. I hauled in the sheets and we were off, silently and gently, across the calm harbor, past a seemingly huge ferry which plied to and from Majorca.

Soon we were secured amid a small fleet of ancient wrecks. There *Cresswell* was to wait patiently, guarded from the hard winter winds by useless, worn-out old Ibizan sailing schooners. They were all big vessels, up to 140 feet long, and their crumbling masts towered over tiny *Cresswell*, while their old, tatty rigging whispered of their lost, romantic youth. In the southeasterlies of the night, the fleet could be heard complaining—a groan from a hull half-full of rainwater, the creak from an unbraced gaff working on a rusted parrel; and less clear sounds, the low moaning and cursing of damaged ships. In the morning we would find them silent and innocently forlorn, motionless in the sunshine, like a fleet of sunken relics thrown up from the seabed by some passing catastrophe.

Our berth among the hulks, even though it was sad for me, was very close to the center of town, with the umbilical post office and the Alhambra Cafe below the Hotel Montesol, where the foreign colony met. It was a strange mixture in town—rogues and angels, refugees, revolutionaries, ex-Nazis, unfrocked Jesuits, frocked Calvinists, hippies, retired civil servants, tobacconists, writers who had never written, others who did nothing else; con-men and con-women, painters, sculptors, gentleman farmers, stock-and-bond investors, gamblers, idlers, lady schoolteachers of a dozen nationalities, some still active; whores and gigolos, all still active; cynics, opportunists, drug-dealers, and alcoholics; heterosexuals, homosexuals, bisexuals, trisexuals, ambisexuals, omnisexuals, asexuals, and transvestites; introverts, extroverts, retroverts, detectives, defectives—you name it, they were all at the Alhambra by eleven a.m., rain or shine. There, on Tuesday forenoon, I waited for Sissie to go to the airport in an ancient taxicab and meet her brother Willie.

It was about lunchtime when Sissie returned. The well-off foreigners were all sharpening their appetites before seeking to increase their girths, and the hustlers and hucksters were sharpening their eyes and ears as they sought to increase their ill-gotten gains.

Sissie was accompanied by a short, chubby, red-cheeked gentleman of about sixty. His hair, under his Panama hat, was silver. He sported muttonchop whiskers and a wart on one side of his nose, which was slightly hooked, so that it looked as if it didn't belong to the rest of his face. He wore a priest's collar, a black shirt, and an immaculate beige tropical suit over plain black shoes. Despite his age and his chubbiness he walked bouncily, like a gymnast who is absolutely certain that God is on his side.

As the pair came along, their faces (apart from his nose) conclusively demonstrated that they had emerged, although years apart, from the same mother—back in the dim, and, in his case, obviously distant past, when the world map was almost wholly red, and fat, jolly Teddy-boy sat on the throne of England.

Excitedly Sissie wended her way through the strange congregation in the Alhambra, dragging the somewhat disoriented cleric by the sleeve to my table, where I sat, my week-old copy of the *Times* now discarded, with the crossword only half-solved.

"Tristan, *dahling!*" she screeched.

Only one of the blanket-bundled bevy of bearded bums at the table next to mine winced. The others all continued staring glassy-eyed, as if they had already glimpsed their prospects fifteen years ahead, and were in some Siberia of the soul.

"*Deah*, dahling Skippah! You simply must . . . I'm simply *delaighted* to introduce to you my brothah, *deah* Willie."

We shook hands. Willie's felt like a freshly landed dab. His grip fluttered. He smiled broadly.

His voice boomed like a great cathedral organ. It was a very loud, round, fruity, mournful, sincere voice, and each syllable he boomed seemed to emerge from his generous mouth like a tennis ball being backhanded across the net. At the end of each phrase the tone rose, so that he always seemed to be asking a question. His voice reminded me of the bass section of a choir rendering a Gregorian chant.

"Awf'ly nice to meet you?" he chanted. "I've read so much about you in Sissie's letters?"

"I hope she didn't say anything bad," I said.

"Oh, no," he chortled.

I'd never really known what the word "chortle" signified until I heard Bishop Willie Saint John do it that noontime at the Alhambra. The chortle issued from his lips like wine burbling from a suddenly unbunged barrel. The sound reminded me of the mating call of the walrus, or the noise a flock of penguins makes when the whole bunch decide to change the direction of their comical waddle. As the liquid, bubbling chortle escaped from Willie, I decided that it came either from an over-goodwilled innocent or from an evil demon. Another brief glance into Willie's bright blue eyes convinced me that the former possibility was more likely.

"Oh, no, nothing at all, Captain," he chortled again. "And I do hope you will address me as Willie?"

"All right, but for Chri . . . for goodness' sake, don't call me Captain. It's a mode of address for a paid functionary."

"Ah, yes. Quite so."

He turned to Sissie. "Miss Benedict is playing in the croquet finals at Windsor?" He turned to me again. "Miss Benedict is my housekeeper?"

The bishop's accent was not nearly as "refined Kensington" as Sissie's. It was good, plain, straightforward Victorian-style upper-class English, with all the vowels said as they *look.*

"Oh," I nodded, wishing I'd finished the crossword.

"Otherwise, I mean if it weren't for the croquet match, I could have had her accompany me to Ibiza?"

Sissie's face cracked. "How simply *spiffing* that would have been! *Deah* Miss Benedict—oh, I *do* hope she wins something. She tries so *terribly* hard."

I cocked my eye at Sissie. "Yes, we could have taken on the local police team."

The bishop looked at me with genuine interest. "Really?" he asked in a sharp tone. "Do they have a croquet side here?"

"So I'm told," I replied.

"Well, in that case, I'll bring her with me next year?"

"The only thing is," I continued, "the Spanish croquet balls are made from ossified bulls' testicles.

The bishop's mouth opened. "Really?"

"Yes—they call them *cojones*," I informed him.

"How very interesting? How very original? *Cojones?*"

Several passing peasants turned and stared at Willie.

"Yes, in fact croquet is known in Spanish as *conmiscojones*, and if you want a game of croquet here the phrase you use is, *Quieres jugar conmiscojones?*" I was really enjoying myself.

"Really? Let's see . . . What does that mean?"

"Do you care to play croquet," I replied, slowly.

Sissie, blushing like crazy, compressed her lips together and shook her head slightly as she stared at me—but not a flicker crossed the bishop's face.

"*Quieres* . . . ?"

"*Jugar*," I prompted him.

"Ah, yes, got it, old chap. *Quieres jugar conmiscojones?*"

All around him now the devious denizens of a dozen dens of depravity, collectors of things and people, were silent. They stared, fascinated, at Willie the Bishop as his voice rolled and thundered the question out along the crowded terrace of the Alhambra. Over and over he repeated it.

Willie and Sissie took off to visit the cathedral at the top of the steep hill. I headed for a fisherman's bodega for a lunch of yellow peril washed down with San Miguel beer, with which I toasted Miss Benedict's success in the forthcoming croquet tournament and her absence from the island.

Sissie told me later that day that Willie had kept repeating the Spanish phrase—all the way up the hill to the cathedral, all the way through that venerable building, and most of the way back to the Hotel Montesol, before some English-speaking Spaniard (rare in Ibiza, then) had, after gently tugging him out of Sissie's earshot, informed him what it meant: "Will you play with my testicles?"

Horrified, Willie recalled that he had asked the question several times of the verger in the cathedral.

"I'll bet he's really pissed off with me," I said to Sissie.

She laid a calloused hand on my arm. "Oh, no, not really, deah. You see, Willie's used to choirboy pranks and all *thet* sort of jolly rot."

"Do you think I'd better come with you to that bloody tea party tomorrow, then?"

"Why *of course,* dahling Tristan. Willie *knows* that at heart you're simply *supah.* And anyway, he must forgive you out of Christian charity. You simply *must* come to Elmyr's tea party. It will be *eb*solutely spiffing. Deah Willie and I passed his villa on our way back from the cathedral. It's simply *awf'ly* naice—you've simply no idea. I'm practically *bursting* with enticipation . . . "

Sissie disappeared up the companionway ladder on her way to her sleeping den under the forward dodger. Soon after there came the tinkling of a Booth's London Dry Gin bottle against a secretive glass and the rustle of Bible leaves being turned; then all was silent onboard the good ship *Cresswell,* and I slept the sleep of the justified.

After breakfast the next day I went ashore, crossed the road, and had a beer in a tiny fishermen's bar. Sailors, longshoremen, and fishermen—anyone to do with the sea—can always use a good bar. It's probably because people who live on and by the sea like the friendliness that booze brings on shore. Maybe it's the salt air.

As I waited there while Sissie changed into her best clothes aboard *Cresswell*, I visualized my friends very clearly and drank to their health. I could even hear their voices as if they were present. Imagination seems to have a fourth-dimensional quality in a voyager, especially one who has spent long periods alone. He learns to use his solitude to sharpen his ability to remember events long past, and so live his life several times over. Some voyagers can—and I have so often heard them—conjure up scenes and people in a manner almost unknown to shorefolk. They are the practitioners of a special art, which will never be lost as long as there are vast spaces and people to cross them.

When Sissie turned up to collect me at the bar before meeting Willie, I hardly recognized her. She had on a white dress with red and blue roses (*blue* roses?), a wide-brimmed white hat with a light blue ribbon around and a great bow to one side, real nylon stockings, and a pair of elegant-looking white shoes—all of which Willie had brought with him from England. She was transformed. Of the Sissie I had known, only the steel-blue eyes, the frizzy hair, and the accent remained. She trotted into the bar, empty apart from an old crone and me, and, holding a white leather handbag out with one hand, pirouetted around. I stared. I gawped. I gaped in astonishment.

"Like it, dahling?" she crowed. "Oh happy, *happy* day!"

I quickly finished my beer and grabbed Sissie's arm. "You look like . . . like . . . *Ascot*," I told her.

Pleased, she slipped one of her arms, bare and sun-burned, into mine, and seemed to purr like a cat.

We went outside, with me feeling like a beach bum escorting the Queen Mum, and made our way to the Hotel Montesol to meet Willie, who treated us to lunch there. We then set off for a car-tour of Ibiza. The driver, a young New Zealand woman, was good-looking and very pleasant, and Willie was so friendly to me that no one would have suspected that I had played such a cruel trick on him the day before. I was so impressed by his courtesy that I invited him to go for a sail with us the next day, even though he was a preacher.

Just before four o'clock the New Zealander duly dropped Sissie, the bishop, and me in front of the by now somewhat jaded-looking hustlers, hucksters, pimps, and pushers at the Alhambra, and we waited for another car that was to take us to Elmyr the Art Collector's villa.

We sat in the afternoon sun, Sissie and I content subjects of the bishop's munificence, sipping Courvoisier brandy (nothing but the best when *deah* Willie was around), and Willie with ice cream and coffee, which he enjoyed the Spanish way by dipping the ice cream in the coffee and eating it so, with the hot, bitter tang exactly complementing the cold, bland sweetness.

By now, after a bottle of wine with lunch at the Montesol, two brandies as chasers, and now another two brandies, Sissie, splendid in her new outfit, was aglow. She and Willie kept up an incessant conversation about Miss Benedict and other friends, acquaintances, relatives, and servants, dead or alive, and, for all I knew, yet to be born. Sissie's screech was the tune; Willie's booming was the descant, and soon every rogue within twenty yards of our table was completely familiar with the domestic arrangements, business affairs, sexual scandals, sporting abilities, regenerative achievements, and secret proclivities of everyone who lived within the environs of the cathedral town of Southchester. But the Courvoisier was good, Sissie was in blossom, and the bishop was a *stout fella*. Then the red car showed up.

It was a Corvette Stingray. As it pulled brazenly alongside the terrace of idling wait-ers and waiters, it was followed closely by an ancient Ibizan taxi. Now a venerable taxi anywhere else means simply an old taxi. In Ibiza such taxis looked as if they had been constructed before the precocious infant of Frau Benz had learned to walk. Behind the Corvette it looked like an elderly orphan who had been adopted by a film star.

As the red Corvette, the very spirit of rodomontade, pulled up, a cry rose from a dozen voices along the terrace. It was as if the car had just won the Monte Carlo rally.

"Elmyr!" The raucous bellow came from a young Frenchman wearing a dozen silver bracelets, a string of beads, no shirt, a tight-waisted jacket, and bell-bottoms.

"Elmyr!" A screeching howl from an elderly figure of indeterminate sex, which had been huddled all day before an empty coffee cup as it nervously tugged at a mink jacket around its shoulders with heavily ringed, long-fingered claws.

"Elmyr!" A bass boom from a dark, heavy-set man in a black leather jacket, whose build and thick mustache reminded me of a circus lion-tamer.

"Elmyr!" In unison from two blond males in their early teens, their faces so smooth and effeminate that you could see their mothers in them. Both were wearing pink satin suits, with obviously nothing under them but slim boys' bodies.

"Elmyr!" The American tones of a huge woman bar-owner, sitting with her great pudgy arm around her dark, sparrow-like, bespectacled female companion.

As the voices hollered, Sissie, the bishop, and I watched a display of sycophancy unrivaled since the days of the Caesars. The object of all this adulation was relaxing casually behind the wheel of the low-slung Stingray, which, although it was supposed to be the very last word in sports cars, looked to me like some great blood-gorged insect. He was, when he alighted, quite short—no more than about five and a half feet. As he glided over to our table I saw that he was *dapper*. His hair was obviously dyed, jet-black, and it had the horse-hair look of an old sofa's stuffing. He wore around his neck a gold chain, from which a gold-rimmed monocle dangled over a cashmere sweater. When he languidly stretched out his hand to raise Sissie's and kiss it, six gold rings, heavy and thick, and one diamond ring, attracted the eye of every impecunious being in sight, including me.

"Elymr," said Sissie in a fainting voice, "how *naice* of you to come."

"Charmed," said the art collector as he gently lowered Sissie's wilting hand.

"My brothah, Bishop Saint John."

"Sir, Elmyr Dore-Boutin."

"And my deah, *deah* skippah, Tristan."

Elmyr's eyes, large and brown, self-pitying, yet calculating, took in my seaman's jerkin and tatty cap with one swift sweep. He shook my hand cursorily and said, "Yes." I felt as if I had been ordered over the top of a battle-trench.

He turned to Sissie and Willie. "I hope you did enjoy your little trip around our beautiful island?" His voice had the timbre of a wayward elf, and the way he accented his words was strange, as if he had studied English only in its spoken, colloquial form, and never learned where to put the emphasis.

"Oh, it was *delaightful*," gushed Sissie.

"Good, then I better take you up to my studio," said Elmyr.

I had been studying him. He reminded me of someone. It didn't strike me right away, but I soon figured it out. He was stocky. Everything about him seemed to be horizontal. His brow, which was wide and intelligent-looking, his ears, his nose, his mouth; everything, including the faint stripes on his green cashmere sweater was *horizontal*. The only vertical thing about him was the dangling monocle chain. His manners, and his manner, were both perfect and charming, a rare combination. Then he turned his round, muddy eyes on me, focused, and blinked slowly. *That* was it—Mister Toad!

"You will come in my car, Miss Saint John?"

I was startled, for a moment, to hear Sissie addressed by her correct name.

"Oh, perfectly delaighted." Sissie melted before the reptilian eyes.

"And your brother will go in the taxi?" There were only two seats in the Corvette.

"And deah Tristan, too?" Sissie entreated.

The toad's eyes inspected mine for cataracts, my beard for fleas. "Yes, of course, my dear."

So it was that Sissie, in the splendid vulgarity of the Corvette, and *deah* Willie and I in the ancient, hoary, dented dignity of the taxicab, arrived at Elmyr's villa.

As we pulled up at the bottom of a set of steps I noticed the wrought-iron name on the whitewashed walls: "La Falaise." The Cliff.

"Original," I said to the bishop.

"Quite," Willie replied absentmindedly.

Elmyr shepherded Sissie, in her rose-bedecked splendor, up the steps. Willie and I followed. Through the arch of the villa we entered a large, cool, dark hall. On either side were mahogany doors.

Elmyr guided us through the hall like a ballet dancer, sweeping one cashmered arm to one side. "My sleeping quarters." Then the limp, Cartier-adorned wrist to the other side. *"La chambre rouge,"* he said with a sly leer at me. "Sleeping quarters of my . . . young guests."

Willie was staring at the lines of original paintings on the walls, hands clasped behind his back in true connoisseur's style. "Dali . . . Dufy . . . Renoir . . . Picasso," he read them off, his voice low with respect and awe.

Elmyr escorted Sissie and Willie, with me traipsing after them—an embarrassing presence, like a dose of influenza that had found its way into the villa—up a tiled stairway and into a huge living room. Its walls, too, were covered with the works of half a hundred masters of modern art.

We all sat down to tea, which was served in the finest Delft-ware on a solid silver tray by a strikingly good-looking, fair-haired, green-eyed youth of about nineteen, with broad shoulders and a street swagger. I could sense that every step he took was being paid for by Elmyr. He wore a spotless white shirt and thin, bright yellow pyjama pants, under which his crotch bulged so that Sissie was constrained not to notice him.

Elmyr introduced him. "This is Henry."

Henry's mouth moved slightly in the direction of a smile, but he must have realized the smile was not going to be paid for by us, so it hovered halfway to realization, then died.

"Henry did come from Nebraska, did you not, Henry?" said Elymr.

The frozen face nodded. He was handsome in a tailor-dummy way, with dirty blond hair and regular features. But his eyes were sly.

"Henry is a student, are you not, Henry?"

Again a slight nod, and a shift of the eyes.

"A student of biology, are you not?"

The sly eyes and yellow-covered genitals retreated toward the kitchen, leaving the fourth question, the one that was silent in my mind, only too-well answered.

Elmyr was a well-traveled man. He described his days in Rio and London, New York and Hong Kong, Tokyo, and just about every well-known city. Always he had met the people who mattered. In Paris it was Gertrude Stein and Ernest Hemingway and Lady Malcolm Campbell, the wife of the holder of the world land-speed record. In between Sissie's oohs and aahs and the bishop's cries of approbation, Elmyr held brilliant court. He told us, as we sat in wonder at his feet, about his meetings with the Aga Khan and Zsa-Zsa Gabor, and Anita Loos and the Duke of Kent. Elmyr didn't drop names; they just flowed from his lips and fell, used and exhausted, into our laps. He had haunted the Café du Dome and the Rotonde, the famous literary hang-outs in Montparnasse. He knew everyone in Manhattan, in Zürich, in Berlin . . .

Suddenly a strange noise broke the spell of Elmyr's monologue. It was a loud, high-pitched yapping. Elmyr strode over to the ceiling-high French window, which let out onto a flower-bedecked patio with a kidney-shaped swimming pool overlooking the ocean from the high cliff on which the villa was built. He opened the door. "Fifi!" he shouted in a peeved voice.

A small white poodle, only inches tall, with a green ribbon around its neck, dashed into the room. It dodged Elmyr's startled grab. It raced around the room, over the leather sofas and poufs, until the teamaker and I trapped it in a corner. We both grabbed for it, but I beat the teamaker to it and picked the squirming animal up. By now Elmyr was back in the room, away from the French window.

"Outside?" I asked him as I passed by.

Elmyr seemed a little flustered. "Er . . . Yes, outside, please."

I went to the door-window, opened it, and happened to glance at three deckchairs with their backs to me, facing the pool. I saw a part of a leg and a foot raised from one of them. Curious, I strolled over almost to the side of the pool before I released the poodle and turned around.

There were three males in the chairs. One seemed about thirty, with fair hair and sharp eyes; another was about twenty-two, with a face and fawn-like brown eyes so pretty than any young woman could be jealous of them; and the third was a stripling of no more than sixteen, with wide blue eyes. They were all laid out, bathing their already deep-brown bodies in the sun, with drinks beside them. They all looked ineffably bored, they all held hands, and they were all stark naked.

When I returned to the living room Elmyr seemed downcast. It was soon obvious that he had ascertained that *deah* Willie was not in the market for paintings, nor for anything else.

Shortly thereafter Elmyr escorted Sissie to the gate and made his parting. We three made our way back down the hill, the bishop's voice booming and echoing from the white walls of the tiny houses, all hung with garlic and fish, through the gloomy arch of the fifteenth-century walls, down to the lower town and the realm of ordinary mortals, with both Sissie and the bishop commenting on what an *"awf'ly* nice, *splendid* fellow" Elmyr was.

In good King Charles' golden days,
When loyalty no harm meant,
A zealous High Church man was I,
And so I got preferment.
To teach my flock I never missed;
Kings were by God appointed,
And lost were those that dare resist
Or touch the Lord's anointed!
And this the rule that I'll maintain,
Until my dying day, sir,
That whatsoe'r king may reign,
Still I'll be the bishop of Bray, sir!

First verse of a seventeenth-century English Anti-Established-Church song.

7

The Ship that Almost Died of Shame

Early next morning, just after Sissie and I had finished breakfast—she once again domesticated in her dark blue gym slip and an inch-wide pink ribbon around her russet hair; and Nelson, as usual at that hour, under the cabin table, banging his tail against my leg in morning greeting—the bishop hailed us from the roadway. "*Cresswell*, ahoy?"

As soon as she heard Willie's voice, Sissie shot up the ladder. "A *teeny* tick, dahling—Ai'll pull the jolly old boat in for you."

From the shady gloom of the cabin a portrait print of Her Majesty admonished me to no incivilities. I gazed up as Sissie hefted a heavy black Gladstone bag down into the cockpit. The Gladstone, which was almost covered with little hotel labels from places as far apart as Colombo and Coventry, was soon followed by a scampering, bouncing Willie.

As Sissie let go of the stern line *Cresswell* creaked against the hull next to her, as if she were complaining, and the ancient work-worn schooner gave off rustling sounds as if she were comforting *Cresswell*, saying, "Cheer up, love, it's only for one day, after all!"

I ascended the companionway ladder. There was *deah* Willie, balanced precariously on the poop whaleback, holding onto the mizzen boom with one hand, grasping the handle of a wicker picnic hamper with the other. He beamed at me with a smile of benediction so wide that it looked as if his muttonchop whiskers would never find each other again. As Sissie took the hamper from him he chanted, "Good morning? Good morning?" Then he looked upward, as if sending a plea to heaven.

I studied Willie as he gazed up. He had discarded his clerical mourning shirt and collar, and was now resplendent in a bright red sports shirt (shades of Elmyr's Corvette), and khaki shorts which reached down to his white, knobbly knees and made him look as if he were just about to surrender the Southchester Cathedral to the Imperial Japanese Army. On his lower legs he wore short black nylon socks, and on his feet spanking white tennis shoes. With his red face, freshly roasted even under the rather weak November Mediterranean sun, and his peeling bald pate and gleaming silver whiskers, he looked, apart from his clothes, like one of those merry, well-fed squires depicted on fox-hunting prints, or on Christmas cards which show early nineteenth-century coaches wallowing through three feet of snow. He looked as if he'd stepped straight out of the pages of *The Pickwick Papers*. Before I, too, turned my glance to the heavens for signs of a breeze, I *knew* that God was up there, and all was right with the world. Willie's face told me so.

"Morning, Willie. Not much of a wind yet—in fact none at all. We're a bit early . . . It won't pipe up for a good half hour," I told him.

"We shall be blessed in the good Lord's time?" said Willie.

"Oh, golly *whizz!*" Sissie screeched, behind me now. "Then Ai'd bally-well bettah make some *tea!*"

In the good old British tradition, sanctified wherever the sun (once) never set, it was Sissie's immediate reaction to any crisis. I think that if *Cresswell* had ever been on the point of foundering into the dark deeps, Sissie would have gone down with a teapot and sugar spoon clutched to her breast. Humming merrily to herself as Willie, surprisingly agile for his age, clambered and slithered down into the cockpit well, Sissie marched forward to her dark, poky hideaway below in the forward dodger. There her huge traveling bag slumped to one side like a fat old Pasha leering in the gloom. She emerged within seconds with a sparkling white tablecloth clutched in one hand, and a box in the other. Once Willie was safely below, she laid out the tablecloth with a grand flourish over the oil- and salt-stained weatherdeck. She took a tinkling tea set out of the box and set it out on the cloth. Immediately *Cresswell* was transformed from a semi-exhausted workaday converted lifeboat into Cleopatra's Barge.

As I wordlessly watched the transmogrification of my vessel into something which looked as if it had strayed out of Regent's Park Canal at Bloomsbury, the bishop beamed at me. "Decent library down here?" he boomed. "I suppose they keep you company when you're on your own?"

"Yes, I learn a lot about myself from them," I replied warily. It was hardly the hour for a literary conversation, especially as I had seen a slight movement of a lamb-like cloud over the cathedral high atop the Ibiza Old Town hill, and hoped there was a bit of a breeze rising.

"Yes?," Willie said, "Many a hunted heart may flee to a good book and find peace and solace there?"

"Oh *deah* Tristan simply *adores* reading, don't you dahl-ing?" observed Sissie.

"Right, especially when I'm on a lee shore, with a bloo . . . a great gale blowing its head off, and the book is the Admiralty Pilot for that particular stretch of coast."

"Ah, yes? You have your pilot and I have mine," said Willie, "but I suspect it's the same pilot for all of us?"

"Only if it's amended and brought up to date," I maintained.

Willie's querying look was puzzled but benign.

"Tristan means that he has to keep all his jolly old charts and pilot books and all *sorts* . . . simply *oodles* of papers and *meps* and things, *eb*solutely up to date, up to the *awf'ly last word*, don't you, dahling?"

Sissie poured the tea—no common Lipton's for Willie, no indeed. This was genuine Fortnum and Mason's *Burma* tea, from a secret stash in the sinister traveling bag.

I tiptoed carefully over the tea set and made my way forward to single up the mooring lines. Nelson was now laid out on the foredeck, on his belly, with his head on his one front paw, gazing aft at the morning breakfast tea-party now in progress. When I bent over to tickle his ear he looked up with his one eye and heaved a great sigh. "Yes, I know, old son," I told him.

As I singled up the forward mooring line, *Rosalinda*, the old schooner which *Cresswell* was tied up to, seemed to shiver in the early morning haze, as if she knew that her little friend, which had been holding hands with her for four days, was about to abandon her, to leave her once more in the sad, sad company of her softly grumbling, night-complaining companions. I felt this, and reached over to pat the hulk's scarred, gray, rotting bulwark. Just then the bishop's voice psalmed, "I see you have all of Shakespeare?"

I didn't reply. The parting of *Cresswell* from the dying *Rosalinda* was too melancholy for me.

Sissie chimed in. "Oh *deah* Tristan simply *worships* Shakespeare, don't you, dahling?"

"I find a repose in the Bard?" Willie intoned in a voice that seemed to make the teaspoons rattle. "When I read him, all questioning ceases for me?"

As I unshipped the mainsail tiers I glanced at him. He held a tea cup in one hand. The other hand was pressed against his chest. His voice thundered on. "All my difficulties . . . all the complexities of life . . . they all seem to lose their importance. I am a novice before an archbishop who knows all my fears, but who smiles at them?"

I slid aft past Willie and let go the after mooring line, then trotted again to the forward line, let go of that, and heaved mightily against *Rosalinda*. Silently and slowly *Cresswell* slid over the oily surface of the harbor and away from the ships' graveyard. All the while Sissie was gazing at *deah* Willie, a smile, half of wonderment, half of revelation, on her face. As I passed her I shot her a quick, dark look, and she bent to clear up the tablecloth.

The bishop's voice reverberated on and on. "My main reason for being glad that I was born English is that William Shakespeare was an Englishman?"

Sissie hauled up the working jib and I heaved up the mainsail. As the mainboom clattered across the boat in the dead calm air, it almost caught Willie under his ear, and I was a little disappointed to see him duck out of its way just in time. Then a slight whiff of a whisper of wind caught the sails, and my attention was wholly taken up with working out across the flat waters of Ibiza harbor. Then I was, for a brief respite, only dimly aware, somewhere in a remote part of my hearing system, of the bishop's voice, which, instead of resounding, now seemed to be a mere mumble. Such are the charms and demands of a sailing vessel and a shy zephyr to work her with, that for one blessed moment I forgot *deah* Willie.

Cresswell reluctantly, and at a rheumatic snail's pace, crept forward. Then the fickle breeze, to taunt us, died away. Only yards from the silent schooners *Cresswell* was left with sails empty and drooping, as embarrassed as an actress who has forgotten her lines. Some seabirds, out on their early-morning foray, glided over with the intention of jeering at us, but as soon as they heard Willie's voice they changed their minds and headed away again to search for a fishing boat. It would be more profitable to them; they would not risk having their eardrums damaged, and they had the wisdom to know that seven in the morning is not the time for a lecture on Shakespeare. In the evening, with a bottle of rum on the cabin table, and the oil-lamp's golden glow on the cabin bookshelves, by all means—but in the middle of a harbor, with all sails up and no wind, Shakespeare is definitely *out*. Conrad or Kipling, maybe. Shakespeare, never. The fact that Nelson, still lying on the foredeck, had seen the seagulls' intent and snarled at them surlily might also have warned them off.

The bishop sat on the coachroof now, with his red shirt, white knobbly knees, black socks, and red face. His mouth kept opening and closing as he droned on with his sermon, shattering the silence of the harbor.

" . . . and being alone a lot can, of course, lead to the discovery of one's self?" The fruity boom carried clearly through the still morning air and over the murky water. A hundred yards away a deckhand who had been asleep on the deck of a fishing boat shook his head and stared at us. On the town quay, 150 yards away, the fishwives and their few early customers stopped haggling as the roaring notes of the cathedral organ, in all their tonal splendor, rolled over them and away up the narrow alleys toward the Old Town walls half a mile away. I stared at the walls for a moment, wondering if we were about to witness a repeat performance of Joshua's remarkable feat before Jericho. But Ibiza's Old Town was fortunate. The walls held firm against the detonating timbre of Willie's monologue.

" . . . but perhaps we need solitude to find other people? Even the Saviour Himself reached mankind through being alone in the wilderness?"

I silently gazed around the harbor. I stared at the sky. I gawped east, west, south, and north as *deah* Willie's voice clanged and pealed and rang, shattering the holiness which comes before the wind's rising.

I looked at Sissie, who was busy adoring Willie. "Might as well put the breakfast dishes in a bucket," I said. "We'll wash 'em in seawater when we get outside the harbor. *If* we ever get outside the harbor."

The mainboom crashed across again. Again Willie ducked just in time, but he didn't miss one word of his sermon. "It must be wonderful to be content in solitude? Content with one's self? At peace with one's self? And especially, I suppose, when there is a definite task to be accomplished, as, of course, there is in a small vessel crossing an ocean?"

"No wind," I mumbled to him from behind the steering wheel, which moved slack and non-resistant in my hand.

"Ah, the wind and the weather?" he fog-horned down at Sissie, who was now in the galley. Then his head came upright once again and he clasped his hands behind his fishbelly-white knees. "What a joy it must be to be a man of the weather? What happiness must a man . . . sound in body and with peace of mind, mark you," he beamed at me, " . . . what happiness he must have to live for and with the weather? For such a man there can be no *bad* weather? Every sky, no matter how threatening, must have its beauty? Every storm which makes his heart pound and his blood race, surely, makes his heart pound and his blood race more vigorously?"

"Not a breath," I said. "Not a bloo . . . not a capful of wind."

"Poor, *dahling* Tristan. He's so jolly *patient*," Sissie's voice rose from the galley. "More tea?" she yelled at the mizzen.

"Not a fiddler's far . . . Not a fiddler's farrago," I muttered, and spun the wheel both ways in frustration, so that the cable stops smashed against their U-bolt limiters down below in the after dodger. "Not a fu . . . fudge . . . Not a fuddle of breeze!" I complained.

"I say, what a topping expression? A fuddle of breeze?"

I peered around in the misty morning sunshine. I stared toward the harbor entrance a half-mile distant and beyond at the open sea, iridescent and shimmering. But there was a leaden hue to it, and it was quite obvious to me that all four winds, and all the western Mediterranean, now they were sure that *deah* Willie was trying to embark in, under, over, and upon them, were *sulking*. It was as if the gods of the wind and the sea had shut up shop and gone golfing for the day. There was a sudden deadness abroad. I expected to see a coffin come drifting around the seawall

head at any moment, with the very dead Lady of Shalott
dangling one arm over the side.

"No wind, dahling? Not one teeny weeny *bit?*"
screeched Sissie from the galley.

"Not a sausage," I snarled back. "And the sky's as
dead as a bloo . . . bludgeoned dodo."

"The good Lord will provide," Willie bellowed, and
just as he did the mainboom swung over and caught him
smack on the ear.

Feeling better, I said, "Careful, it might swing across
again."

"Ah, accidents will happen in the best-regulated families." His voice was somewhat pained and a mite lower in
volume now, as he quoted Queen Victoria.

"Are you all right, dahling?" yelled Sissie.

"If pain did not exist, we should never experience
happiness," roared Willie.

"Ai say, how simply *brave* of you," Sissie screeched.
"How simply *splendid.* Just a jiffy, old cheppie—Ai'll have
tea ready in a tick or two!"

Forward, Nelson heaved and sighed; then, as if fascinated by Willie's performance, he nestled his head once
more onto his paw and stared at the bishop, blinking every
now and then. I looked around me. *Cresswell* was stopped
stone dead. The sails hung like a sailor's pockets after a
night ashore. The sky above and the water around us
looked as if the world had decided never to turn again.
Halfway up the hill, brazen morning sunlight shone on the
Old Town walls, which reflected rosy-gold above the
jumble of white cottages of the lower town. Seaward there
was not a sign of any whiteness on the sea—no crests, no
troughs, no undulations of the horizon. Everything seemed
to have stopped in adamant indignation at the sound of
Willie's voice.

It was like charity flag-day in Aberdeen. It was like five
minutes before opening-time in a London pub, with
Cresswell, Nelson, Sissie, Willie, and me the waiting, shaking, desperate patrons, gazing in despair through the

gloomy Edwardian windows at the far wall of the saloon, trying to see if the pub-clock hands were indeed moving, or if it was merely a mocking, painted face that stared back at us, begrudging our very existence.

I turned back toward the companionway to see Sissie's Sheffield-steel-blue eyes now melted in utter sympathy. "Oh, *deah* Tristan—tea?"

The mainboom swung again. Willie ducked again. The clatter and squeak of the mainsheet block jeered and made sport of my frustration. The dull thud of the working jib up forward poked malicious fun at my hand on the wheel. The houses on the hill, the tower of the cathedral, the fishing boats alongside the town quay, the leaden water, the deadened sky, and the sound of the bishop's voice as it hollered and squalled, yelled, belled, and vroomed, all chorused accusingly the twelfth commandment of the sailorman: *"Thou shalt not take to sea with thee the man in black!"*

Willie by now was onto a subject obviously close to his heart—Cheerfulness. As I glowered at the sails and the sky, he roared on. "Of course we must thank the good Lord for any little blessings we have? When we count them we must remember that we do, in fact, suffer along with the rest of mankind? We must not think it is a sin to be cheerful?"

Sissie cooed as she handed me my mug of Lipton tea. "Why don't we start the jolly old engine, dahling? At least we shell get out of this *dreadful* harbor."

On *Cresswell* it was an unpardonable sin to initiate talk of the Iron Judas which lurked below. But now, with the burden of sin safely on Sissie's shoulders, I perked up.

"I've only got a gallon or so of diesel left," I told her, "But at least we've got enough to get us outside the seawall. We might just find a bit of breeze out there."

"*Jolly* good idea, dahling. Shell Ai start the dratted thing, or shell you?" Sissie stood there like a tense messenger before a Spartan general at Thermopylae.

I cocked an eye at the bishop, who for once was silent. I certainly didn't want him to know that I let Sissie swing the obstinate little bastard of a starting handle in the impossibly confined space below the weatherdeck. It was to me as if she had asked if she should let an imaginary idiot brother, drooling, out of the forward dodger, and thus divulge a dark family secret. But the bishop was still beaming at me, and God, whom I had thought had gone away for the holidays, was back in heaven.

"No, we'll do it like we always do," I growled, giving Sissie a look which would have silenced Kublai Khan. "You take the wheel. Head for the entrance. I'll start the fuc . . . fucated engine."

"Fucated engine?" roared Willie.

"Yes, it means painted . . . We painted it the other day, in Formentera."

I heaved up the engine hatches. Almost in tears with shame, humiliation, and frustration at not having sailed *Cresswell* out, and with the old schooners still only yards away, I stared round my boat again, like a madman trying to figure out which way he should head after climbing over an asylum wall.

Now that she had her hands on the wheel (a rare treat), Sissie was becoming romantic again. "Oh, *deah* Willie," she gushed, "I *do* so wish that Miss Benedict were heah! She would have enjoyed herself so *bally* much. Oh what a *rotten* shame. I do hope she wins the tournament."

"I'd rather not talk about croquet just now," boomed Willie. "After all, we are out here to enjoy a rattling good sail, aren't we?" He watched me in silence—the miraculous silence that always falls just before a sailing boat's engine is started and after it has been stopped.

I spitefully rammed oil into my old enemies, the two cylinders. I pushed down viciously my old antagonist, the decompression lever. I attacked with brute malice my old adversary, the starting handle, even as Willie roared the words, "Reminds me of the good old days, out with Algernon and Bertie, punting down the Thames at Windsor . . . ."

"*Deah* Algernon, how awf'ly sweet he was . . . He used to dandle me on his knee . . . *awf'ly kind*," Sissie screeched.

As I attacked the handle for the third time, sweat now pouring from me, the engine sensed my fury and decided to surrender to my wishes. With at first a sort of burp, almost apologetic, then a cough, it spluttered to life. I dropped the now-free starting handle. I leaned over and hissed at the loudly exploding engine, "Now you bastard, if you stop before half a bleedin' hour's up I'll unbutton you and you're for the deep-six!"

The engine missed a stroke, as if it were swearing that it wouldn't dream of letting me down, then roared away again.

"And I don't want to hear that bloody voice up there for at least half an hour! Understand?" I kicked the front casing of the engine, then poked my head above the hatchway. Unbelievably, Willie's voice could still be heard. I bent down again, and with a spanner soon unslipped the throttle-limiting attachment so that I could get more power and, hopefully, more noise out of the engine.

It was to no avail. Even with the throttle wide open and the hatches left gaping, *deah* Willie boomed out still over the very best the engine could do. Resigned to defeat, I made my way up to the foredeck, where I sat alongside Nelson and let the working jib flap away at my head. Its noise, combined with the engine, the spattering mainsail, the creaking sheet-blocks, and the slapping of loose halyards, helped to drown Willie's, but not quite. His voice, like an aura, like an odor, penetrated everything.

Willie was now lecturing Sissie on Art. She must have mentioned the visit to Elmyr's villa the day before. " . . . And of course works of art are the only means whereby we can truly communicate with one another, completely and unhindered?"

I stared aft as *Cresswell* slid through the glassy harbor. Sissie was replying to her brother, tilting her head to one side and squinting. Her lips moved, but I couldn't hear her.

Then his voice chanted on. "Well, of course, the problem of art and morals . . . the relationship between them, my dear Cecilia . . . ." (*Cecilia?*) "is that it's too often mooted that the problem only exists on the side of art? Our type of people too often assume that our moral standards are satisfactory and appropriate, at least in the theory if not in the fact? We seem to question only in what ways art should conform to our ideas of morality?"

Willie droned on and on. I lay down and buried my head under Nelson's neck. He lifted his head and licked my ear. I groaned. I lifted my head and grinned at him. He grinned back. I groaned again. Nelson whimpered in reply. Even the passing harbor water looked exhausted.

When *Cresswell* was a mile offshore the sea was still as flat as a baker's tray. It was obvious there would be no wind all day. There would be no lifting to the sea-swell, no zizzing of the wind in the shrouds, not even any crafty jiggling to a soft breeze. There would certainly be no beating into the wind, with spray whizzing into our intent eyes; no sudden gusts to frighten Willie into startled silence, even momentarily, as had been my hopeful consolation until now. *Cresswell* would feel no ground-swell, nor the proud wonder of her first heaves over them, the same every time it happened, now as the very first time, way back in 1908. Today her hull would not tremble as she ran out from the protection of the jutting headland. Today she would stay a dead, inanimate collection of bits of wood and metal, put together by men's hands, like a house ashore. Today there would be no sense of heart and spirit, the soul and dream which had been built so truly and honestly into her. Today she would not send the spit of the seas playfully over her shoulder, hosing spray aft at us. She would not communicate to us the soaring *praise of life* from the sea and every living thing in it.

I stopped the engine. *Cresswell* sorrowfully slowed down and stopped dead in the dead water. She wallowed.

"No point in going any further," I mumbled, as I crawled up out of the engine space. "We've only got enough diesel oil to get us back in again. . . . Unless you want to row."

Willie was now in the midst of a descant on Satisfaction. " . . . And the amount of satisfaction that we get from life largely depends on our own ingenuity?"

"Oh, dahling, not to fret one teeny bit. *Deah* Willie's *awf'ly* heppy."

" . . . Those of us who sit around waiting for satisfaction to overtake us . . . ."

"Well, we'll have to sit here. It's not too bad. Maybe you can talk him into going over the side for a swim."

" . . . .usually find only boredom instead?"

"Oh, Ai say, what a *splendid* idea!"

"Yes, if I were you I'd get him over the side as soon as possible, just in case a wind comes up. You never know."

" . . . And, although one can be satisfied with one's circumstances, of course one can never be satisfied with one's attainments?"

Willie was in the ideal circumstance of a preacher who has achieved his highest earthly attainment: He had a captive congregation. The only escape was over the side. Either me or him. It wasn't going to be me—I can't swim.

Soon Sissie, in her black one-piece swimming suit, which made her look as if she were a contender in a 1922 beauty contest, and the bishop, who had doffed his shirts, socks, and tennis shoes, were clambering down *Cresswell's* rudder as Nelson and I watched them gleefully. Once in the water, Willie, although he spluttered at first some declamation on how fine and good it was, spoke little, and then in low tones to Sissie. For an hour or so, after I had told them there were shoals of all kinds of exotic fish by the headland a mile to the east of us (which there weren't), they stayed over there, well out of earshot, and I lay down in the sun on the weatherdeck to relax my frayed nerves. After a while there came a soft padding on deck and Nelson lay down beside me. And so we spent a sunny, calm forenoon.

As the sun reached the meridian, the rolling, vrooming voice, like a slow-moving squall, relentlessly approached *Cresswell* again, and, to Sissie's occasional murmur of comprehension and approbation, lectured to her and five wheeling seagulls on Disappointment. Presumably they had searched hard for the exotic fish.

"... And Belloc wrote that he had a friend who told him in early life that he was determined to expect the worst always? For thus he would receive no ... (splutter) ... disappointment? Belloc wrote that he watched his friend living by that doctrine and finally discovered his friend to be abominably disappointed?!"

Sissie crowed a laugh. "Oh, *deah* Willie ..." Her head rose over the rudderpost simultaneously with my heart dropping into my deck shoes. "... So very clevah, so terribly, *awf'ly* funny!" she said as she passed by, dolloping seawater from her thick, dimpled thighs onto the decks and over me.

There was consolation, though, on that windless day off Ibiza. Willie handed up the hamper he had brought with him. Sissie opened it and revealed an Aladdin's treasure of culinary delights. There was *pâté de foie gras*, which we smeared on some bread that Sissie had made only two days before; a fine Wiltshire ham, applesauce from Warwickshire; cheddar, Lancashire, and Caerphilly cheeses; Keiller's marmalade and Robinson's jam; clotted cream and Eccles cake—all of which we washed down with real scrumpy cider from Cornwall. It was an epicurean tour of the cathedral towns and cities of England, Scotland, and Wales, and we all ate in precious, almost absolute silence, except for Willie's thundered comments on Appetite.

"It is somewhat humiliating for me ..." (another large ham sandwich disappeared into the maw of the cathedral organ) "... to realize what a controlling influence the intestines have on the thoughts and ways of humanity?"

As I handed Nelson a long string of ham fat I reflected that heaven might or might not be for Sissie and Nelson and me, but that this world was certainly for the clergy. And I thought of what an ancient fisherman had once said to me in Ireland: "It's a strange priest, beJasus, whose pig dies of starvation."

After lunch *Cresswell* was still floating absolutely still in the water, as ashamed as an abandoned bride, so Sissie and Willie took off again swimming over the side for a pair of hours. This time they did not swim far, so instead of sleeping in peace I was treated to commentaries on various subjects.

Enjoyment: "It takes a good, clean mind to know how to enjoy the bright and worthwhile things in life?"

Happiness: "It has been said, my dear Cecilia, that the moment when one realizes true happiness is when one distinguishes the idea of felicity from that of wealth. But I think that can hardly be true—consider Prince Elmyr, for example?"

Heroism (this after Sissie had spent a good ten minutes telling Willie how *awf'ly*, terrific'ly *brave* I was): "Well, of course, Cecilia, the only thing that gives bravery and heroism—I mean the physical sorts—any kind of meaning, is *death.*"

This cheered me up no end, as you may imagine.

But even the best of days draw to their ends, and by three in the afternoon Willie and Sissie, both rather exhausted and a lot quieter now, returned onboard. I started my mortal enemy, the banging Iscariot below; it clattered away at my first hate-filled, sweaty exertion, and *Cresswell*, like a scorned woman, her hull tense and furious, slunk back to the old hulk's berth. As she slid in gently alongside the ancient *Rosalinda*, the hoary schooner seemed to tremble. The slight bump we gave her made the broken wires hanging from her rotting gaff jiggle and dance, as if the old girl was pleased that her little friend had returned to keep her company once more during the long nights of wistfulness over glorious days never to return.

Except for Willie's voice, though, *Cresswell* was silent, with her sails lashed and all her loose gear stowed by Sissie. Willie, now with his sports outfit re-donned, stuck out a fluttering flounder at me. "Thanks for a wonderful outing, old chap?"

"Pleasure. Sorry about the wind."

"Oh, think nothing of it. Can't expect everything, can we, and your company's been marvelous?"

"Thanks, Willie." I turned to check the mooring lines.

"*Deah*, dahling Willie," Sissie murmured behind me. It was like a litany in church, with Sissie intoning the replies.

"Yes, I say, do come along with Sissie and me for dinner tonight. Perhaps we can have a drink or two afterward?"

"Glad to." (Never turn down comestibles or booze.)

So went the only time I ever sailed with a clergyman.

We have done with Hope and Honour, we are lost to Love and
   Truth,
      We are dropping down the ladder rung by rung,
And the measure of our torment is the measure of our youth.
      God help us! For we knew the worst too young!
Our shame is clean repentance for the crime that brought the
   sentence,
      Our pride is to know no spur of pride,
And the Curse of Reuben holds us till an alien turf enfolds us
      And we die, and none can tell them where we died.

We're poor little lambs who've lost our way,
      Baa! Baa! Baa!
We're little black sheep who've gone astray,
      Baa-aa-aa!
Gentlemen rankers out on a spree,
Damned from here to Eternity,
God ha' mercy on such as we,
      Baa! Yah! Bah!

"Gentlemen Rankers" (last verse)
—Rudyard Kipling.

The Whiffenpoofs of Yale University changed the words to
this poem and put them to music.

8

Little Black Sheep

BY SIX o'clock in the evening Sissie was again bright and effulgent in her rose-bedecked white frock and wide-brimmed hat. I had changed into my corduroys and a clean tee-shirt—the only one onboard, as it happened. It was dusk, and time for mutual admiration.

"Deah, dahling Tristan, *mai*, how perfectly, *eb*solutely adorable you look!" Sissie gushed at me, fishing for praise herself.

"And you look like a . . . a *coronation!*" said I. That got Sissie so flustered that she could just about stop her handbag from sliding over the side into the mucky old-wreck berth as she heaved *Cresswell's* stern line. In some miraculous way she had done one of those things that women do with their hair, so that instead of looking like the frayed ends of a live 10,000-volt electric cable it shone aureate, a golden glow around her blue eyes, like sunset in a rose bower. Her new high-heeled white shoes made me again wonder at what marvelous solutions of engineering stresses are to be observed in women's feet. As Sissie grabbed onto the mizzen topping lift and tensed to jump to the jetty, I had a vision of the Eiffel Tower balanced upside down on its television mast. I swiftly concluded that there must be some sort of levitation involved; surely those slender, delicate heels could never, on their own, support a whole 170-pound English games-mistress? This was obviously the question that the small, dark fishermen were asking themselves as they crowded to the door of the bodega opposite the old-hulks' berth, and jammed themselves, stretching, straining, and craning in wide-eyed Latin wonder, to watch as this vision of blue-eyed pulchritude flashed by them, chatting away to me, like a full-rigged sailing ship sending semaphore signals by the dozen, and smelling of something that brought to mind the offshore breeze from Antibes.

Willie was waiting for us, his face a beaming, rutilant red, in the Hotel Montesol foyer. "Cecilia, my dear?!" His roar made the counter staff—a man of about ninety and a boy of about thirteen—jump almost to the ceiling. It was as if General Franco himself had just marched into the hotel. They sprang as much to attention as they could; then, recovering their wits, pressed just about every bell within reach, so that in seconds we were surrounded by a hovering flock of penguin-suited waiters, all staring at Sissie in her finery.

The bishop had undergone yet another transformation. Now he was resplendent in a white confection, worn over a light blue shirt and round collar.

"*Deah*, dahling Willie! How *terribly* naice to *see* you again!"

It was as if the pair had just returned from the ends of the earth; she from the back reaches of the Kalahari desert, he from a mission through the Canadian arctic. You would never have dreamed that they had, only three hours before, been swimming out in the bay. I stared in wonder, and with a touch of sadness. Now, in the midst of this Continental display, I knew that the British Empire was finally finished.

Willie turned to me, his pate gleaming under the foyer chandelier. "And Tristan?" He clapped one ecclesiastically benign flounder on my shoulder and, taking Sissie by her chubby elbow, led us gently but surprisingly firmly into the hotel dining room. There, at a snowy white table gleaming with china and silverware, the bishop did us proud. There was no waiting for service with Willie's voice around. He had only to mention the weather and right away three waiters and the wine-server were around us, as if they had been suspended on wires, awaiting the commands of *"su honra, el obispo,"* his honor the bishop.

It was obvious that the dining room staff cared not one whit that Willie was Anglican; he could have been a Catholic, a Methodist, a Seventh Day Adventist, a California prelate of the Mother Church, or even a Buddhist—he wore a round collar, and that was enough. The word had obviously been passed to the kitchen and wine cellar, for the food and drink were superlative and the after-dinner brandy excellent.

When we stepped out into the street our stomachs were replete with good food and wine, and our ears with Willie's maxims: "One forgets how unsophisticated, how . . . indeed, how crude life remains outside the universities? Talk of television shows, cinema shows, the latest gadgets, sport; everyday anecdotes, what occurred at the office that day—that type of thing? No real talk at all? One is amazed that life goes on at all? People not caring much for anything that really matters at all?"

As we wended our way through the narrow streets Willie's voice reverberated from the whitewashed walls of the little shops and made the raffia hats and mats hanging outside shiver and shake. As we passed the Ibizan families out for their evening constitutionals, or to display their offspring (of which there were plenty), the women turned their eyes, wondering, toward Willie, but didn't move their heads under their black shawls. All the men, of course, were too busy gazing at Sissie to be bothered by the booming chant.

Willie was now holding forth on the subject of Children. "To children, childhood holds no particularly striking advantage? Their wants and desires are eternal, and they never seem to yield to the passing of time?"

"We'll go to the George and Dragon," I murmured to Sissie.

" . . . A child's life is full of tedious questionings— Where have you been? What makes this work? How is it

made? The only answer, of course, is another question—
Why do you want to know?" The bishop was in full swing.

Sissie gave me a questioning look.

"The terrible thing about childhood," the bishop
droned, "is that we were taught that we ought to admire
people who are good, when all we cared about was
whether they were kind?"

"It's an English-style pub," I hissed at Sissie, "up
toward the town quay. It's run by two London blokes—
brothers. I was in there the other day. They've got Wat-
ney's beer and Bass ales." So runs an exiled sailor's mind.

" . . . To talk to a child, to really fascinate him, to hold
all his attention, is much more difficult than holding a
whole congregation with a sermon, but it's also much more
rewarding, I feel?"

"Oh, my *deah* Tristan, how jolly *splendid* of you to think
of finding an English place for *deah* Willie and me!" Sissie
squeezed my arm like a nutcracker crushing a shell.

"It has been said that to enter heaven one must become
as a little child?" Willie chanted.

I decided to converse. "I should think that to enjoy any
heaven yet invented it would be best to remain a child."

But *deah* Willie was not biting. He thundered on.
"When a child is good I do not love him because he is
good, but because he is a child?"

"Oh, deah, *dahling* Willie." This, of course, from Sissie.

"But children know when they're being patronized," I
said, as we reached the steps leading down into the George
and Dragon. "They know, and they go straight and immediately on the defensive against you, against anyone who
treats them as strange beings—against someone who loves
them simply because they are children."

My dander was up now, fortified by the strong odor of
Bass ale slops rising up the steps. "It's a sort of insulting
discrimination to treat young people as if they were a
different sort of animal. Children are people!"

I raised my voice above the wailing of some California
song by the Mamas and Papas. It occurred to me in a flash

that it was highly appropriate that young adults—practically children—should name their group of childishly whining voices after the soppy pseudonym of parental authority. *"Children are people!"* I repeated loudly just as the music stopped.

For a blessed moment there was a golden silence in the dimly lit, tiny, crowded bar. Then a throaty voice from a dark corner shouted, loudly and drunkenly, "Children should be seen . . . and fuckinwell *exterminated!"*

As the music recommenced I made my way to the bar and peered into the dark corner whence had been hurled the harsh remark. A blond lady who sat at a barstool called over her shoulder in a low, ripe, fruity English voice, "Take no notice, darling—it's only Steel. He doesn't really mean it. He's had one too many, that's all."

The lady turned her head toward me. She was ancient. I don't mean elderly, I mean *ancient*. From behind, a quick glance at the shapeliness of her back and her hair had given me the impression that she might be thirty or so. When she turned I saw immediately, even in the dim light, that she was at least eighty. I discovered later that she was in fact eighty-nine. Her face was heavily made up, with flat white powder liberally patted over her wrinkles, and gleaming red lipstick. Her eyes, under drooping lids, were dark blue, and looked straight into mine.

I decided it was a good, honest face. I smiled at it. It cracked. The cigarette dangling from her lips lowered its angle and sent smoke up into her eyes, so she shut them momentarily as she continued. "Steel's a writer, and you know how *they* are." She lowered her head and flicked cigarette ash from the sequined bag lying on her lap.

I grinned again and said, "Yes, of course. Not to worry, love."

I peered again into the corner. Sitting there was a stocky man with a large, leonine head covered with dark curls, which fell around his ears. His face was heavy and his jowls fell from each side of his nose, which had a rounded Jewish cast. At first, as I stared at him, he was slouched with his chin down into the collar of his Astrakhan overcoat. His eyes were shut. Then one eye opened. It gleamed back at me, a mischievous button. The other eye opened. A generous, sensitive mouth grinned, and the first eye winked at me. I laughed silently and winked back. At least he had shut up the bishop momentarily.

I turned back to the ancient lady, who was squinting at me, studying me. Next to her a young Ibizan, about twenty-two and well-dressed, leaned against the bar. He eyed me with what I took to be hostility. I immediately sensed that he was the ancient lady's escort. I smiled at him and greeted him in Catalan to put him at ease. Right away his anxious tension dissipated, like gas escaping a collapsed balloon.

There were horse-harness brasses all along the low, black beam over the bar; a touch of home, even if they weren't genuine. The bartender was a thin, hurried, anxious-looking young man, with curly black hair and sharp, darting eyes. He dashed around the minute space behind the bar as if concerned that the very last ship was departing the island with all his customers, and he needed to get rid of all his stock before the imminent sailing.

Deah Willie's sonorous tones almost drowned the Beatles' music now issuing from a large tape-deck on the bar shelf. "A large Scotch and soda. Brandy or Scotch, Cecilia? Tristan?"

"Oh, *deah* Willie, gin, please. Booth's," simpered Sissie, standing close behind me.

The ancient lady had been glaring at Sissie; then, just as fast as the sun breaking through clouds in the Trades, she smiled. "I hear you're English," she said throatily. It was a statement to lesser breeds without the Law, and to the world in general. She stuck out one white-gloved hand toward me. "I'm Lulu," she whispered hoarsely.

I introduced myself and Sissie.

"And this is Eduardo," said Lulu, nodding backward toward her young companion. "He doesn't speak English, but despite that he's awfully nice—you know, in *their* way."

As Sissie took Eduardo in with her steely North Sea eyes, he seemed to cringe visibly, yet at the same time put himself on offer to her. He reminded me, at that moment, of a snake farmer I had once seen trying to trap a cobra.

"Awf'ly naice to meet you, old chep!" Sissie screeched at Eduardo.

Behind Sissie, *deah* Willie was bellowing something about the dartboard, which, obviously pristine and never used, was hanging proudly on the back of the bar door. In that bar there wasn't room to swing a cat, much less play a game of darts.

"Put a man in a room where he can play darts or dominoes," droned Willie, "or read a newspaper in peace, or have a rattling good talk, and one observes that he will not drink as fast or as deep, or as strongly as he otherwise would? I'm very pleased that there are facilities here for other activities beside drinking? There should always be other things to do in these establishments beside drinking? What does a man drink for? To amuse himself? And to forget all his troubles and the woes of the working world?"

"Bullshit," roared the voice of Steel the Writer, from the dark corner. It had the flat yet tangy New York flavor to it. "Bullshit. For that he goes to a goddamn whorehouse!"

For a moment there was no reaction. Sissie, startled, turned to me, smiled a quick smile, then flung the rest of the smile to Miss Lulu's escort, the smoky-eyed Eduardo. Taking in the bishop, wincing as Willie let loose again, then side-glancing at Lulu and me, Eduardo decided that the whole match was too much for him. He retired from the fray and gloomily studied the whisky for which Miss Lulu had just paid from her sequined bag. The snake farmer, too, I remembered, had mounted his jeep in disgust and taken off in a cloud of dust, back home through the bush.

I looked at Steel the Writer. His big, handsome head was still bent forward, resting on his chest. But his eyes were gleaming, wide open, studying the bishop with a taunting leer. I grinned at him. He raised his glass, drank it off, and slammed it back down on the tiny table in front of him.

Willie threw the congregation another maxim from the pulpit: "It's the privilege of good-fellowship to talk nonsense, and yet have that nonsense respected?"

"*Mary had a little lamb, its fleece was white as snow,*" recited the drunken-sounding voice from the corner. "The guy's a goddamn plagiarist!"

This time I didn't just smile at Steel the Writer. I attended him. There must have been some respect in my look. He watched me for a full second, and something passed between us. He *knew* that I knew that Willie was paraphrasing one of Charles Lamb's letters to his sister Mary. For a moment I was flabbergasted. I reckoned that it was a chance in a billion that anyone east of New York and south of London would know just how very unoriginal *deah* Willie was, but I saw in a flash that Steel the Writer had reckoned up the situation, too.

Steel stood up. He was a big man, bearish in his open Astrakhan coat. He raised his arms above his head and stretched them, almost touching the ceiling of the bar. Then, with a ponderous movement, he slowly pressed his way through the throng crowded at the bottom of the steps, staggering slightly and grinning at me. He winked again, turned his broad back, and slowly, steadily made his groggy way up the steps and out into the narrow, moonlit street. The bar was then, somehow, much emptier, as if London had been deprived of its tower.

Now Willie had the ground to himself. He rambled on. "I'm told that some American writers who have known each other for years have never met in daylight, or when they are sober?"

"What a dreadful, *tiresome* little man!" moaned Sissie, alluding, presumably, to the departed American. Every male she disliked was "little."

I leaned over to her. "The *Thurber* you get from England."

"Oh, Tristan! I didn't know that you knew Lewis Carroll!" She had misheard me. "Oh, I simply adore *Alice in Wonderland*," she screamed at Miss Lulu. "Don't you?"

"No, I prefer Hemingway," replied the ancient lady. "He's much more manly."

I studied Miss Lulu with new-found respect—even a little fondness. She had tried to defend Steel in her own way, but it was no use. She might as well have tried to sink the Majorca ferry with her handbag.

But soon the scotches that Lulu was knocking back like a trouper, and Sissie's gin ("Booth's London Dry, please—I simply cawn't *stend* that dreary Dutch nonsense!") did their work, and both ladies were chatting away at female small-talk, the eighth wonder of the world, while Willie beamed about him and broadcast to the motley audience in the George and Dragon more of "his" views on writers.

"When one says that a writer is fashionable, one practically always means that he is read by people under thirty?" I could almost see a half-starved, tubercular Orwell turning in his grave.

"Of course, most writers are depressives—they need perpetual reassurance?" I didn't know who he was quoting now, but I concluded it must have been some editor or other.

With Willie's organ-voice zooming at me across six barflies, I turned around to inspect the people behind. My eye was immediately struck by one of the most beautiful young women I have ever seen. She was tall and willowy. She gazed at her companion—a small, fat man with thinning hair and the wily face of a bookmaker—as if he were the captain of a lifeboat and she were waiting for him to rescue her from the foundering *Titanic*. She had dark blond hair and a face like a delicately sculpted dream, as if the artist had used a feather and a sycamore leaf instead of a mallet and chisel, and had worked away at the shape of that face for an eternity to perfect it. Set in the face were the eyes of a Siamese cat, gray and gold and green and deep. It's easy to say that her smile brought to mind the Mona Lisa, but it did—except that the perfectly shaped lips were closed because they were wise lips, and not merely to cover bad teeth.

The Vision noticed me looking at her. Her green-gray eyes gazed into mine. The slight smile remained, frozen. She looked into me as I would look into a grave. It was as if she were crying into a void. Desperate. She might have been twenty-four.

I turned my glance to her companion. I had overheard him talking in the cockney accent of the London suburbs. He was shorter than I, and when he turned his watery blue eyes on me he lifted one eyebrow. He was chubby and flaccid, and his skin, in the light of a green lamp above us, was somewhat the color of a melonskin—pale green, with liverish yellow patches. I guessed his age at around forty-five, but he later told me he was thirty-two.

"You English?" he asked.

"Well, Welsh."

"Yeah, my old man was Welsh. Kept a dairy in 'ampstead, he did. Wotcha doin' 'ere, then?"

"Oh, knocking around. My boat's in the harbor."

"Yeah? Used to be in the navy meself. Wanna drink? My name's Alf." He turned and nodded casually at the Vision, who I now saw was dressed neatly in a gray jacket, a frilly blouse with its neckline high and demure, and silk pajama trousers. "And this bird is Louise."

The young woman showed no sign that Alf had spoken. She gazed ahead of her as if she were sleepwalking with her eyes wide open.

"She don't drink," said Alf. "She's just comin' off an acid trip." He smirked at me. "She yaffles it like a bloomin' kid eatin' candy! Her old man's a bleedin' cabinet minister in 'olland, an' 'ere she is, screamin' 'er bloody 'ead orf 'alf the time, when she's not on her back dishin' out khifer to the locals. Them randy sods, they're at 'er like bloomin' kids at the jellybeans, ain't they?" He laughed again, his fat lips slobbering as he pushed between Sissie and me to get to the bar, where Willie was droning on and on at two well-dressed elderly gentlemen, both with soft, smooth faces, who had entered moments before, holding hands.

I tried to talk to Louise. "Which part of Holland are you from?" I asked as pleasantly as I could.

The gray-green eyes never flinched. The perfect mouth hardly opened. She spoke in a low, flat, clear voice. "Fuck Holland."

"I spent the winter there a couple of years back—at Volendam. Do you know it?" I tried to smile.

"Fuck Volendam."

"How long are you in Ibiza?" I continued bravely.

"Fuck Ibiza. And fuck you." Still no sign of any emotion. No sign of any intent, any awareness, any presence, any love. The face, startling in its beauty, showed nothing. No petulance, no dislike, no distaste, no hatred—nothing. Only a cold, cold, beauty. It was like looking at the frozen, ice-shining rocks of Spitzbergen on a calm day. There was nothing sinister in that face. Nothing evil. The eyes did not threaten, or menace, or daunt, or warn, or intimidate. They did *nothing*. They were blank, as if she were blind, as indeed, for a flash, I thought she might be—until I caught a flicker from them as she stabbed a stare at Willie. That was the only reaction that wonderful face showed in the whole hour I watched her eyes, on and off, in brief glances, while I observed the assembly and listened to Alf.

Alf came back from the bar, bearing our drinks. He nodded his head toward Sissie, with whom he had just had a short, joking exchange. "She your old woman?"

"Passenger," I replied.

"Cor, blimey, ain't 'alf a life, innit?" He gulped at his beer, looking at me the while. "Only come down 'ere twice a year," he said.

"What do you do? I mean, do you work?" I asked, as I took in his loud checked jacket, blue shirt, and silver tie done in a wide Windsor knot.

Alf spluttered as he gulped his pint again. "Wot, me work? You must be jokin'! Nah, I backs the gee-gees. I makes enough to come down 'ere every four months, and stay 'ere fer about two or three months, then orf I go, back again, see?"

"What do you do here, then, Alf?"

"Oh, I drinks an' . . . " He craftily threw a leer at the still-staring Dutch lass, " . . . an' I gets me end away, don't I?" He said this last bit almost defensively. "Only it's bug- gered up now. She caught a dose o' siff, an' the local docs won't treat 'er, so she's got to go orf to bloomin' Majorca, ain't she?" He raised his pint again, gulped deep and long, smacked his lips as he put down his glass, and went on. "Still, I don't mind. Plenty more where she came from, eh?"

"You meet her down here?"

"Yeah, she was down on the beach dishin' it out, along with about twenty other birds. They had a midnight party over at Figueretas—Ronnie the Pouf's place. Bloke called Legros stood all the booze and brought about five dollie-birds and three young blokes. He fancies *them*, see?"

"What do all these people do, Alf? I mean how do they live?"

Alf grinned at me after he set his beer down again. "Oh, a bit 'ere, a bit there. You know how it is. Ronnie the Pouf, well, 'e's a sort of barman, but Legros, blimey, 'e's got money growin' out of 'is ears, 'e 'as; 'e's an art dealer—you know, flogs paintings. Travels all over the world. I think 'e's a poufter too, but 'e knows I'm on the other team, so 'e never bothers me. We get on all right. 'E even invites me up to 'is mate's 'ouse for drinks now an' again. They got a swimmin' pool an' all up there . . . up in the Old Town it is."

My ears pricked up. I looked at Alf closely. "Oh? What's his mate do, then?"

"Oh, 'e's a real turn, that one. Another pouf- ter . . . 'E's a . . . what do you call 'em—you know, people what buy paintin's?"

"An art collector?"

"Yeah, 'e's an art collector. 'E's a big noise from Paris. Name's Elmyr."

I looked quickly at Sissie, but she was busy conversing with Lulu and had not overheard Alf. Over all, like the voice of Jehovah, the bishop droned on. I said nothing as I listened to Alf gossip about life on the island which I had heard described as "the Saint Germain des Prés of the Mediterranean," but which others spoke of as "Garbageville sur la Merde."

"See that little bloke at the end of the bar?" Alf did not move his head. "Don't look now, but that's Old Bill. Secret Police, but it's all right—'e don't know one bleedin' word of English."

Later, *deah* Willie, having lost his audience of hand-holding gentlemen, both of whom had nervously sipped mineral water as he fired his maxim gun at them, edged his way over toward Alf and me. His voice drowned Alf's intriguing account of life and personalities ashore in Ibiza, and for another fifteen minutes, as I tried to block off my ear passages, Sissie gazed in wonderment and Alf gulped his beer, in between staring, his mouth open in astonishment, as Willie, seemingly oblivious to everything about him except the presence of an audience, held forth.

"There is nothing we like to see more than the gleam of pleasure in a person's eye when he knows we have sympathized with him and understand him? When he realizes that we are genuinely interested in his welfare? At these times something rare and spiritual passes between two dear friends? These are the moments that make life really worth living?"

As Willie's voice jiggled the horse brasses and shook the bottles at the bar, Alf leaned close to me. "'Oo's that?" he asked in a whisper.

"The bishop of Southchester—a right toff," I replied in a low voice.

"'E's a real card, ain't he?"

"Ah, he's all right. Got a touch of verbal diarrhea, that's all."

"'E's with you?"

"Yeah, he's that lady's brother. We went out sailing today, but there was no wind."

Alf eyed the bishop. "Makin' up for it, ain't 'e?" he said. "'Ere, let's take 'im round to the Tierra bar. I know a bloke 'round there, supposed to be a painter. French bloke . . . But 'e's really an acid dealer. Brings it down from Switzerland. If I pays 'im a thousand pesetas 'e'll slip some into 'is booze."

"Come off it, Alf," I muttered, and saved the bishop for England.

"Well, it's only a suggestion, i'n it?" Alf slugged his pint.

Willie was still rambling on. "It takes a lot of patience, of course, to appreciate domestic happiness? Some volatile souls actually prefer unhappiness?

"Although I love a holiday, of course, I do actually prefer my own surroundings; they mean so much to me, especially when I'm feeling miserable? Alas, this holiday seems to me to be so short, but I am getting the holiday feeling a little more each day? I have almost rid myself of the ever-imminent sense that I am neglecting some spiritual duty to others when I am away from my diocese?"

And so on, all the while with Sissie staring at him in holy wonder and Miss Lulu nodding her ancient head wisely, in between taking great draughts of Scotch and soda. Eduardo, by this time, had leaned his head on the counter and appeared to be fast asleep. Everyone else except the Dutch statue, Alf, the anxious young bartender, and me, had departed. The bishop had a congregation of only six people, with a seventh probably asleep—until three newcomers descended the steps.

A young man and woman, both about twenty, both blue-eyed blonds, both expensively dressed, both good-looking, bounced in merrily, then stood aside to let a thin, ascetic-looking man, also well-dressed and handsome, pass by them toward the bar. There, as Willie's voice rolled around his ears, the ascetic man bought drinks. Quickly the three newcomers, very privately among themselves, saw off their drinks and left as fast as they had entered.

"They didn't stay long," I observed to Alf in a quiet way.

"No wonder, is it?" Alf replied, eying Willie. Then he leaned toward me conspiratorially, and whispered, "That bloke 'of just left is a millionaire an' only thirty. 'E invented something to do with printing'. Nice bloke, only 'e's a bit bent, see?"

"Bent? You mean he's homosexual?"

"Nah, he's not *that* way," replied Alf. " 'E's a what-jacallit . . . one of them people what likes to see other people gettin' it away?"

"A voyeur?"

"Yeah. Well, an' them two others, they're German, an' they're always with 'im. He watches 'em an' plays with 'imself while they're on the job, see?"

"Well, that's one way of passing time, I suppose," I said. "As long as they're not hurting anyone. And those two seem to be doing pretty well for themselves."

"Yeah. They're bruvver and sister, and they reckon he pays 'em fifty quid every time."

It was midnight when *deah* Willie and Sissie and I, shaking hands all around in good-fellowship, departed from the bar. The bishop was still ranting away. "But the release of holidays abroad cannot, of course, dear Cecilia, make up for frustrations at home? As a matter of fact, the reliance on holidays to accomplish that often destroys them? By expecting too much one gets less from the holiday than otherwise? Only an emotionally satisfying life, even within a hard-working existence, can be enriched by holidays which are then equally though differently satisfying, as, indeed, this holiday is to me?"

"Oh, *deah*, dahling Willie!"

Soon we were all back at the Hotel Montesol. An obsequious porter glidingly guided Willie into its luxurious interior, and Sissie and I wended our way back onboard *Cresswell*, to the welcomes of Nelson's wagging tail and the jingle of *Rosalinda*'s frayed rigging.

"Oh, *deah* Tristan, thenk you *so* much for such a lovely, ebsolutely *spiffing* evening!" Sissie called from the forward dodger hatch.

"Think nothing of it, love. G'night!"

Nelson crawled under the cabin table and laid himself down alongside my berth. Then I was happier, and fell asleep knowing that tomorrow my crew and her *deah* brother were off to Majorca for three whole days, and that from there the bishop was due to return to the Land of Hope and Glory.

Now as I was a-walking down Ratcliffe Highway,
A flash-looking packet she happened my way,
Of the port that she hailed from I cannot say much,
But by her appearance I took her for Dutch.

Chorus: *Singing too-roo-lye-oora-lye-addie,*
        Oora-lye-oora-lye-aye!

Her flag was three colors, her masthead was low,
She was round at the counter and bluff at the bow,
From larboard to starboard and so sailed she;
She was sailing at large, she was running free.

She was bowling along with her wind running free;
She clewed up her courses and waited for me.
I fired my bow-chaser, the signal she knew,
She backed her main tops'l and for me she hove to.

I hailed her in English; she answered me clear,
"I'm from the Black Sheep, bound for the Shakespeare."
So I wore ship, and with a "What d'ye know?"
I passed her my hawser and took her in tow.

I tipped her my flipper and took her in tow,
And yardarm to yardarm it's off we did go.
Then she took me up to her lilly-white room,
And there all the evening we drank and we spooned.

The first five verses of "The Ratcliffe Highway," a hauling chantey very popular on the crack clipper ships which plied the Western Ocean in the second half of the 19th century. A "packet" was the term used for ships which ran regularly between certain ports. They were considered the elite. The Ratcliffe Highway was just by the East London docks. The Black Sheep and the Shakespeare were pubs frequented by "easy ladies." The chantey goes on, of course, to tell how the sailor was robbed by the "flash packet," and ends with a warning to young sailors who might be tempted into similar situations.

9

On the Highway

Sissie was up and about even earlier than usual. Before the Majorca ferry departed she prepared breakfast, washed the dishes, had a last, hurried scurry around the galley to make sure it was clean. She also made out a list of groceries for me to buy before she returned.

I had been reluctant to shop, at first. To me it was a petty chore—the haggling in Catalan, all the sniffing and weighing and tasting, the rituals of rejection and reluctant acceptance; the small, dark, dingy places full of bags and boxes and black-shawled elderly ladies of limitless girth and age, who looked upon men-shoppers with disapprobation and disdain. In the past I had been forced into demonstrations of fumbling, uncertain *machismo* which would have made even a ballet dancer look like a heavyweight boxer. Then the old ladies would stare at me and slowly melt into matronly helpfulness and condescending expertise. They had even, in some cases, undercharged me.

In Spain, shopping was *women's* work. So was every other type of labor, with the concrete exceptions of fishing, plowing, building tourist hotels, waiting at table, drinking, and begetting the next generation. This was not a case of female exclusion or male exclusivity; woe betide any man who strayed into the preserves of traditional female activities. But foreigners, all of whom the Spaniards at that time looked upon as being somewhat crazy (understandably enough), could sometimes get away with shopping if the old ladies knew them, or if native menfolk were around to hiss through their teeth, as the women started giggling, to subdue their mirth.

Now, over breakfast, I repented my reluctance to shop. It wasn't only that Sissie had hardly any time to do the shopping before the ferry left. It was something else, although of course I didn't tell Sissie what it was. I let her imagine it was because I was thinking of her, helping her, being considerate. A bit of flannel goes a long way, sometimes, with a woman in a frenzy of preparation for a trip.

The real reason I agreed to do the shopping would be, to landsfolk, probably much more mundane, much less romantic.

Sea voyagers on the move for years, as I have been, have a difficulty in really getting to know the people of the countries and islands at which they call. In the main, they seldom have much interest in what lies beyond the waterfront and its denizens. This is not surprising; they probably get a much more genuine sense of a port, if only of its repair facilities and drinking dens, in just one day, than the normal tourist gets in a couple of weeks. But sailors rarely get to know much else—*unless they shop.*

The average sailor's needs may be simple (tending, in some cases, towards crude) and they are not always satisfied—but at least they give the sailor contact with others, even if some of those others would never be ordered to tea at Buckingham Palace, or invited to address the Ladies' Guild. The ordinary sailor—I'm talking about deckhands and cooks, not the peaked-cap, blue-blazer brigade—seldom wants to explore much beyond the waterfront or burden himself with historical facts and ancient dates, so as to be a bore at the end of his voyages. It may be a pity, but there it is. The average sailor is not too interested in having his snapshots disturb the native air or undermine the locals' peace again, just that little bit more.

In any case, if a landlubber—especially a tourist—should sneer at this attitude among deckies, he should consider that he sees very little more, since he himself is harnessed and constrained by his determination to "see everything," and his view is severely narrowed by his almost slavish dependence on the machinations of commercial tourism interests. Indeed, I met many tourists in Ibiza who, except for the sun and the sand, might just as well have stayed at home. It would have been cheaper, and for them probably as culturally rewarding.

There's not a lot wrong with commercial tourism. The world belongs to everyone, and everyone should have the right to go wherever they want to, and see and experience whatever they need to. But tourism does wreck the natural scheme of things. It does turn sturdy fisher-lads into simpering, avaricious, crawling hotel waiters; it does change bonny peasant lassies into harried bedroom cleaners; and it does carry with it not only the seeds of its own destruction, but those which can destroy every true value it touches. Tourism usually turns self-supporting areas and people into limpet-dependents of the industrial economies, which is all very well while the industrial areas are booming, and while wealth is growing. But when the crunch comes . . .

These were my thoughts as I ate the breakfast which Sissie had set out for me on a clean china plate, and as Nelson brushed my leg with his tail. He was pleased. I could feel it in the quiver of his tail and the rapid panting of his body against my foot. He *knew* Sissie was leaving *Cresswell*, for a while, at least.

Still in her gym slip, with the early-morning light all rosy-red, streaked across the sky above the companionway, over her frizzy ginger mop with its pink ribbon, Sissie delved into the galley cupboards and shelves, all the while keeping up a running commentary on what needed to be restocked.

" . . .And peas and beans . . . and, oh *drat!* We've no tomatoes. And this dried fish is smelling to high heaven . . . must chuck the jolly lot out . . ." She scrabbled up the fish corpses and jumped to the companionway ladder.

"Where're you taking that?" I asked, my mouth full of bread, butter, and tea. "Leave it—I'll use it for bait when I get back on the outer mole. There's some fine mullet coming into the harbor.''

She turned and slapped down the brown, rotting fish on the table in front of me. She expected me to object to this, but I carried on chewing. I'd had far worse things on my breakfast table than a few stinking cod.

She stood for a moment, studying me; then, with a shiver of her chubby body, she sighed. "Oh, *deah* Tristan, what *shell* I do?" she wailed.

I glanced up at her, still chewing. "What's up now, lass?"

"Well . . . oh, *deah* . . . You're so jolly *callous* about things. Ai mean you just don't seem to bally well *care* about yourself, and I'm so worried . . . Ai'll be in an *eb*solute fret about you while Ai'm away. Oh, I simply should *nevah* have offered to go with *deah* Willie to Majorca!"

"Oh, I'll be all right, girl. I'm a big boy now. The only thing I'm concerned about is getting the boat away from these bloody hulks and this damned roadway. These cars roaring past . . ." (there was about one vehicle an hour passing the stern of the boat) " . . .are sending me off my rocker with all their bloomin' noise."

Sissie slammed her shopping pad down on the galley shelf. "Then Ai shell jolly well *stay*. I simply *cawn't* leave you heah all alone!"

Nelson's body stiffened against my foot. I stopped chewing my breakfast. I looked at her. "No, you go, Sissie. I'll be all right, I tell you. Willie needs you far more than I do. If he goes to Majorca alone and those bloody sharks over there get hold of him, there'll be an international incident."

"You're sure, darling? Honestly? *Eb*solutely sure?"

"If I'm to do the shopping I'll need some money," I said, by way of showing her I was sure.

"Oh, *deah*, of course!" Sissie turned around and bounced up the companionway, her dimpled thighs quivering as she pounded the rungs of the ladder with her ditchdigger's brogues. Soon she was back, looking downcast and almost apologetic. "Ai've only 300 pesetas left with me," she said. "*Deah* Willie's paying the fare to Majorca, and I'll collect some more money tomorrow."

"That's all right. Leave it here," I said majestically, as if I were doing her a favor. Three hundred pesetas were worth about six dollars.

Sissie was supposed to be paying me a guinea (two and a half dollars) a day for her board and keep. It was all terribly English; all arranged over a handshake nine months before, and we had, of course, kept no records. But I reckoned she owed me money.

Soon, as the morning sky changed to blue and the early breeze sprang up out of the east, Sissie was once again transformed into something recognizably feminine. Once again she shone in her white, rose-covered dress. Once again her new white hat, with blue ribbon, was perched atop her whiskey-colored hair, and her eyes shone like the engine-room guardrails onboard the royal yacht *Britannia*. She stood at the top of the companionway, holding her new white handbag.

I took another swig of tea and made my way up the ladder. "Right, let's get you ashore, then."

Her body seemed to soften as she laid a hand on my arm and pulled me around so she could face me. For a moment I looked into her eyes. It was like looking lengthwise down a roll of freshly manufactured barbed wire. Suddenly a great tear dollop sprang from each eye and hovered there. I stretched the sleeve of my sailing jerkin down over one hand and reached up to wipe away the tears.

She pulled away from me. "No, Ai'm all right. Ai *really*, truly *am*, dahling."

The hovering teardrops obeyed the eternal laws of gravity and water-level, and fell. Momentarily, involuntarily, I glanced down at my feet, as if to make sure that the teardrops had not damaged the weatherdeck paint we had applied only a few days before in Formentera.

I made my way aft to heave on the stern-lines, with
Sissie tottering behind me on her high heels. Gallantly, as
another pair of teardrops fell onto the poop whaleback, I
took her proffered handbag, at first making sure that no
fishermen were peering out of the tiny bar across the street.
Sissie leaped. Still watching the bar door, I handed over her
bag. As the boat slid out again to the extent of the stern-
lines she gazed at me.

"You'd better get cracking," I said. "Willie will be
waiting."

"Oh, *deah* . . . Well, if you're sure you'll be *awf'ly* all
right . . ." Sissie's face looked doubtful. I was reminded of
the first time my mother left me at the infant's school, so
long ago, so far away, where the wet west wind whistles
over the coast of Merioneth.

"See you, Sissie. For Christ's sake, cheer up. It's only
for three days. Anyone would think you were a bloomin'
foreigner, the way you're carrying on! I'll see you. I'll be at
the outer mole."

I turned and, without looking back, skittered down the
companionway ladder and picked up my mug of tea while
Nelson whimpered and stuck his old head on my lap.
"Bloody women!" I said to him.

Nelson waved his tail and licked my free hand as I
gulped the tea and silently toasted my regained freedom.
Once again I was master, under God, of all I surveyed.
Even the feel of the cabin woodwork seemed to tell me that
Cresswell knew it, too. We were three again, a holy trinity—
three, the old magic number of the Celts. I had the same
sense of exultation that my forebears must have had each
and every time, throughout the ages, when they swept
away the blinding trappings of an alien religion and, for a
few magical days each year, wallowed and revelled in their
own unregenerate *mire.* I looked up through the companionway hatch; even the sunbeams seemed wilder and freer.

After letting Nelson lick the breakfast plate to clean it
(and save fresh water), I made my way again topsides. I
looked first over to the town quay. The Spanish powerboats

were still there, with their crewmen busy wiping and pol-
ishing and generally justifying their otherwise seemingly
decorative existences. I glanced at the cathedral atop the
Old Town. There was a slight movement of breeze, no
more than a candle flicker. It would soon be enough to
move the boat. I gazed at the outer mole, almost a quarter
of a mile away across the wide harbor, and saw a boat
moving out, away from the wall. No sooner had I seen the
movement of the departing boat, whatever she was, than I
had *Cresswell*'s mainsail tiers off, her working jib hanked on
the forestay, and her mooring lines off. With a great shove
against the silently weeping *Rosalinda*, we were off. Nelson
padded softly to his usual sailing station on the poop
whaleback, and lay down with his head on his paw to
supervise.

Soon the mainsail was hoisted. Even though there was
no breeze to speak of, and the gaff was swinging
unenthusiastically, and the mainsail hung listlessly for most
of the hour it took to work our way over the dead-calm
harbor, *Cresswell* felt, under my feet, as if she were joyful,
and she slowly slid along over the oily water like a young
girl shyly intent on some mild mischief.

Mooring to a jetty stern-to—which is the invariable
custom in Mediterranean waters—is sometimes a very difficult thing. For novices it can result in anything from a
stove-in stern to a busted rudder or snarled anchor, to a
bitter argument in six languages with half a dozen other
irate skippers and crewmen. The way you do it is first to
pick out the spot on the jetty where you intend to insert
your stern. Then you try to make sure that no other
anchors or anchor lines will be snagged by yours. You drop
your anchor way out from the jetty (at least six of your own
boatlengths, as a rule of thumb); then, if you're lucky
enough to have an engine, or the fuel to run it, you wangle
your stern in between the other boats that are moored up
until you are close enough to throw someone a line—if
there's anyone around. If there isn't, then you get your
stern close enough to the wall to be able to jump ashore

with a mooring line so you can secure it to a nearly ringbolt or bollard.

Of course, this is all theory. In practice, the underwater part of the jetty will probably be encumbered by rocks or sunken wrecks or other hazards sticking out from the jetty along the harbor bottom for twenty feet or so. In practice, the two vessels between which you are mooring will be production fiberglass eggshells, which will split open as soon as your boat's hull merely brushes them, and, unless you can afford insurance, bring claims down on your head large enough to ensure that you will spend your old age in abject poverty.

This time I was lucky and everything went without a hitch. I slung my car-tire fenders over *Cresswell*'s side again as she approached the anchoring spot. The mainsail came down with a rattle. I gazed around calmly for a spot to anchor. I kicked the anchor over the bow. The chain went down with a louder rattle. Then, as I waited for the anchor to sink into the sticky mud of the harbor bottom, I made myself a cup of tea. All around was quiet. The seawall was still deserted, even though it was almost seven o'clock.

I had already chosen my new neighbors. Indeed, I could choose no others—there was no space for *Cresswell* anywhere else on the outer mole. One neighbor was to be a Spanish fishing vessel; but she was obviously a conversion, because a cabin and a stubby mast had been added onto her, and she was far too clean and well-maintained to be a working vessel. On the other side would be a dumpy, squat, steel boat about twenty-five feet long, which, after staring at her for a while, I decided was a converted ship's lifeboat. She was painted battleship gray and had two short, squatty masts added to her. She was filthy with grease and dirt, and her topsides were loaded with heaps of junk—an old mattress and such. In other words, she looked *interesting*. All the more so because drooped over her stern was a huge, tattered British Red Ensign, which was so soaked in black goo that it looked as if it had been used to clean the boat's bilges. I stared at the name crudely painted on her in huge letters with red-lead paint, and grinned to myself: *Dreadnaught*.

"*Dreadnaught!*" I hollered a couple of times. No reply. I shouted a few times; then, seeing that "no answer was the loud reply," I hustled my little rubber dinghy off the coachroof into the water, scrambled over into it with the mooring line, and paddled myself away to the outer mole wall. I secured the dinghy, clambered up the mossy, oily wall, and then hauled in my mooring line from *Cresswell*. When the mooring line tautened up I heaved the boat's stern in slowly and carefully, taking my time, as we say, by the dockyard clock. As soon as the stern was close enough I leaped aboard, quickly shortened up the mooring line—and there she was, all taut and cozy, moored stern-to. No fuss, no palaver, all done in almost complete silence. Satisfied that all was well, congratulating myself on a difficult maneuver accomplished with professional aplomb, I returned to my tea.

Then the toothache started.

For the ocean voyager there are many terrors to be overcome. Most of them can be defeated or circumvented by simple reasoning, or by guile or force of will. Some cannot. Among the most serious of these are bodily complaints which might leave one either physically incapable or mentally exhausted, too weak to struggle on. Of these unknowable, unforeseeable ailments, probably the most threatening, given otherwise good health, are appendicitis and toothache. To those who intend to make small-boat voyages, and especially those who intend to make them alone, the first thing I would advise them to do is have their appendix out, and with it all their teeth. In my years of voyaging I could not do this, simply because I could never afford the cost.

My appendix was no problem; I ate too much rough and ready food for that. But my teeth—my Celtic, inch-long-rooted teeth—with them I have suffered the tortures of the doubly damned. I had once sat alone, 1000 miles from the nearest dentist, with a raging ache burning up along my jaw, up along my nose, spearing itself in savage stabs into my brain, into my very soul. I had cursed every curse known in five languages and gripped my jaw, my head, my ears, the nearest bit of boat or rigging, trying to squeeze, force, wring, and *tense* the life out of it. I had ranted and roared and cried tears of rage. I had howled to the empty, bitter reaches of the uncaring ocean. With the boat pitching and tossing, and my tooth's burning root seeming to stab down into my heart, I had damned every sea that rolled and trundled past in the darkness of the ocean night, summoning up the courage, the will, to break out the mole-grips and somehow get the great ridged-tooth jaws onto that *bastard* of a tooth and lock the pliers onto the crown. I had then, in utter agony, worked away with both hands on the pliers, twisting and forcing, pulling and pushing this way and that, until, after a seeming eternity of twinging, wracking, griping, nipping, creaking, stabbing, and gnawing misery, the tooth loosened. Then, in desperation and anger garnished with the strength of a madman somewhere deep within me, I had pulled the bugger *out*. Finally, amid a welter of broken bone-bits and roots, saliva, and blood, and feeling a wild, triumphant joy, I had hammered the rotten-stumped tooth, still locked in the mole-grips, against a ringbolt, trying to extract from it some degree of the misery, the hell, which it had bestowed on me.

Now, although I cursed at the first sudden stabs of pain, I was not in the throes of despair I had felt at sea, alone. Here it was simple. All I had to do was go ashore and get the thing pulled out. No messing about between me and my teeth—at the first sign of mutiny, out it comes, and over the side. No root-canals, no fillings, no petting and cosseting and pampering and poncing about. Get the bugger *out*. Give him the deep-six!

A tooth which once has had its way and yet has not been jettisoned is like a once-disaffected crewmember: Listen to him, slap his wrist, let him off, tell him to be good, and send him forward to the crew's quarters—and before you know it you'll have the whole fo'c'sle raging with all sorts of weird ideas, like democracy and equality for all, and soon the whole slew has gone bad and the ship is aground or foundering, and there you are, swimming strongly for England and bugger the Olympics.

I grabbed Sissie's raffia shopping bag, but it was decorated with little embroidered flowers, so I flung it on the starboard berth, and charged ashore without it. I wasn't going to have the fishermen at the bodega door staring at me and a be-flowered bag—not Rory O'Boggarty, the Playboy of the Western Approaches, either. As I jumped, with the starboard side of my face in a fury of pain, over the stern onto the jetty, Nelson whimpered and stared after me in sympathy.

It took about fifteen minutes to reach the dentist's office. It was on the second floor of a big, decrepit building at the rear of the Hotel Montesol. Its walls, all discolored and black-streaked plaster, looked as miserable as I felt. I raced up the wide, dirty staircase and passed the usual black-shawled, chubby, elderly woman on them.

"*Dentista!*" I shouted at her.

"*Cerrado*," she gummed back at me, her black eyes gleaming with unexpected enjoyment. "Closed. He opens at ten o'clock."

"Is there another one nearby?" I pleaded.

The harridan smiled gently as she turned the knife. "No—he's the only one in Ibiza," she said slowly, savoring every lisped word.

I dashed back down the street, still holding my jaw. It was only eight fifteen. What to do? What to *dooo* . . . I moaned softly as I tensed my midriff, trying to prevent my soul from escaping through my jaw. I would be British about the whole thing, I told myself sternly. That's what I would bloody-well do! None of this Continental nonsense, this damned foreign self-pity, this Frenchified indecency! Keep a stiff upper lip, that's what I would do. Straighten my spine, stick my chest out, look everybody in the eye, and be so self-controlled that Her Majesty would be proud of me.

I would do the shopping. Yes, that was it, the shopping I would do. Business as usual. Everything stops for business—even a toothache. Keep the home fires . . . But *God*, there was nothing about the home fires burning in my mouth. Sweet Jesus, hear my plea, I prayed as I stamped each step hard into the ground, as if trying to take revenge on the earth itself for my having been born into this life of misery and pain. Get a-hold of yourself, man—don't forget that England expects every man to do his duty, I admonished myself as I reached a tiny grocer's store, a mere hole in a cottage wall.

Inside was the customary black-shawled lady. She was knitting behind the counter. She threw me a look of consternation as she wondered what a foreigner was doing in the preserve of small, dark women with huge broods and small, dark men with huge thirsts. I went to the bar immediately to show her that I was, in fact, a man, even though not Ibizan. With a shaking hand I took out the 300 pesetas that Sissie had given me earlier, just as a wizened gnome with a face the color of cured mahogany stepped through a dark curtain behind the counter. He was about eighty-five, and wore a brown woolen cardigan over a collarless gray-and-white-striped shirt. On his head was the requisite black fedora, which, even in my agony, I was surprised to see did not have a pointed crown.

The gnome-patriarch gauged me for a moment. "*Señor?*" he said.

"Please, quick, *señor*, I have a toothache. Please give me brandy. Two glasses!"

As the head of the gnome family poured out two measures of brandy the old lady clucked her tongue in sympathy. I turned to her; she shot me a look of intense pity. I raised the glasses swiftly, one after the other, and poured the stuff down. "Another, *por favor, señor*," I wailed.

This one I didn't swallow; I rolled it around and around the offending molar with my tongue. The pain dulled momentarily and I got on with my shopping, being careful not to be too finicky as I slammed down sugar and flour, peas and beans to be weighed, lest the old lady should question my masculinity to herself.

By the time I had pointed out all my needs, and the men had weighed them, and the women had bagged them, it was almost ten o'clock (slowness is a virtue in Ibiza), and I, ostensibly to be *macho*, but actually to dull the toothache and basically because I *liked* it, had quaffed yet another four glasses of cognac.

Now, as I paid the bill—185 pesetas into the half-drawn claw of the old woman—I felt a hundred times better. Now the toothache was a mere annoyance.

What's a minor ache and pain now and again to a hearty sailor? I asked myself as I stepped outside into the bright sunshine. In fact it's almost gone now—maybe it doesn't need to come out at all? Then a sudden stab of hot fury from my upper jaw told me that I must be terribly *British* again, and face the music. Right, I told myself—you go in, Tristan-bach; bear the standard of the red dragon on high, and remember the loins from which you sprang!

Up the stairs I went, past the same old crone I had seen earlier. To my relief, and to her obvious disappointment, the dentist's door was half open.

"Would you like . . . what are you, English?" asked the small, dark dentist. He had a toothbrush mustache and shiny hair, which looked as if it had been polished by a boot-black. "Do you want . . . anesthetic, *señor*?" (Women's stuff, anesthetic—it almost pained him to pronounce the word in front of a man.)

"How much is it—the extraction, I mean?"

"A hundred pesetas plain. A hundred and fifty with . . . anesthetic." His eyes dropped again as he mentioned the unmentionable.

Quick calculation. Only 115 pesetas left. "Well, I don't need anesthetic, of course." Oh, God, why did I spend so much on groceries? I asked myself.

"Ah, *bueno!*" The dentist smiled widely as he sighed with relief. Now he knew he was dealing with a *man*. Now there would be no problem with delicacy or gentleness. Now the beast was loose. He grinned again, as he suddenly tipped the chair back, and I was flung down to an almost horizontal position. "*Bueno.* Of course not. Naturally. I beg your pardon, *señor!*"

I will not speak protractedly of the anguish, the agony I went through in that little dentist's chair in Ibiza that fine November morning. All I will say is that during the hour and a quarter it took him to prod and probe, tease and tug the molar out, I wished again and again, a thousand times an hour, that I was alone at sea with those bloody mole-grips.

But all things come to an end—even torture, slowly and steadily applied by a gloating tailor's dummy with a toothbrush mustache. Eventually I was able to flee the room groggily and speed past the ancient hag who had been relishing my Calvary through the open door of the office. Even in my shock, the knitting she held brought to my numbed mind visions of the Reign of Terror and the guillotine.

Swallowing blood, I hared around to the grocery *tienda* to collect my earlier purchases. The ancient lady was still there. So were the two men. The gnome-patriarch in the cardigan sprang to attention with his eyes as he saw me enter the shop. After about a minute's swift silence, to me an eternity, he said, "My God! What happened to thee, *señor?*" (I was *in* with them now—Pappy had *theed* me.)

"Quick, brandy!" I croaked. My mouth felt as if it had been clawed by a tiger, which indeed it had been. Blood had dripped all down the front of my tee-shirt, and was caked on my hands.

"*Por Dios, pobrecito!* By God, poor little chap!" muttered the ancient lady, pulling her shawl closer around her comfortable breasts, as if to ward off evil spirits.

The patriarch grinned at me, and it immediately became obvious that he knew very well what I had been through. He had only one tooth.

He placed a tray of small glasses on the counter. There must have been a dozen glasses—maybe two dozen; I was too agonized to count them. He took a bottle of *Terry* brandy from the shelf behind him, all dust and grimy silk tassles. Without pausing to lift the bottleneck he poured the golden liquid into all the glasses, so that they were almost brimming. "From God and us," he intoned gravely, as his grubby hand swept the tray toward me, "to you and God, *señor.*"

I was already fishing nervously in my pocket for the fifteen pesetas. The patriarch reached over the counter and held my arm. "There is no payment, *señor,*" he said. He turned his eyes sideways in the direction of the dentist's office. "You have already paid the devil. We can take nothing from you. Drink!"

By the time the old gentleman had finished speaking I had already tossed three glasses of cognac down my throat. Then, after I had coughed and spluttered blood over my paper bag of purchases, I set to on the others. "*Señor, Señora!*" I raised my glass to each of them, "I thank you and wish you good health, many descendants, *hiccup,* and long life. I wish you *hic* pesetas and love *hic* and the time to *hic* enjoy them!"

The three gentlefolk beamed at me. The dignified patriarch poured a drink for himself and his companion, who may have been his son, I wasn't sure. They gave the lady a warm lemonade bottle from a box under the counter. (Men's work, drinking booze.)

By the time I'd seen off all the glasses of cognac I felt like Derby Day. Pain? What was a little pain? "Pain is not for a man, *señor,*" I told the patriarch.

"*De seguro, señor. Es solo por las mujéres, no?*" he cackled, showing his tooth again. It was as if he'd been reading my mind. "Sure, pain is only for women, isn't it?"

Then, with the patriarch holding one arm and his son the other, and the old lady carrying the bag of supplies, I made my way through the door and out into the sunshine again.

"Go with God," said the gentle patriarch as he took the bag from his good wife and placed it in my numbed arms.

I staggered along the street. All I could think of was getting back onboard my boat and sleeping off this dreadful morning. I remember slightly weaving down the town quay. I recall hazily being halted by a big, fat Civil Guard sergeant who sternly demanded to know what I was doing drunk at that early hour. Apparently my bag broke as I fell forward against his bulging stomach, sending a cloud of fine white flour over his immaculate uniform, a stream of sugar into his boot-lace holes, and a dozen egg yolks dripping down his sharply pressed trousers. These things I do not remember. Later I was assured time and again by fishermen acquaintances who witnessed it, that all this did, in fact, happen. They assured me on the lives of their mothers, so I know it must be true.

What I do remember, though—and this memory will never leave me—was waking up that night to find myself safely onboard the dark *Cresswell*, tucked into my berth. Most of my purchases—those that had not been lost in the unfortunate accident—were on the table in front of me. Also on the table was an unopened bottle of red wine, with a note scribbled in Spanish: "For when you arise. Your dog is tied up. Sergeant Alfredo Lopez, G.C."

One man in a thousand, Solomon says,
Will stick more close than a brother.
And it's worth while seeking him half your days
If you find him before the other.
Nine hundred and ninety-nine depend
On what the world sees in you,
But the Thousandth Man will stand your friend
With the whole round world agin you.

'Tis neither promise nor prayer nor show,
Will settle the promise for 'ee.
Nine hundred and ninety-nine of 'em go
By your looks, your acts, or your glory.
But if he finds you and you find him,
The rest of the world don't matter;
For the Thousandth Man will sink or swim
With you in any water.

His wrong's your wrong, and his right's your right,
In season or out of season.
Stand up and back it in all men's sight—
With **that** *for your only reason!*
Nine hundred and ninety-nine can't bide
The shame or mocking or laughter,
But the Thousandth Man will stand by your side
To the gallows-foot-and after!

from "The Thousandth Man"
—Rudyard Kipling

Editor's Note: Chapters 10 and 11 were originally combined in a single story entitled "*The Saga of Dreadnaught*," which appeared in slightly different form in Tristan Jones' *Yarns*, a collection first published by SAIL books in 1983, and reissued by Sheridan House in 1990.

10

The Thousandth Man

SUNDAYS are what you make of them. They can be days of holiness and gloom if you go to chapel, sacrifice and misery if you go visit your in-laws, a sports day if you think that chasing a ball around, or watching it being done, is the acme of human endeavor—or you can rest and read. Not being Scottish, Irish, English, or Continental, I decided on the last pursuit on the day following my visit to the diabolical dentist.

That Sunday was to be, I thought, ambrosial. Despite the cavernous hole on the starboard side of my upper jaw, when I awoke I was elated. It was the first time in months that *Cresswell*, Nelson, and I had been alone, to do as we pleased. I could lounge around in my underpants, without having to sluice my face in the water bucket; I could burn the bacon and eat an egg raw in milk and throw my pillow playfully at Nelson, and he could jump around as best he could on his three legs, with his tongue hanging out, and pant and grin at me, and not worry if his tail brushed a damned china cup off the table. By the time breakfast was over we had, both of us, sloughed off, in half an hour, months of weary fair manners-at-table, and Oh-deah-we-really-jolly-well-ought-to-buy-a-decent-bally-tea-towel, which was Sissie's plaint every breakfast time. Now Nelson could hop onto the starboard berth, which had been his favorite lounging place before the days of Nemesis, in the shape of the bishop's sister, had overtaken us in the vineyards of France. Now he could lie there, with his head on his paw, grinning at me, until I gave him my tin bacon plate to clean with his eager tongue before I restowed it, by throwing it at the stove and letting it find its own resting place, just like the good old days.

After breakfast and the daily exercise just described, as it was yet cool topsides, I chose a book to enjoy. Shakespeare isn't for the morning, and Boswell's *Life of Johnson* I decided to save for the next day. Conrad's *Nostromo* tempted me, but in the end I settled for my old friend, *The Oxford Book of English Verse*. I made another pot of tea and subsided onto my berth, with my head on piled pillow and oilskin jacket, my back to the hatchway, whence came the daylight. Now, after I lit a cigarette, I was in my own version of *paradise*. Here was bliss, a quiet ecstasy, perfect contentment, supreme happiness. Now I was as near to Avalon or the Fortunate Isles as I could ever expect to be in this life—and probably after. No one had ever told me, in those days, that a "man of action" was not supposed to enjoy poetry. No one had ever tried to insinuate into my consciousness that poetry and action were completely inimical, one to the other. In my Welsh innocence it never occurred to me that poetry was anything else but the expression of action, nor that action could be other than the expression of poetry. True, years before, in my navy days, when Hollywood films had been shown on deck to the lads in the less-cold Arctic nights of Heflavik fiord, I had sometimes wondered why none of the heroes ever seemed to look at a book, unless it was a cattle-baron totting up his profits and losses; but this I had put down to the ignorance of the film-makers.

As for real life and as for sailors, I've never met a real sailor yet who wasn't, at heart at least, a poet—and as a general rule, the more of a rough-and-tumble scallywag he was, the more of a poet. They must have been poets-at-heart; none of them ever had any *justification* for doing what they were doing. I'm not saying that sailors are all working poets—God saved us from that debacle by making most of them mute; but I never met one of them, no matter how roguish he was, who did not have a sense of the rhythms of the ocean, of life; the mystery, the ineffable surging song that is born wherever and whenever a boat meets the water of the sea. No one could live the life we live without being a poet at heart, at least not for long, and certainly not happily. Those who try to, exist like aliens in a strange land, trying to speak and understand an incomprehensible tongue, an insane babble. They cannot fathom that the very act of sailing is an act of pure poetry; that the sanity of sail is not, cannot be *presumed*, as is the sanity of the land. At sea it either *is* or it *isn't*, and there's nothing in between—and nothing can be saner than that.

That morning, turning the pages of Wyatt and Spenser, Byron and Donne; tasting and savoring each spicy morsel, in between winks at Nelson and sips of tea, I imagined the shadow of a landsman on my shoulder, asking the eternal question that landsmen have always asked of voyagers—*Why?* I looked around the cabin again, all gray paint and smoky from the stove-smuts. I saw the shining brass oil lamps jiggling in their gimbals every time a fishing boat rumbled past, entering port from her night labors, with the crew (I knew in my mind's eye) already changed into their best black suits for church. I gazed at the pictures on the bulkheads—Nansen and Scott, Shackleton and the Queen; they stern and intrepid, she smiling. I felt the warmth of the sun as it slowly climbed into the sky and the rays streaming into the cabin, and their angle, without my even looking at them, telling me the time as precisely as any clock ever made, even as I read. I heard the low groan of the mooring lines and the anchor rode every time the boat was disturbed, and I heard a voice . . . from the direction of my new neighbor, *Dreadnaught*.

"*Cresswell*! Hello there!" It was a high-pitched halloo. Nelson started. He jerked his head up and stared at the companionway, his tongue hanging out. Again the voice. "Anyone home?"

I stuck a teaspoon in the page I was reading and quickly donned my pants. It was a man's voice, but you never knew if there were women around at that late hour of the morning—or any hour, come to that, especially on Ibiza's outer mole. I made my way up the companionway ladder, and gazed around and saw him.

"Morning," said I.

He was a stocky man with a round, red face, which was decorated with one of the biggest mustaches seen around since General Kitchener was a lad. It was black-gray and *huge*. It was so big and droopy and magnificent, with its ends curled up, that the first impression I had was that the mustache was wearing *him*. At each end of the mustache were ears which stuck out from his head as if they were about to flap as soon as the mustache whirled into a propelling motion. Under the mustache, so far as I could see, all he wore was a pair of overalls, so begrimed that if he'd doffed them I think they would have stood up on their own. His feet, black and grimy, were bare. On his head he wore a white-covered peaked yachting cap. It was the only clean thing about him. That cap was *pristine*. Its gold badge gleamed in the morning sun. He looked like a cross between an admiral, a British army sergeant (Boer War vintage), and an unshod, overworked omnibus-workshop mechanic. I scanned his face and guessed he was about sixty-five.

"Ah, yes, 'morning, old chap," he said in a Midlands accent. "I was just making a cup of tea, as it were, and I wondered if you'd like a drop? I saw your boat yesterday over the way, there . . ." He threatened the old-hulk berth, far away on the other side of the harbor, with his mustache. The mustache appeared to resent being pointed at the hulks and trembled in seeming anger. Then, as it was pointed at *Cresswell*, it subdued its annoyance. "Lovely old girl, isn't she? Royal National Lifeboat Institute?"

I nodded, both to the mustache and the man. He was standing on a once-blue-and-white-striped mattress, which was now gray and black and sodden with rain and damp,

and which lay thrown across the foredeck of the tiny
Dreadnaught.

"Must introduce myself, as it were . . . Amyas Cupling."

"Tristan Jones."

"Yes, I know . . . I met your mate Peter Kelly in
Monaco."

He gets around, I thought to myself in a flash.

Amyas Cupling looked up at *Cresswell's* masthead,
then as he spoke he slowly took in every inch of her rig and
hull. "Beach-launched heavy weather rescue vessel. Lovely
jobs . . . real engineering. Put them together like steamers,
like battleships, as it were." Both he and his mustache
smiled with genuine pleasure. "Let's see, let me guess her
year . . ." He frowned. The mustache drooped in deep
contemplation as it followed the line of *Cresswell's* forestay.
Suddenly his blue eyes smiled. The mustache lagged a little
behind the eyes, as if waiting for an order over the ship's
telegraph. Then it, too, curled its ends up even further, an
order was somehow passed, and the ears wiggled. I fully
expected to hear the tinkle of a telegraph bell, and the roar
of an accelerated forced-draft fan, followed by the whine of
whizzing steam-turbines. "Hmm.. let's see, couldn't be
before oh-five . . . they had the thirty-footers until
then . . . I'd say oh-seven or oh-eight."

"Dead right," said I. "Spot on, Amyas." I would have
congratulated the mustache, too, had I known its name.

"Thames Ironworks?"

"Absolutely hundred-aye-one," said I, truly impressed
with his knowledge of small craft.

"Marvelous craftsmen," said Amyas Cupling. "Really
knew their stuff, eh?" Without waiting for my comment he
went on. "Double diagonal mahogany on grown oak frames?
Goodness me, they really took their time, as it were. Do you
realize that if you take into consideration the years it took to
grow the oak frames into the exact shapes needed for . . ."

Amyas checked my boat's name again. *Cresswell*, as he
leaned over to read the name on the lifebelt hanging on the
port shroud, seemed to purr. By now Nelson was at the top

of the companionway, staring at the mustache. He looked as if he'd at first imagined it was some kind of tomcat perched on Amyas' upper lip.

Mister Cupling went on. "Ah, yes, *Cresswell*. Named after a place in Northumberland, eh? Yes, it took them about eighty years to grow those oak frames into shape, as it were. They had plantations in Portugal, you know, and that means . . . let's see . . . she really started building in about 1828! That's when they planted the oaks for the frames, as it were."

"Amazing, isn't it?" I said. I already knew what he was telling me, but I didn't want to be impolite. He was evidently enjoying himself and his view of *Cresswell*.

Amyas Cupling and his mustache both looked at Nelson. My dog shook his shoulders for a second in consideration, as if he expected the mustache to leap onto the jetty and race away toward the town.

"Your mutt?" asked Amyas.

I introduced Nelson. Amyas approached close to *Dreadnaught*'s guardrail, which consisted of one rusty wire that undulated around the ship as it passed through stanchions which leaned this way and that, like drunken derelicts around a hostel door.

"Lovely boy," said Amyas. Nelson wagged his tail in pleasure at the wagging of the mustache. "Had a dog myself until a few months ago—of course not a thoroughbred like yours, just a little old sort of cross between a wire-haired terrier and a King Charles spaniel, as it were. Found him in an alley in Tangier, and those blessed brutes were kicking him and throwing stones. Couldn't let them get away with that, could I? Boxed their ears, as it were, and brought the poor old thing home to *Dreadnaught*. Had him for a year. Nice little chap. Teddy, I called him . . ."

Amyas meditated for a moment, until a high-pitched whistle broke into our requiem for Teddy. Amyas Cupling and his mustache immediately perked up. "Ah, there's the kettle singing. Do come onboard. I'll have tea made in a jiffy. No need to remove your shoes . . . I'm refitting, as it were. Bring the dog if you wish," he called as he lowered himself down through a rusting steel hatchway at the after end of *Dreadnaught's* rusting steel coachroof.

Nelson, of course, would not accompany me. He was very jealous of his duty to guard *Cresswell* whenever I left her. It would have taken a whole panzer division to have shifted him once I was off my boat. How the police sergeant had gone onboard the previous day was still a wonder to me, except that Nelson must have known that I was ill and incapable. But he must have had an ugly attitude to the sergeant, else why would he have been tied up?

As I scrambled over *Cresswell's* taut, shining guardrails and *Dreadnaught's* rusty, drooping wire, I inspected the one sail that was still bent on the rusty steel lifeboat's black, unpainted, half-rotten, stubby mainmast. The mainsail was in the same state, and half its parrel clews had been ripped away from the canvas. It looked as if it had been savaged by a drunken pterodactyl. I gingerly danced over the damp mattress on deck, scrambled across and through a jumble of rusty one-inch wire cable, picked my way through a collection of oily cans and barrels, all rusting, and finally reached the hatchway.

The scene below was almost indescribable. It was as if I had been hiking on the Yorkshire moors, and had come across the wrecked relics of some early Victorian underground workings—a tin or copper mine, which had petered out and been abandoned long, long ago.

Down in the gloom, in the dim yellowish light of one small electric bulb (there were no portholes) was a mass of dismantled machinery—eccentrics and connecting rods, valves and tappets, pistons, nuts, bolts, oil pumps, water pumps—all dead bone dry and rusty; electric wires sprawled every which way, all ancient and discolored; batteries—a battery of them—all dirty black and dusty; and tools—spanners, socket wrenches, drills, pliers, screwdrivers—scattered everywhere, mostly corroded. In the center of the rust-streaked steel cabin, with condensation sweat gleaming on all sides and dripping from the roof, was Amyas' obvious pride and joy—a gray, rust-patchy box with great thick black cables sprouting from it and disappearing into the dark gloom of the forward end of the boat. I stared at the box until, just as my foot slipped off a rusty cylinder-head lying at the bottom of the rusty steel ladder, I figured out that it was, in fact, a portable welding set.

Recovering my balance, I peered around. Apart from the engine bits, tools, batteries and electric cables, welding set, the steaming kettle that Amyas, beaming, held in his hand, and Amyas himself, everything in the cabin seemed to be *welded*. The cabin table was a steel plate welded onto two bent steel pipes that were welded onto the steel hull frames; the berths, one piled with rusty engine pieces and tools, were steel plate welded together and to the boat; the shelves, all quarter-inch steel plates, were welded to the damp steel ship's sides.

I spotted the library shelf. Fully expecting to find rusting steel books welded to the shelf, I clambered my way over to it. I inspected the titles: *The Sea Engineer's Manual*; *Emergency Repairs at Sea*; *Marine Engines and their Maintenance*; *The Marine Engineer's Practical Handbook*, and so on.

I turned from reading the book spines to see both Amyas and the mustache smiling at me. The whole scene, in the dim glow of the one tiny bulb, was as if the manacles workshop in some gloomy corner of Dante's inferno had gone on strike some five years before, and was now in the custody of a benevolent Victorian ironmaster. If Isambard Kingdom Brunel had come aboard that moment, I imagined, he would have doffed his top hat and for once in his life smiled.

Amyas was now pouring tea into two rust-spotted metal mugs on the steel table. He cocked one bushy eyebrow and the mustache at me. "Like it, eh?" Without waiting for my response he went on. "Of course, I'm refitting at the moment, as it were. I started this one in Gibraltar. Of course I don't stay in one place while I refit; sort of sail around anyway, as it were. Been to Sardinia,

Corsica, Malta, Greece, Yugoslavia, Italy, south of France, and Majorca while this refit's going on. Can't stand to be in one place for too long. I was in the merchant service for thirty eight years . . . got to second engineer. Then Suez came along and the old Line folded up and sort of left me high and dry, as it were."

As he spoke he doffed his immaculate white-topped peak cap and hung it on a rusty steel bolt over his berth. His graying hair, rather long and lanky, fell all around his head, making him look like a happy walrus who has just surfaced from below a patch of long-stranded seaweed.

"That must have been quite a wrench?" I punned.

"Worst of it was, I lost my missus in the same year," he said. The mustache drooped for a moment, then picked up again. "But anyway, we can't mope around, as it were, can we? So I decided to go to sea for a change. The Line was now defunct and the brokers had sold my old ship, *Princess of India*. Good old girl she was. Made the London-Bombay run four times a year, rain or shine, for sixty years, and I managed to get hold of one of her lifeboats—sort of rescue it, as it were. This is it."

"What, *Dreadnaught*?"

"Of course, old chap. She was the forward lifeboat, starb'd side. Officers only. I used to take her 'round Bombay harbor for trials in the old days. Great fun. Used to take the lads for a spin, as it were."

"So how did you get here, then?" I asked, fascinated.

"Oh, I bought her in Inverkeithing, in Scotland, three years ago. But she was in a terrible state. They'd let all the lifeboats go to wrack and ruin."

"Did you refit her there, in Inverkeithing? I know it well . . ."

"Oh, no. It was autumn, you see, and what with the weather and the Scotch mist it would have meant a longish delay, so I slapped the masts in and sailed her direct to Gibraltar and started the refit there. A bit warmer, as it were."

"But that's well over a thousand miles!"

"Yes, she was a bit sluggish at first, but the wind picked up off the Bay of Biscay. Only took us six weeks. Well, just under seven, as it were."

"How did it go in Gib? I mean the refit?"

"Oh, I couldn't stay there long enough to finish it. The harbor mooring fees were too steep for us, so we took off on a little bimble into the Mediterranean, as it were. Went to Malta, first, but it was cheaper in Greece, so we went there."

"But that's another thousand miles . . . more?"

"Only took eighteen months. Of course we didn't hurry. I mean the Med's too interesting for that—so varied, as it were."

"When did you get the refit done, then, Amyas?"

"Well, as you can see, I'm still at it. There's no point in hurrying, unless, of course, it's an emergency, as it were. No engineer that's worth his salt wants to botch a job, you see. I know it might seem a little slow to some people ashore, but three years is not such a terribly long time, especially when you're alone on a job, is it? She sails quite well, even if she's a bit slow compared to *Princess of India*, for example, so I haven't missed much of the Mediterranean. Been in Spain, Italy, France, Malta, Morocco, Greece, Yugoslavia . . . No, little *Dreadnaught* and me, we've been refitting all over the place. Fixed quite a few other boats' engines, too. Of course I always help the local fishermen out before the yachts. I mean, they're working. They've their families to feed, as it were."

"Do they pay you?"

"Oh, no, I wouldn't dream of asking for money. After all, I'm a professional ship's engineer, and the golden rule . . . if someone's in a fix . . . as it were."

Amyas and I finished our tea. I had looked around his galley. It was such an incredible mess—rusty steel pans hanging over a rusty steel stove; and an ancient Colman's mustard can, so patchy with rusty brown that it would have given Escoffier a fainting fit. I invited my engineer friend over to *Cresswell* for fish stew.

"That sounds jolly good," he said, accepting my invitation. "After all, it is Sunday. One really shouldn't do too much on the Sabbath, as it were."

We finished our fish stew. Nelson avidly cleaned our bowls. Replete, Amyas and I adjourned to *Cresswell*'s cockpit. There he talked of refits and gudgeon pins as I watched the Sunday afternoon parade, a procession of Ibizan locals out for their weekly *paseo* along the seawall. It was always a spectacle. Whole families, all together, from grandpas and grandmas down to minute week-old babies in costly perambulators resplendent with silk tassels and sunshades and shiny chromium wheels, and all the mature adults soberly dressed in black suits and black dresses with black shawls. The older women wore their best jewelry and the older men tried their best not to follow the younger women with their eyes. All the younger women, the single ones, promenaded in tight-knit groups of five or six, all flashing eyes and white smiles for each other. The younger men also trooped in tight-knit groups until they were within a few feet of the knots of nubile women. Then the young men's groups dissolved into a file, and a straggle of unspoken questions were shot at the women as they were passed. The young women duly giggled, and some even turned their heads to follow the youths, but you could always tell which young woman really fancied one of the men. That one kept her head still as she walked on, straightfaced, eyes front.

It was fun, watching the oldest game in the world. The West End and Broadway could do no better when it came to a show. The locals never seemed to notice the foreign boats or the people on them. This game had been played before the first boat floated. It was as if we did not exist. Which was as well, for Amyas Cupling and I had front-stall seats, and could enjoy the sights and sounds of the promenade without any embarrassment.

Amyas dealt with compression ratios and propeller pitches and a lot of other engineering esoterica, most of which was, and still is, a complete mystery to me. It was poetic, all the same. What could sound more helpful than "camshaft?" What could ring more solid than "block-lining?" Amyas' words, like "induction," "compression," "ignition," and "exhaust," sounded so much more romantic than my terms for the same things—"suck," "squeeze," "bang," and "blow." Amyas was an engineering poet, a poet-engineer, *as it were.*

Toward three o'clock the little converted Spanish fishing boat, on the other side of *Cresswell* from *Dreadnaught*, moved slightly toward the jetty. I turned around to see if someone was playing with the mooring lines, and saw that it was a little old man in a black suit, just like the hundred other little old men who promenaded along the jetty that Sunday. As I looked up in his direction, the little old man bowed toward me slightly, with true Castilian courtesy. Somehow I knew he was the boat's owner.

I jumped up, just as Amyas was explaining some intricacy of third-stage expansion, and scrambled over *Cresswell's* stern onto the jetty. I heaved the little old man's mooring line to bring the boat closer, and helped him cross safely over the narrow gap between the mole wall and the stern of his little craft. Safely onboard and down in the cockpit, he turned and smiled at me, and bowed again. *"Muchas gracias, señor,"* he said. "Alfredo Ramero Gonzales Rodrigues de Valdez y Compostella." (Or some such name; it sounded more like the Real Madrid soccer team than one person, to me.) "Please accept my deepest thanks, on behalf of myself and my vessel, *Estrellita del Mar!"* His Castilian was of the purity of a mountain stream.

I introduced myself and Amyas Cupling to the little old man. *"Little Star of the Sea*! What a beautiful name, *señor,"* I said.

The little old man bowed again. "Thank you so much," he said, now in perfect English, Oxford accent and all, but with slight Spanish undertones. "If you have any need of me, please accept my invitation to come aboard and I shall make my best endeavors to be of assistance to you gentlemen." He turned and unlocked the tiny main hatch of his boat, and went below.

I smiled at Amyas, who raised an eyebrow. We said nothing until I was back onboard *Cresswell*. Then I spoke in a low voice. Sound carries much more between boats than anywhere else.

"Funny little fellow," I commented.

"Looks quite well-educated, as it were," replied Amyas, also in hushed tones.

"Nice little boat, though. Looks converted when you first see her."

"But she's not," whispered Amyas.

"No, she's been constructed like that. Copy of a Majorcan fishing vessel, built as a yacht. Nice job they've done of her, and she's very well kept. Jesus . . ." I remembered that I had not heard Amyas blaspheme. "Sorry Amyas," I said.

"That's all right, old chap. I know you're not taking the Lord's name in vain. Don't forget, I was at sea for thirty-eight years."

"I mean," I continued, "just look at that paintwork. You can see they took their time with it, whoever painted her. And look at that gold-leaf trimming around the coachroof coaming. Holy smoke, it must have taken them a whole month to get that line around her alone!"

"Yes," said Amyas Cupling. "Actually, I intend to do *Dreadnaught* much the same way." He meditated for a minute. "When the refit's finished, as it were."

"Yes, it wouldn't really make sense to paint her before you get her shipshape, would it?" I said, as I glanced around and over at the saddest-looking, dirtiest, scruffiest, rustiest tin-pot of a vessel I had ever clapped eyes on outside of a coaling depot. Under my glance, poor old *Dreadnaught* seemed to flinch and move as if she were protesting that it wasn't *her* fault. What did Amyas Cupling expect after the glories of *Princess of India* . . . Tommy Lipton's *Endeavour*?

We went down into *Cresswell*'s cabin again for me to show Amyas my library, so he could borrow one of my books. As he browsed through the titles there was a low rumble from out in the harbor. Amyas turned to me questioningly. "It's all right, Amyas, it's a powerboat coming in. Plenty of people up there to give him a hand. Take your time. I'll put the kettle on for another cuppa. Take whatever book you fancy."

A minute or two later Amyas commented, "Well . . . I think I've read all of these, as it were."

"Shakespeare?" I asked.

"Oh, years ago. I used to read him on the night watches, when I was third engineer on the old *Princess of Burma*." Amyas dismissed the Bard. "But I'll tell you what, old man, as long as you're not using it today or tomorrow . . ."

"No, I've got my book for tomorrow. Verse. It's over on my bunk. You can borrow any book in the library," I offered.

"Well, it's not in the library. Look, it's on this berth." He held up my oil-stained engine handbook and read the title. "*Volvo-Penta MD2 Owner's Manual of Operation and Maintenance*. I'd really like to read through this, if I may borrow it, as it were."

I was just on the point of saying "By all means," when *Cresswell* lurched so violently that the steaming kettle was jerked out of my hands and clanked into the after cabin bulkhead. Amyas froze. I shot up the companionway ladder. Angrily I glared around. In the split second it had taken me to reach open air I already knew what the cause of the shock was. Now I saw I was right.

A great monstrous powerboat, eighty feet long, all gleaming white and silver, had backed right into the little old man's converted fishing boat, *Estrellita del Mar*. As the monster had backed stern-first into her, the tiny boat's anchor chain, a thin, quarter-inch one, had snapped, and the fishing yacht had smashed into *Cresswell*'s starboard side. Now, *Cresswell*'s sides, being constructed like the walls of Durham cathedral, would not give way as the motor yacht continued backing into the small fishing boat, crushing her against *Cresswell*. Something had to give. The laws of force and motion demanded it. *Cresswell's* anchor chain obeyed the laws and, although it was three-quarter-inch galvanized steel, it snapped like a piece of knitting wool even as, horrified, I watched. Then, as the big, bruising bastard from Barcelona continued racing his engines at full-speed astern, *Cresswell* smashed into *Dreadnaught*. It was no good yelling; the roar of the eighty-footer was far too loud for any voice to be heard. Then I saw the line.

The monster had secured a long, thick nylon mooring line from her port stern right across all three bows of *Estrellita*, *Cresswell*, and *Dreadnaught*, onto the jetty bollard, and was now, as well as shoving with all the might of a thousand horses, hauling in the nylon line with his after capstan! It was as if a great big bully was not only pushing his way into a line of little old ladies, but was crushing them to death with his stomach as he drew himself to the wall behind them with hawserlike arms.

Aghast, I glanced up at the bridge of the killer. There were three figures up there, one in a flowered shirt with dark glasses. The owner, I told myself swiftly. Another in a white hat and dark glasses—the guest. And one in a white cap and jacket and dark glasses and toothbrush mustache. The "Captain." Not a trace of expression on any of the faces, except that of haughty might and right.

It all took place in seconds. I shot up the ladder, took in the scene, bent down . . . and then I did something that I had never done before, and which I sincerely hope I shall never have to do again.

I grabbed my double-bladed Royal Navy deep-sea diver's knife—it was more like a Roman short-sword—from its brass "Siebe Gorman" sheath just inside the companionway, and I flew ashore. I don't remember leaping, or scrambling, or clambering, or climbing. The next thing I knew I was ashore, with my diver's knife at the throat of a large, dark, white-jerseyed seaman who was standing by the straining killer-hawser. He ran, wild-eyed. I sawed through the thick nylon line with the wicked edge of the knife. The line twanged and shot back into the harbor water with a *zuzz*, just as *Dreadnaught* smashed her stern against the cruel stones of the quay. Something went bang, even over the roar of the killer-craft's engines, and *Dreadnaught*, as Amyas, now on *Cresswell*'s deck, staring aghast, started to sink by the stern. We both shot wild looks at one another. In an flash we both knew that poor *Dreadnaught*'s propeller had smashed against a rock, and that her propeller shaft had been bent so badly that her stern gland had been ripped open, and that filthy harbor water was now pouring into the wretched little boat just as Amyas' life-blood was pumping wildly through his heart.

I tore down the jetty, knife at the charge, toward another gin-palace crewman who was standing, flustered, at her starboard mooring line. As I raced for him I saw out of the corner of my eye that the powerboat's stern was swinging clear now of *Cresswell*, but had taken my bowsprit with it.

I lunged at the crewman, I must have been screaming my head off, but if I was, I didn't hear it. The noise of the killer's engines was too high. A moment before I reached him the little crewman, his eyes bulging at me, threw himself into the harbor. I slashed the other rope just as the killer's engines died. Then, as he swung round slowly to face the east wind, I shouted up at the men on the monster, "You great clumsy bastards! You come ashore and I'll cut your bloody balls off!"

Then I came to my senses just as quickly, it seemed, as I had lost them. To this day I think I did the right thing. If I had not cut the lines, all three small craft would eventually have been crushed against the wall and probably sunk.

The little old man on *Estrellita* was now on deck. He was staring calmly, sternly, wordlessly, at the ruin and carnage around him. Amyas was still on *Cresswell*'s deck, holding onto her guardrail as he wept silently and stared down at the filthy harbor water, into which *Dreadnaught*, with a gurgle, had completely disappeared. I, too, looked down to see the last of her air bubbles reach the oily surface and pop. For a minute I looked silently at Amyas. He was like a broken man.

A voice came from the killer ship. It boomed out tinnily across the harbor. They were using their loud-hailer. "I have reported you to the local harbormaster and the chief of police on my radio. Do not move from where you are . . ."

I cupped my hands around my mouth. "Get stuffed!" I shouted. *"GET STUFFED, YOU SODDIN' GREAT OAF!"*

"YOU ARE TO REMAIN WHERE YOU ARE—POLICE ORDERS!" yelled the voice.

"POLICE BULLSHIT!" I roared at him, and climbed back onboard *Cresswell*. At least if I were to be arrested it would now be onboard a British-registered vessel, I thought. Let them pick the bones out of *that* bastard!

Amyas threw me a look of abject misery. He slumped down onto *Cresswell*'s side-deck, his head in his hands. I put my hand on his shoulder. "Bugger 'em, Amyas . . . Oh, sorry, mate. I got a bit excited."

"It's all right, Tristan," his voice sobbed. "I understand."

"You can stay onboard *Cresswell* if you like, mate, until we figure out how to raise *Dreadnaught*," I said.

I looked around me again. The haughty figures on the bridge of the killer ship were all three gazing in my direction, the two civilians with their arms over the bulwarks, folded, and the skipper inspecting me through a huge pair of binoculars. Still enraged, I threw him a British two-finger sign, then an Italian three-finger sign, then a French four.

I turned to look for the little old man, but he had gone below again, probably, I thought, to check the hull of his tiny fishing boat to make sure she wasn't leaking. That reminded me to do the same, even though I knew that *Cresswell* was as tough a nut as ever there was.

Leaving Amyas, his head still in his hand, on deck, I hurried through my boat, inspecting her frames, checking the bilge-water level to ensure that her keelson had not been strained; and her coachroof beam knees, her futtocks, and her ribs, to see that they had not shifted. Even if I was headed for the jail, I thought, I'd make sure that *Cresswell* was all right, and Amyas could look after her for me until Sissie got back from Majorca.

As I set my plans, a harsh, imperious voice yelled out from the jetty. "*Cresswell!*" it shouted; then, in Spanish, "Come on deck with your hands up. You are under arrest!"

That's it, I thought. I stretched my hands up in good old Texas style and headed up the companionway, telling Nelson softly to stay where he was. As I ascended the ladder I saw, crowded all around *Cresswell's* stern on the mole, about twenty Spanish navy seamen and their young officers, and a dozen Guardia Civil in their black leather hats and gray uniforms. Every one of them, except the officers, had a rifle or an automatic gun of one kind or another, and every one of those pieces of armament was pointed directly at my heart. I froze on the weatherdeck, silent.

"You are to come with us. You are under arrest!" A naval lieutenant addressed me, glowering as darkly as his twenty years or so would allow. Behind him all the sailors and policemen stared sullenly, threateningly. The lieutenant then waved his pistol at Amyas. "You, too!" he ordered.

Amyas had just started to rise from the deck when suddenly there was a commotion among the four officers on the jetty. Startled, the young lieutenant who was doing all the arresting, was arrested himself. He jolted upright as if rammed stiff by an electric shock, and saluted. As he did, he hollered "*Marineros, aten . . . ción!*" Seamen, attention! All his uniformed minions sprang to attention and saluted as their guns clattered to their sides. All the Guardia Civil were now heels-together and eyes-front, facing the little fishing boat. I turned to look at what had caused this transformation. It was astounding. You could have feathered me down with a knock!

The little old man was now in the *full dress uniform of a general of the Spanish Army!* It was complete with sword and a great sash thrown across his shoulder. Around his hat was a red band under a badge so big and so golden that it looked like a pride of lions.

The little general's Spanish was far too rapid for me to understand exactly, but I caught the gist of what he said as he languidly gestured with a white-gloved hand across his shoulder at the drifting powerboat: "Lieutenant, you will arrest that offender—that offender against the laws of God, the dignity of man, and the rules of common decency. You will place an armed guard onboard his boat, and you will hold him here for as much time as it takes to salvage the vessel of this *caballero*." He gestured, again languidly, at Amyas, who, surprised as I was, gaped at him.

The little general continued. "You will attend all three of us, tomorrow, early, to ascertain our estimations of damage sustained by our craft and ourselves by the actions of that *moron*." Again he flicked a white glove at the power-boat. "And you will multiply that sum by three. That will be the amount of the fine which you will levy against that *animal*. After our repairs and the salvage of this gentleman's boat have been effected, you will then ensure that the surplus of money is donated to the local orphanage. Is that clear?"

"*Si, Señor Gobernador-General . . .*" The lieutenant hesitated, nervously, still rigidly at attention.

"Well, there are problems?" the little general snapped.

"There is no salvage firm on the island . . . It will take a long time for them to come from Barcelona."

"Time is essential. That boat must be raised tomorrow or the day after!"

"But . . . ?" The lieutenant was shaking by now.

I turned and addressed the general. "*Perdoneme, Señor General . . .*"

The general turned to me. His face softened. "Yes, my friend?"

"Er . . . there is a salvage firm on the island . . . but it's foreign-owned."

The general smiled. "I don't care if it's owned by the Russians! I want this thing cleared up before I leave Ibiza! Anyway, where is this firm, and who owns it?"

"It's right here." I reached over and slapped my hand on Amyas' shoulder. "Cupling and Jones, Limited, Marine Engineering and Salvage Company. British, *señor*," I told the general as his eyes gleamed with amusement. "Branches in Chatham, Portsmouth, Plymouth, Hong Kong, and Singapore!" I left out Gibraltar; it was a touchy subject at that time in Spain.

The little general threw his head back and laughed. On the jetty all the sailors' and policemen's faces relaxed, and they started to grin. Then the general's face turned serious. "Do you think you can do it? Do you think you can raise *Señor* Cupling's boat?"

"Yes, sir, but we'll need the Port Captain's permission to use certain pieces of equipment and property which are lying in the harbor."

The general gave an impatient wave of his hand. "No problem," he said. "He's having dinner with me tonight. Write me a list of whatever you need. This young man here . . ." he flicked a hand at the navy lieutenant, "will be responsible that whatever it is, it is provided for you, and that you are afforded whatever other assistance our marine authorities can give you."

"Thank you, *señor*."

He bowed slightly. "*No hay de que*. No need. It is I who am in your debt after you helped me onboard earlier today, *Señor* Jones. You see, courtesy is not merely its own reward . . . And by the way . . ."

"*Señor*?" I grinned at him.

"When you proffer that estimate for repairs and salvage, bear in mind that the orphanage here is not very rich. I was there before I came onboard this morning. I think you may as well make sure that at least some little good comes out of the evil events of this afternoon . . ." As he said this, one of his dark eyes flickered just a tiny bit. Or was it a wink?

From my dinghy I recovered *Cresswell*'s anchor chain with a grapnel, and secured her well again. Then, over supper of beef kidney and chips, Amyas cheered up. We now had a plan. Tomorrow we would set to and raise *Dreadnaught* from her grave.

"What was it that officer called him? It wasn't just general, as it were?" Mister Cupling asked me.

Nelson whoofed. He loved kidney.

"No, Amyas, it was *governor*-general. He's the boss of all the bosses in all the Balearic Islands. It just goes to show, you never know who it is you're meeting, do you, as it were?"

I'll fire this trip, but I'll fire no more,
Chorus: *O-ho, O-ho ho!*

I'll take my money and I'll go ashore,
Chorus: *Fire down below!*

Miss Nancy Bell, oh, fare you well,
I'll pay my money and I'll go ashore.

A bully boat, and a bully crew,
And a bully-ragging captain, too.

The possum jump and the panther roar,
I awoke this morning at half-past four.

I crept out safely from my hive,
And took a dram at half-past five.

Says I, "Old boat, let's have no tricks!"
Her boiler burst at half-past six.

So now we travel under sail,
'Cos Jonah's the man that swallowed the whale.

I'll fire this trip and I'll fire no more,
I'll pay my money and I'll go ashore.

—"The Sailor-Fireman"

This is probably the first of the very few stoker-engineer's songs, sung when the first engines were fitted onboard sailing ships. It originated, it appears from the inclusion of the word "possum," in the United States, probably in the mid-nineteenth century.

11

The Sailor-Fireman

THE LITTLE general was up and about very early the next day. I heard him padding about over onboard *Estrellita del Mar* before dawn. He accepted an invitation to join Amyas Cupling and me for breakfast in *Cresswell*. Eggs and kipper, scrumptiously fried to a turn by Amyas, who was now rigged out in my spare pair of working jeans and one of my tee-shirts. He had washed his feet.

After discussing with the general his little boat for a while, I asked him how long he had been cruising about alone.

"Ah, *Señor* Tristan, I have been sailing much more ever since I fell off a horse. Had a bad injury, you see. I used to love horses—still do, in fact, but I can't manage it any more. I'm seventy-three now. So I sail around in my little boat. I don't do too much sailing; she has a good engine and I only sail on the calmest of days. I love it."

The general, again in his black suit, thought for a moment, as if dredging words from his subconscious. "It's the . . . very antithesis of army life in a lot of ways—the informality, the camaraderie with all differing types of people. And yet in some other ways it's very similar to the military—the need for order and some kinds of regulations to keep the vessel in good . . . " He looked as if he were searching for a word.

"Fettle," I prompted.

"What's that word?" The little old man screwed up his eyes.

"Good fettle. It's the Saxon equivalent of the opposite of chaos, of anarchy. It's having things shipshape, the way a sailor likes it; the way it has to be for the sea to let him survive. What do you think, Amyas?" I looked at Mister Cupling, offering him a share in the conversation.

Amyas looked serious. "Order? I should think that sums it up in one word, as it were? After all, can't sail a boat around for long that's not in good order, can we?"

A vision of *Dreadnaught* hobbling from Scotland to Greece, under a continual refit, passed through my mind. "No, you're right about that, Amyas," I replied.

The young naval lieutenant, along with a burly petty officer and two ratings, arrived just after six-thirty. The lieutenant seemed at first flustered and disappointed to see all of us old men up, about, alive, and awake before he arrived. Then he perked up and dashed onboard *Cresswell* like a lad arriving at a fairground, all pink cheeks, gray-green eyes, and enthusiasm.

"Must be from Galicia," the general muttered, "and anxious to succeed."

Then, down in *Cresswell*'s cabin, the lieutenant caught sight of the general's face. He froze to attention. So did his men.

The general looked up, stern-faced, but with a twinkle. "Well, lad, don't just stand there! Say something! What's your name?"

"Francisco Alvarez Dominguez . . . " etc. etc. etc. The name went on for about a minute, like a ship's passenger list.

"Well, lieutenant, *Señores* Cupling and Jones. . . . *Limited* . . . have worked out what they will need for the repairs and salvage operation. They've discussed it with me, and I've approved the plan and the charges for the work to be done and the equipment to be employed. Now, I'm flying to Barcelona today, and I'll be back in three days.

When I get back I'll expect to see *Señor* Cupling's boat afloat again!"

"*Señor!*" Lieutenant Francisco's head jerked upright.

The general strolled to the companionway ladder and handed Francisco a piece of paper. "Now when you relieve your armed sentry on that floating *pig-sty* out there, you give him this. Tell him to pass it on to the *animal* who drives that *thing* around, and to inform him, *from me*, that he has exactly forty-eight hours to get hold of this amount and to hand it over to *Señores* Cupling and Jones here. If he doesn't, you can tell him I'll have his boat taken to Palma cavalry barracks and mashed up with the horse bran!"

"*Señor!*"

"Good. Now, get together with these two *caballeros* and see that they get whatever they need!"

"*Señor!*"

The general mounted the ladder and passed over to his own boat. Before he went below he turned again to the young lieutenant, who was still standing at attention. "Oh, and one other thing, son. Make a good *Spanish* job of it, eh?"

"*Señor!*" shouted the young man. When the general disappeared he looked down at the piece of paper. Softly, he whistled. He looked at me. "My men are ready, *señor*, all ready. What do we need for this operation?"

I introduced Amyas and myself, to put the lad at ease. He introduced himself again. Then, after Amyas had handed him a cup of tea, and a flaskful for his men on the jetty ("Cheer them up a bit, as it were, eh?") I clapped my hand on the lieutenant's shoulder and started reading off the list that Amyas and I had worked out the evening before, over supper. When I started reading the list and describing our intentions, Lieutenant Francisco's face was clouded; then, as I rambled on and made swift sketches on the back of an old chart, his expression lightened, became intrigued, enthusiastic, and finally amused—so much so that he at last laughed.

"Marvelous!" he said. He looked at me in my Breton smock, tea mug in hand, a mischievous gleam in my eye. Then he stared for a moment at Amyas and his mustache, twitching and grinning as they hovered over our shoulders. Suddenly the lieutenant straightened. "*Señores*," he intoned gravely, "you know I'm beginning to think you really *are* professional salvaging experts!"

"Actually for salvaging spirits, as it were," Amyas murmured, with a wink at me. The mustache twitched in agreement.

"Yeah, Johnny Walker Black Label, preferably," I muttered. "Come on, let's get *Cresswell* and *Estrellita* out of the way."

I suppose some people must think of sailing vessels as mere collections of inanimate objects, like planks of wood and bits of iron and nails, wire, and canvas. They may be right, but if they are, then the old, dying hulk *Rosalinda* and her next-door neighbor must have been the most deliciously excited bits of inanimate matter that ever existed when they felt Amyas and me jump onboard them.

As we had walked along the town quay toward the hulks, they had looked sulkily depressed, as gloomily miserable as ever, like old ladies with migraines, too pained to bother to fix their hair, too old and worn-out to have it done for them.

As soon as my feet hit *Rosalinda*'s deck, and Amyas' directly afterward, I felt a transformation in the old derelict. Some people will say that it was only the vibrations as our weights descended onto her rotting decks that made her tattered halyard wires jiggle and tremble, and that it was merely an odd squally gust which fluttered the ragged tatters of her moldy mainsail as Amyas and I headed for her cargo-hatch coaming and gazed down into the murky water, still and clammy, in her hold. Others will say that the voices I heard, as we discussed getting the water out of her, were only the echoes of our own words bouncing back at us from the great oak frames in the ghostly shadows of the side-decks. Others will say that sailors are superstitious creatures, and anyway, all small-boat voyagers are a bit dotty and liable to let their imaginations run away with them.

But I say—I swear—that as Amyas and I boarded that old derelict her pulse leapt; it seemed that the spirits of every man who ever sailed in her jumped for inexpressible joy. We had not lowered ourselves down on her deck like curious sightseers. We had no cameras slung around our necks. We were not looking for quaintness or bizarre curiosities from the distant past. We had little thought in our heads about the "romance" of sail. We were not dreaming of her past voyages—*and she knew it*. The moment we bowled onboard her that old girl's fainting blood *raced*. She knew that we were gauging her remaining strength. She knew we *wanted* her. She knew that, in some way, she was still useful. As we stared down into her hold she heaved and sighed, welcoming us—but it was only a passing fishing boat's bow wave that did that, of course.

Her next-door neighbor, an even more ancient, stump-masted ruin, which had been merely fidgeting as we inspected *Rosalinda*, seemed almost to faint entirely away with anticipation and excitement as Amyas clambered over her decayed bulwarks. He first walked back to her stern and peered over her counter. "This one has no name, Tristan. Sort of nameless, as it were!" he called.

I plunged my knife into *Rosalinda*'s mainmast. It was sound enough. "Good," I sang back, "then we'll call her *Bloody Neverbudge*!"

Amyas grinned as I hopped onto the nameless wreck. "*Bloody Neverbudge*—she certainly looks it," he said. "Hasn't moved in years, I'd say, but she must be built like Gibraltar, as it were. Hardly a drop of water in her. About a foot—probably rainwater."

"That's a wonder, Amyas, because she's got dropsy," I replied. I meant that her keel was hogged; that is, it dropped down from the horizontal forward and aft. *Bloody Neverbudge* seemed to take that as a compliment. Her rotten gaff boom, which was swinging loosely over my head, suddenly moaned as if in pleasure.

After Amyas and I had prodded around the hulks' mooring posts and their bulwarks with our knives, seeking out the rot and marking the sound wood with great chalked crosses, for about an hour, the Spanish navy turned up. It brought two commandeered fishing boats. One of these belonged to Josélito, my local fisherman friend. I waved at José as his boat slowly chugged up to the hulks. He grinned back at me hugely. He was obviously pleased. He would be paid well for his labor, and it seemed he was remembering my Halloween visit to the graveyard with Rory O'Boggarty, Ireland's Hope and England's Dread. I winked at him.

Both fishing boats had portable diesel water pumps on deck. Both had twenty fathoms of two-inch chain laid out. Each had a Spanish navy scuba diver, both of whom were already donning their rubber suits in a welter of joking about how they were going to manage to make it with the mermaids, dressed so.

By the time *Rosalinda* and *Bloody Neverbudge* (even the Spaniards were calling the ancient ruin by her new name now) were pumped out, Amyas and I, with the help of a couple of seamen, had one end of each long chain secured around the bases of both mainmasts, and the fishing boats were securely lashed alongside both of our hulks. With the amount of water taken out of *Rosalinda*, her hull had risen a couple of feet out of the harbor. Now both old ladies drew less than three feet under their bows.

Soon our little squadron was ready to get underway. Before we cast off the shackles of the hulks' imprisoning mooring lines, Francisco, as I had requested, planted staffs, with Spanish ensigns bent to them, on the sterns of the two hulks. The old ladies shivered with delight and seemed to be charmed at being invited out by a young, good-looking officer of their very own navy—but of course it was only the vibrations of the fishing boats' engines. Let no one ever think that they were thrilled almost out of their keels to be stepping out again, pretty new red and yellow shawls over their shoulders . . .

With a great roar as the fishing boat engines accelerated, and a mighty swirl and churn of mucky harbor water, the hulks moved off, shy and reluctant at first; then, as the fishing boats gently, courteously insisted, and as the lashing lines took up their strain, and after the old ladies and we had glanced around nervously to make sure their slips weren't showing, the whole fleet moved steadily in the forenoon sunshine across the dead-flat water of the harbor. *Rosalinda* and *Bloody Neverbudge* felt the wind in their hair—what was left of it; the jagged, torn, rotted bits of sail still aloft. They sighed with pleasure and delight. I was in *Rosalinda* and Amyas was in the more ancient ship. There was no point in our trying to steer the hulks—their rudders had dropped off, or been removed, long before.

"See you in Miami, Amyas," I shouted.

"After I've had a look around the Bahamas, as it were!" he sang back over the yards of passing water between us. Both the old ladies jolted at this, as if they imagined we were serious—but of course it was only our passing over the bow wave of a ferry from Formentera. Of course boats don't imagine; of course they don't dream; of course they don't *know*. Any sensible landlubber knows that! What do these sailors, these wandering fools, think the folks of the towns and cities are? Idiots? Romantics?

By the time we got both the hulks' bows alongside the sunken *Dreadnaught*, and both of the long chains into *Dreadnaught*'s main hatch and out through her forward hatch, and back to the hulks; and both hulks' cargo holds so full of water that their keels both rested on the harbor bottom; and both chains tautened up around the masts, and the portable pumps again sucking water from the sunken old ladies, it was time for lunch.

Amyas, Francisco, and I, all three of us filthy shipmates, strolled over to Antonio's bodega. We took one of the seamen with us to collect sandwiches for his mates, who stayed and watched the water gush from the diesel pumps, and the two hulks' hulls slowly, slowly rise again, and the cables from the sunken *Dreadnaught* slowly, slowly tauten. Francisco ordered the petty officer to stop the pumps as soon as the cables were dead taut, and to await our return. Such is the life of the owners of a salvage company and a naval officer.

It was obvious, when we reached Antonio's, that the events of the day before, and of the morning, were now common knowledge, but of course distorted out of all proportion. From the loitering ancients outside the door we learned that "communist swine" had "made an attempt on the life of the governor-general, and ought to be castrated." Antonio insisted that a bomb had been planted in *Dreadnaught*, which the foul murderers had mistaken for *El General*'s boat. From Rory O'Boggarty, who sat, as usual, in the back of the bar, in gloomy shadows, a customary bottle of beer in front of him, we received a quote from W.B. Yeats: "Sure, *the center cannot hold . . . and the ceremony of innocence is drowned . . .*"

"Oh, for Christ's sake, Rory, stop getting on my soddin' *wick!* Is it nothing better you have to do but spout bloody poetry at hard-working poor sailors?" I retorted. "Here we are, only come in for a quick beer and a bite, and you're covering us with your damned Bloomsbury gloom."

"It's an old Celtic tradishun," he slurred, "for the bard to be welcoming the warriors."

"Along with the women," said I. That shut him up. Very conscious of sexual roles, they are, in County Limerick.

A half-hour later, when we arrived back at the salvage site, the pumps were still running, but soon the chains tautened and, as the stumps and masts of the two hulks took the strain of *Dreadnaught*'s ten tons, the mooring wires and anchors holding them in place strained and squealed, moaned and groaned. This was the crucial moment. We stared down into the murky harbor water, at the spot where *Dreadnaught* lived out her agony. There had been a fresh southerly wind during the night. While it had not blown the oily muck away from the outer mole wall, it had piled the harbor water on the northern shore of the bay, and this had drawn a lot of the gunge with it, so we could just see *Dreadnaught*, the mere shadow of her, as she lay with her deck five feet underwater.

Suddenly, as we peered down, as if gazing on some exotic sea monster, the shadow moved. Only a short jerk, but it moved. The chains jerked and slumped back again. The seamen on the hulks' decks again tautened them up with their chain-ratchet tauteners, their "bit-nippers." The pumps roared on.

José was sitting on the steps of his wheelhouse, eagerly consuming a fish pie his wife and brood had brought for him. As his eldest son, the pig-sticker, waited for him to finish with his lunch pail, I turned and saw the fat baby. It was waving that damned rattle and frowning at me. It looked like Churchill in 1940, even though it was being drooled over by Amyas, Francisco, the petty officer, and its mother.

I stared down again at the shadow of *Dreadnaught*. Suddenly, with a grating and grinding, a cracking and straining, the shadow disappeared, the hulks heaved and groaned, and all the positioning cables were brought up rigid, like the holding wires of a circus Big Top tent. The fat baby was forgotten now, except by its mother, of course. Every other eye was now watching the wires and the hulks. Francisco and Amyas were at my side. By now the jetty was crowded with well-wishers. The *swine* on the arrested killer boat glared at us.

"We got the bugger!" I said. "Look, the chains are almost vertical now. We pump out another few tons of water and she'll start to rise."

"To come back to life, as it were," said Amyas.

"*Felicidades*," Francisco said. "Congratulations!"

"Not yet. It's too early," I told him. "Softlee, softlee, catchee monkee," I added in pidgin English.

Even as I spoke, both *Rosalinda* and *Bloody Neverbudge* heaved upward slightly. Again the chains slackened off.

Again they were tightened by the sweating seamen. Then, as we watched like worshipers seeing the Host being raised in slow motion, the two hulks rose. In silence, almost breathlessly, everyone watched—everyone except the fat baby, who was now forgotten and howling its fat head off behind us.

Slowly, inch by inch, the freeboard of the two hulks increased. Inch by inch . . . six inches . . . eight inches . . . foot by blessed foot . . . one foot, two feet, three, four, five, six . . . until, at long last, to the rousing cheers and *olé*'s of everyone present, the dirty gray top of *Dreadnaught*'s rusty-steel coachroof broke the water surface. Soon her deck was awash. In minutes, Amyas was onboard his beloved boat, hanging over the stern, bashing a rag-enshrouded wooden chock into the damaged stern gland. Soon, when *Dreadnaught*'s deck was a mere inch above water level, one of the pump hoses was dragged over and plopped into her. After a few more minutes she floated again. A hundred spectators of a dozen nationalities, all cheered.

Dreadnaught's exterior looked to me only a *little* sorrier than it had before she had been sunk. The mattress was only a little damper, and the oily ensign dripped harbor water, but apart from that, and the busted stern gland, I couldn't see much difference at all on her exterior. Of course the crowd and the seamen, most of them, didn't realize that, and so there was a long spate of ooh's and aah's of commiseration and pity for Amyas, even though he himself was now grinning like the Cheshire Cat, as the last mucky liquid came from *Dreadnaught*'s insides, spurting out the pump hose. When the last burbling gush was over, he hauled *Dreadnaught* close to the wall and stood looking at me. The mustache ends were again cocked.

I squatted down. "OK, Amyas? Think she'll be all right now? We'll get you over to the hauling railway in a while, when the hulks have been returned." I said this quietly, in case the hulks should hear me. "Everything all right down below?"

"Oh, fine. Of course, there's a bit of mess and everything will have to be dried out. The stove jets will need to
be changed, but otherwise everything's about the same, as
it were," he replied, quieting his voice, for while he spoke I
had lifted a finger to my lips. Spanish hearing is very acute.

Soon the crowd had melted away. Soon the hulks were
sadly but, it seemed to me, proudly being escorted across
the harbor to the graveyard. They were still wearing their
new ensigns as the fishing boats pushed and tugged them
across the calm waters. Now there was something indefina-
bly *different* about them. It was as if they now had a fresh
story to tell to the other condemned hulks when the soft
night breeze disturbed their broken rigging wires and the
tatters of their ancient sails. They were like old folks going
back to the home after a day out with the lads and lasses.
They had a new lease of life. They knew they had been
useful, and had helped another of their kind—and they
knew that they and others would remember the story, and
that they might be called upon again, to help their own
little world keep turning. But of course they were only two
rotten, moldy, ruined hulks which had been used as pon-
toons for a few hours . . . that's all.

But not quite. Francisco had promised me that he
would leave the ensigns rigged. One of his minions would
raise and lower them every morning and evening. Amyas
had painted, in big red-lead letters, a new name on the
oldest vessel—*Bloody Neverbudge*. It was daubed all across
her stern, where passing people would see it plainly. And
under her new name he had written, in white paint, "Res-
cuer of *Dreadnaught*—November 1965."

By dusk *Dreadnaught* had been hauled up by the horse-
driven capstan onto the schooner repair slipway, over by
the road to Santa Eulalia. She was safe and drying out
slowly.

After supper Francisco took Amyas and me to Antonio's for a couple of beers at the table next to where the
slumped O'Boggarty was fast asleep in his corner.

"You might as well sleep onboard *Cresswell*," I told Amyas. "Sissie—she's my mate—won't be back for another day, and anyway, she won't mind if you sleep onboard then; too bloody bad if she does."

"Oh, that won't be necessary. I'd be grateful if I can stay tonight," he said, "but tomorrow I'm going to go 'round *Dreadnaught* with a blowtorch—I'll soon have her dried out again, as it were."

"How about your welding set? Do you think it's knackered?"

"Oh, I can fiddle around with it, as it were, sort of fix it up. Give me something to do . . . " Amyas' mustache wiggled.

Then, at Francisco's prodding, we talked about the war; about the convoys and the battles in the Arctic. Amyas, it turned out, had been less fortunate than I. He'd had six ships sunk from under him. "Of course, now I suppose I can claim seven ships sunk?" he said, as young Francisco gazed at his face, fascinated, and I grinned.

The following day I accompanied Amyas over to the slipway and gave him a hand getting all his sopping gear—his blankets, books, tools, engine bits, cooking utensils, food, and clothing—out of his boat. We laid it all out to dry as best we could in the sunlight. It looked a sorry collection. A bit like a scrapyard. In the afternoon it started to rain, so we threw a great tarpaulin over the lot and retired to a little boatyard workers' bar across the road. That's one thing sailors learn—never fight the weather. Always go along with it, especially on shore. If we didn't, we'd be drooling lunatics before you could say "nice weather for ducks."

"Of course I don't mind being on my own," said Amyas over our third beers, "but I do miss having my missus with me. We'd planned to cruise around together for years before I returned, only she wanted a wooden boat, so I suppose it's just as well, really. She never did understand metal . . . and she hated engines. I used to fix up the neighbors' cars and lawn mowers and such while I was home on leave . . . Well, if someone's in a jam, as it were . . . and she used to do her nut. Never wanted me to take her out to the cinema and such . . . Stay at home with my slippers on in front of the fire. She was a good girl, but a real homebody, as it were. I don't know if she really would have liked *Dreadnaught* . . . What do you think?"

"Well, women are a bit funny. Some of 'em like steel boats, some don't, I suppose," I replied.

"Yes, they are strange creatures. I suppose you never really get to know them until you've been living with them for a while?"

"My old biddie's not too bad," I said. "I keep her in the for'd dodger when there's nothing for her to do, and when I've got something on, I send her ashore, shopping and all those things. Gets her out of the way and keeps us happy. Bloody dog can't stand her, though. It's like he thinks she'll commit barratry any day; you know, pinch the boat while I'm ashore. But really she's all right, at least when she don't talk too much . . . "

Amyas laughed. "Oh, that's pretty usual. Seems they're mostly like that, I'm told, after they get to know you, as it were. Actually I find that type of thing sort of refreshing. At least it makes a change from the Old Man continually complaining about not getting enough revolutions . . . enough speed, or the steam-winch breaking down . . . "

He was silent for a minute, then he said, "Yes, I suppose the ladies are a bit like Scots captains, really. You just have to put up with 'em, I suppose. Still . . . "

He sighed.

Suddenly I had a bright idea, but it half-faded away again. "Anyway," I said, "I was going to offer to pass Sissie on to you. She's not a bad hand; she loves hauling in the anchor and heaving mooring lines, especially when there's a cold wind and it's raining—she laps it up!"

Above our heads, the pouring rain battered the tin roof of the shanty bar. Amyas looked at me, interested.

I continued. "Problem is, she's leaving for Morocco in a few months." I paused for a moment. "Anyway, I'll put it to her when she gets back from Majorca. See what she says."

Then our talk went back to boats, and Amyas wound up giving me a full hour's run-down on the working of gas-turbine engines.

Lieutenant Francisco was onboard *Cresswell* early next day. In his hand he carried an envelope. He gestured over his shoulder as he slid down the ladder. "He's waiting on the jetty," said he, after he had sung out a greeting.

Amyas was frying cod's liver and chips for breakfast. With Sissie absent we could relish sailors' favorites again. None of your bloomin' sickly pale eggs and underdone bacon now. I sat on my berth scratching Nelson's ear. I looked up at Francisco. "Who? Who's waiting?"

"The powerboat owner. Look, he drew the money yesterday. All four banks had to pool together to raise it. He wants a receipt."

I stood up and looked over Francisco's shoulder. On the jetty was the man in the peaked cap, toothbrush mustache, and dark glasses. His face was expressionless as the glasses stared my way. I felt like charging ashore with my diving knife. Instead I reached under the galley stove, grabbed a roll of toilet paper—Spanish, a bit like wrapping paper anywhere else—and ripped off a sheet or two. I scrawled a receipt over the paper and thrust it into Francisco's hand. He looked down at it and read: "Received money for salvage of *Dreadnaught* and repairs to *Cresswell* and *Estrellita del Mar*." Then my signature.

"You haven't written the sum of money, *señor*."

"Oh, Christ . . . " I grabbed the paper again, with my hand still shaking in anger at the thought of that sod on the jetty. "How much is it?" I asked impatiently.

"One hundred thousand pesetas . . . I have it here," he replied.

"Right . . . One . . . *What!*" I almost collapsed against Amyas, who dropped his frying pan, fortunately onto the stove.

"One hundred thousand pesetas, *señor*. That's what the general wrote down on your estimation, after he'd seen what you needed and the work required."

Quickly I scrawled in the sum over the receipt, as I reckoned to myself . . . 2000 dollars . . . divide that by three . . . my hand shook even more . . . that's 660-odd dollars for *Dreadnaught*, and over 1300 bucks for the orphanage . . . and the whole operation had cost us only the price of a few beers . . . except for the fishing boats . . . two boats at twenty bucks . . . still left Amyas and me with more than 600 dollars . . .

I rammed the receipt into Francisco's hand.

"What shall I tell him?" the lieutenant asked.

"Tell him to stick it up his nose."

Francisco turned to mount the ladder, wordlessly. I looked at Amyas. He was in a seeming state of shock. His mustache twitched. His hands trembled. I called to the lieutenant. "No . . . tell him thank you and to call again soon!"

Francisco glanced over his shoulder and smiled before he clambered to the stern.

Amyas subsided onto my berth. He stared straight ahead of him, before he looked at me. Then his eyes crinkled up and the mustache and ears followed into the biggest grin imaginable. "Tristan, do you know how much that is?" His voice was hoarse.

I waved the envelope that Francisco had handed me. I tore it open. Out slid a bundle of notes two inches thick, onto the biscuit tin lid that served as a chart table in *Cresswell*.

"Two thousand dollars, my old friend, and 600 of it for you! By Jesus . . . sorry, mate . . . by Jumpin' Jiminy, you can have *Dreadnaught* looking like a bloody admiral's barge!"

"Oh, I couldn't take all our share, Tristan. You did more than half the work. And anyway, it was all your idea."

"No, listen Amyas, you take what's left over after we pay the fishing boats and the orphanage. It'll mean you can get your engine fixed ashore. I'll tell you what; if you like, you can take Sissie and me to dinner one evening next week when we return from Formentera. Fair enough?''

Amyas stared into space for a minute, then he said, "Well, that's very generous of you, old chap, but I simply couldn't . . . I mean, after all, what would I do while I'm sailing around if I didn't have my engine to fix, as it were?''

That knocked the wind out of my sails for a few minutes, while I struggled not to laugh. Then I said, "Well, at any rate, Amyas, you can get the whole bloomin' boat painted and new sails and all, and still have enough left over to cruise for a few months.''

"Oh, I couldn't do that . . . it wouldn't be right . . . honest . . . ''

I lost my patience. "Well, all right then, Amyas, as senior partner in the Cupling and Jones *Dreadnaught* Salvage Company, which hereafter will be considered dissolved, and as director in charge of finance, I'm paying you your fee for your advice in the firm's recent operations and also a bonus upon your retirement . . . OK?''

Amyas' face drew itself up into a certain dignity. The mustache ends curled up. His eyes brightened. "That sounds reasonable enough, as it were," he said. "How much is it?''

"Thirty-one thousand, three hundred pesetas. Here, sign this receipt, please; then I can close the company books.''

I wrote a receipt on another piece of toilet paper, Amyas signed it, and thus was dissolved the shortest-lived salvage company ever.

Amyas said, "Don't forget, bring your lady friend to dinner next week.''

"When we get back from Formentera, Amyas,'' I said.

Sissie was back in the late forenoon. "Yoo-hoo, Tristan dahling!''

I heard her voice from the otherwise deserted jetty. Nelson growled softly. I put down my book of verse— *Paradise Lost*.

I helped her onboard. She was still in her rose-bestrewn finery. Her eyes glowed like new Barlow sheet winches. "*Deah* Tristan!" she bellowed, as I grabbed her arm. "How *did* you manage without me?"

"Oh, it was a bit rough, but we managed it somehow." I took her parcels.

She was glowing, excited, as she passed down the companionway. "Theahs a present for you, dahling Tristan!" she yelled, "and one for *deah* dahling Nelson . . . "

Nelson glowered at her. Sissie turned around slightly, rocking the boat. Her eyes stabbed at the stove. Three pans, treacherously littered with the remnants of kidney, liver, fish, and chips betrayed me. "Oh you *poor* deah. Just look at this bally old galley . . . Simply awf'ly . . . mmm . . . Well, I s'pose you've been terribly *busy* while Ai've been away, dahling?" She plonked her parcels on the spare berth.

"Bit of reading. Filled the water tanks," I replied.

"Heah . . . " Sissie handed me an envelope. "A month's chartah fee. Three thousand, five hundred pesetas, dahling."

"Thanks, Sissie. That'll keep us going until I get another delivery. By the way, Willie get away all right?"

"Oh, absolutely. He bumped into one of his curates in Palma airport. They traveled back togethah." She ripped my present open.

"How delightful for the curate," I said.

"Spiffing!" she said, as she handed me a red-and-blue-striped tie.

"Just what I needed—thank you, Sissie!" I gasped as she pecked my cheek.

"I simply *knew* you'd like it," she murmured.

In calm or storm, in rain and shine,
The shellback doesn't mind,
On the ocean swell he'll work like hell,
For the girl he left behind.
He beats it north, he runs far south,
He doesn't get much pay,
He's always on a losing game,

Chorus: *And that's the Sailor's Way.*

Main chorus: *Then it's goodbye my little Marie,*
We're off to sea again.
Sailor Jack always comes back
To the girl he's left behind!

—from "The Sailor's Way"

This is a capstan and pump chantey, but it was also sung as a "fore-bitter," that is, even when work was not being done—which was rare. This chantey is unique in that the haulers joined in singing the last line of the verse along with the chanteyman.

12

The Sailor's Way

"SO HOW were things in Majorca, Sissie?"
I asked, as she fondly showed Nelson a new bright-red
doggie bowl she'd bought for him. Nelson softly growled at
her and the bowl as though it were poisoned.

"Oh, simply *spiffing!* Deah Willie, of course, just as you
said, dahling, didn't like Palma much, but then neither do
Ai. All the bally *noise* and the *dreary* traffic, and all those
simply *dreadful* little hotels going up. Oh deah . . . " Sissie's
forehead creased as she closed her eyes and shook her
shoulders. Then her eyes sprang open, and she was *British*
again. "Tea, dahling?"

She didn't wait for a reply. Kettle in hand, she went
on. "And those *ebsolutely peasanty* little men on the street—
shocking! Honestly, dahling, one would think they'd nevah
seen a woman before, the way they carry on . . . so persistent, I mean—so awf'ly bally *boring!* Poor *deah* Willie
hardly knew *what* to do."

"They weren't chatting him up, were they?" My eyes
must have gleamed.

"Oh, no . . . Well, hardly . . . " She frowned for a
moment, then half-apologetically smiled. "Well, not until
we got on thet *dreadful* omnibus to Pollensa. Willie did so
awf'ly want to see *deah* Robert Graves' *charming* villa, and
this shocking *harridan*—I mean she was *antediluvian*, my
deah—sat next to us. She was from one of those simply
obscure Scandinavian places that awful chep Ibsen used to

201

write about, and she was dragging around this poor little—well, you reahlly couldn't say *cheppie*, dahling—*person*, who looked sort of terribly *prole*, and he was so *pimply* . . . and his *purple* shirt!"

I grinned over my tea mug. "Don't tell me he felt Willie's knee?"

"Well, my *deah* Tristan, *e*ctually Ai don't know *what* happened. You see Ai was too *dreadfully* preoccupied stopping this dratted *cockerel*—it was in a *bawsket* undah the bally seat in front of me—from pecking at mai jolly old *feet*. But quite suddenly deah Willie simply *insisted* on stopping the blessed omnithing and *alighting*—I mean, dahling, right out in the middle of *nowheah*." Sissie's eyes crinkled as if in pain. "And we had to get a sort of lift in this ancient *farm-lorry*, and when we arrived, dreadfully exhausted, we found thet *deah* Robert Graves was away. Awf'ly naice villa, though . . . oodles of palm trees and things . . . "

"So you got back to Palma—then what?"

"Well, my deah, it was long awftah midnight when the omnithing finally *oozed* back to the city, and *deah* Willie and I couldn't find a taxi-cab, and we had to jolly well *plod* all the way back to the bally hotel, and all these *ghastly* little men simply *scurrying* the streets and all these *dreadful* hussies loitering about. It was all so sort of *primeval*, rawther like something out of one of those *terrible* continental *opera-things*, you know?"

"Carmen?"

"*Eb*solutely!" she exclaimed. "Oh, deah Tristan, how simply *clevah* of you!"

Sissie gazed at the picture of the Queen for a moment, then said, quietly, "It was *rancidly* un-supah, my pet, and *deah* Willie was so *dreadfully* upset, and I had to almost *smothah* him to jolly well prevent him from dragging some of those *sordid* little hussies along to a restaurant for suppah, and all the bally while these simply *beastly* little men were sort of *breathing* at me! Finally one of those *awf'ly* naice policemen of theahs trotted along and escorted us back to our hotel . . . Oh, *deah!*"

I was smiling to myself. "What's up now, lass?"

"Oh, why do those little cheps *do* it? Ai mean, it's not as if theah were no sort of awf'ly jolly *decent* gals around, is it?"

"That's one of the oldest questions around, Sissie. Anyway, I wouldn't wonder at the bloke who does that now and again. If I were you, I'd wonder at the feller who *doesn't*."

Even as I said that, Lieutenant Francisco climbed onboard *Cresswell*. I called to him to come on down. He descended and saw Sissie, who still looked pained. I introduced Sissie to Francisco. He clicked his heels together at the bottom of the ladder, gently took hold of Sissie's brown, calloused, and wilting hand, raised it delicately as he bowed, and lightly brushed it with his lips. Sissie almost dissolved into the paintwork.

"*Señora*, I am at your feet, enchanted," murmured the young officer. Sissie was too breathless to say a word. She seemed somehow to hang in space as her Boedicea-blue eyes glazed at him and her mouth fell half open.

In his fairly good English Francisco said, "*Señor* Tristan, the Mother at the orphanage is ready to receive you, and begs that you and your friend Amyas . . . and the *señora*, I hope . . . " (he flashed sex and slavery at Sissie, who almost moaned in a transport of feminine fluster) " . . . will join her and her staff for lunch at one o'clock?"

"Of course we will," I replied. (Never turn down comestibles and booze.) "Delighted, Francisco. Will you be coming, too?"

"I have that signal honor, *señor*," he said.

Sissie suddenly remembered that she was British. "Would you like *tea*, Lieutenant?" she purred breathlessly.

"*Señora*, your tea will be to me as the drink of the gods," said Francisco, as full of Spanish flannel as a Ganges blanket.

Sissie smiled weakly at him. She glowed in a subtle way; her Saxon reaction to his Iberian charm oozed out of her like red-gleaming iron slag seeping out of a Bessemer blast-furnace. I studied her face for a moment as she stood over the teapot. Her eyes were half-closed. There was a dreamy smile on her lips, and her dumpy chest heaved as she reached one hand up to pat her frizzy ginger hair.

Of course the cat was coming out of the bag, now. Francisco would tell Sissie the tale of *Dreadnaught*—well laced with Hispanic charm and decorated with Castilian embroidery. Now that Sissie was under the spell of a *real* charmer, *deah*, dahling Skippah could go to pot. I silently slid up the ladder and headed for Amyas and *Dreadnaught*, to collect the engineer-poet and bring him back for lunch at the orphanage. I left Francisco to put Sissie *au fait* with the stirring tale of *Dreadnaught*'s demise and resurrection, and to drink "the drink of the gods."

" . . . best *Burma* tea, from Fortnum and Mason's," I heard Sissie purring as I jumped onto the jetty.

An hour later, at the orphanage, where we arrived in Francisco's navy jeep, about fifty kids were lined up to greet us, with four nuns in command. The kids were all ages, from about two up to twelve or so; boys and girls, all dressed in blue uniforms. The girls' gym-slips reminded me of Sissie's. But it was a sad moment as we passed them, at least for me, even though the kids were dutifully smiling and looking their best. The Reverend Mother was gracious and more than grateful for the money which was handed over. I had left it to Francisco to do this, as I thought it would be less embarrassing for the Mother to accept it from the Spanish navy, and from a Catholic, than from we Britons—an Anglican, a Calvinist, and a . . . a delivery skipper.

The meal we had was simple—a salad, broiled fish, potatoes, and afterward a custard pudding. The wine was excellent—a vintage Marques de Riscal. The table had no cloth; the plates and glasses were set out on its clean, well-scrubbed top. The meal was served by older girl-orphans, who looked, although serious-faced, contented with the honor. They did not seem awed by the Reverend Mother at all—in fact their demeanor reminded me of my own sisters' attitude toward our mother, so long before in Merioneth.

The hall where the meal was taken was, surprisingly to me, starkly simple. It was a long, whitewashed place, with a high roof supported by massive timbers. The only decoration was a small, dark wooden cross on one wall. The windows were set high, and were clear glass, through which sunbeams streamed.

At first the conversation was a little stilted. Only the Mother, among the nuns, spoke English, and so we managed as best we could in Castilian, with me trying to interpret for Sissie. After a short Latin grace the Mother was effusive in her gratitude, but I told her she should reserve it for the little general, and that the wooden beams above our heads reminded me of a ship's timbers.

"True enough, Captain Jones. They came from the ships of the Moors, which were sunk here in the harbor in the early fifteenth century," the Mother replied.

"Of course they were great sailors, the Arabs," joined in Amyas, whose Spanish was excellent. "They were the first, really, to manage to head more or less into the wind . . . " He hesitated. I figured that he was trying to think of a Spanish equivalent for "as it were." Then he went on. "Of course, *we* invented steam, though. Good job, really—otherwise we'd probably be speaking Arabic now . . . "

And so we sailors, ignoring Hero of Alexandria, got the conversation rolling, and Amyas managed to mention just about every Spanish shipbuilding yard and engineer of note from the past hundred years of so. After a while the Mother happened to remark that the orphanage water-pump was not functioning too well, so Amyas and I spent a good hour in the cellar after lunch, taking the pump to bits and fitting it with new glands, which Amyas cut from an old leather belt.

As he worked away dexterously he said, "Your lady friend is quite . . . charming, as it were, old chap."

"Sissie's glad to be back from Palma."

"You didn't mention anything yet? I mean what we talked about yesterday . . . about her coming onboard *Dreadnaught*?"

"No, haven't had a chance yet, Amyas."

He looked relieved. "Good, I'm glad," he said, as he tapped a washer home around the pump shaft. "I wouldn't want her to see *Dreadnaught* until she's a bit more . . . cozy, as it were."

There was silence for a moment, except for the tapping of the hammer. Then I said "I think you're right, Amyas. I'll talk to her . . . no, a better idea is if we wait until we see you again when we return from Formentera. I can put up with her for another week or so. No sense in rushing, mate."

"No. We ought to be a bit diplomatic. After all, she *is* a woman. Have to be a bit diplomatic with 'em. Funny creatures . . . Don't want to let her think we're arranging things for her, as it were . . . "

I didn't get a chance to reply. Francisco and Sissie and the Reverend Mother all trooped into the cellar.

"Such delightfully *sweet* children," gushed Sissie. "Oh, what a *dreadful* pity you and Amyas couldn't see them at theah lunch—so awf'ly well-behaved. Oh what a ghastly shame *deah* Willie and *dahling* Miss Benedict couldn't have . . . "

Amyas switched on the pump. It worked perfectly. A mere perspiration of water from the shaft glands, just as it should have been. The pump whined away as Sissie's voice faded. The Reverend Mother beamed as she handed Amyas, Sissie, Francisco, and me a tiny silver crucifix each. I still have mine.

On the way back to the harbor in the navy jeep, in between Francisco's charming the pants almost off Sissie, I told her that we were sailing for Formentera again the next day. "Too bloody dirty in Ibiza harbor. I've cleaned the waterline about ten times since we arrived here, and it's almost as bad now as it was yesterday. I've only to fix the new bowsprit on and *Cresswell* will be all ready."

Sissie somehow managed to drag her eyes and attention away from Francisco. She grabbed my arm as the jeep bounced along into the lower town. "Oh, *dahling*, Ai'm *so* glad. Ai'm *eb*solutely, awf'ly *thrilled!*"

"What about?" I asked. I had thought she would have been sorry to leave Ibiza while there was a possibility of Francisco coming onboard.

"Oh, deah . . . Ai've been so *frightfully* fretting . . . in a *dreadful, awful* . . . reahlly a *paroxysm* of . . . *anxiety*, dahling."

"Oh?" I wracked my brain about this for a moment as the whitewashed walls flashed by. Then I gave up. "Why?"

Sissie turned her head, her hair flying in the wind. Her eyes were damp. She patted my arm. "Oh, silly old me!" she cried. "Ai *do* get these *dreadful* turns . . . Ai reahlly don't know *what* to say, my pet . . . "

"Come on, Sissie, for Chrissake, what's biting you? Is it something here in Ibiza? Is it some bloke getting on your wick?"

She half-laughed, and slapped my arm harder now. "Oh, no. It's . . . " She left the rest unsaid.

"What the heck is it, then?"

"It's poor, dahling *Miss Poméroy!*" she burst out. "Ai simply cawn't get her out of my mind. To think of her in the grubby hands of thet great, hulking *beastly* fellow, thet dreadful *foreign* brute! After all, she is *British*, dahling!"

This was a new one on me. I saw in my mind's eye the tiny blue-rinsed children's author. All I could say was, "Well, girl, you pays your money and you makes your choice," but by the time I'd managed to roll that one out, Sissie was smiling again.

"Ai shell go to see her as *soon* as evah we're back in Formentera."

She said it as if she were Queen Victoria ordering out the Guards, so I knew it was useless to argue further, and kept quiet while Francisco craftily worked his magic on the Dragon of Devon all the way back to the jetty.

We were alone again onboard *Cresswell* by the time I popped The Question to Sissie. I did it as casually as a sailor could. "How do you like Amyas, then?"

She dumped the supper potatoes into a bucket, violently. "Oh, what a dreadful, *boring* little man! I sweah I couldn't understand a word he said. All sorts of piston rods and . . . What was it—bally *gudgeon* bars? Ai'm *sure* it must have simply *tired out* thet awf'ly sweet Mothah Superior merely trying to *comprehend* what the dickens he was *talking* about. I know it did *me*, dreadfully."

I made my way forward to fit *Cresswell*'s new bowsprit. Nelson softly padded along the deck behind me. Both our hearts sank. Albion's daughter was staying with us for a while yet. That was obvious. But so, often, go the best-laid plans of mice and men—and dogs, too, we reflected as, hissing into my teeth, I viciously reamed out a new bolt-hole in *Cresswell*'s foredeck and Nelson sadly looked on. We both knew now that Amyas was going to remain alone for quite a while.

Our voyage to Formentera was short in mileage but tall in experience. Ibiza harbor was calm when we left it, and so were the first couple of miles south, but when *Cresswell* cleared the southern point of Ibiza island, and rounded into the channel north of Espalmador, we found a strong southwest wind—hard enough to blow the devil's socks off. In the narrow, shallow channel, it piled up steep seas. It made them crowd together, impatient to shove past one another so as to reach the deeps to the east. Of course, as the seas shoved each other, and those in the rear cried "Forward!" and those in the front called "Back!" quite a furor was created in the strait, and it took poor old *Cresswell*, who could only sail up to about sixty degrees off the blind eye of the wind, about three hours of bash-and-crash-through, slide-and-glide-off, and hammer-and-stammer-into-and-over the charging ranks of watery panic, to get through.

Naturally, all this was right up Sissie's street. She stayed at my side as I heaved and strained at the wheel, beating *Cresswell* first this way, then that, against the wind, stealing a few yards each time we made a short "board"— each time we made first a zig, then a zag, with the boat rising and dropping down eight feet every four seconds and Nelson panting down my neck as he lay secure on the poop, watching for dolphins. Sissie was in her element in this kind of thing—the "juicy bits," she called it. A sort of orgasmic idiocy crept over her face as she squinted against the flying spray. "Oh, jolly, jolly *dee!* Oh, happy, *happy* day!" she yelled, as another maverick sea picked up *Cresswell*'s bow and flung her to one side with contempt and almost wrenched the wheel out of my straining arms. "Oh, lucky, *lucky* me!" she crowed, as yet another piled-up lump of green, watery malevolence rose ahead in vicious obduracy, up, up, up . . . and *Cresswell* humped the shoulders of her mainsail and girded the loins of her bows for the shock, and as the emerald monster grew before us in the light of the sun behind us, until we stared up at it, until it loomed—a great, lumbering, beautiful bully, which gathered up immense strength in the blue-black heart of it, curling slightly—and smashed down on our bow, sending great whizzing streams of water slashing aft.

All the time this went on, as if it had always gone on, and would always go on, for ever and ever, Sissie sang beside my ear . . . *"Somewheah, ovah the rainbow . . . "*

After about an hour of this, the lotus-eater in me asked the age-old island-sailor's question: "Why sail uphill, against the wind, anyway? Why not take it easy and return to a haven downwind and wait for the wind to change direction? Why struggle? Why not do it the easy way?"

I turned to Sissie. Both of us were wet through, streaming seawater. "This is going to take us bloody hours, getting across this little lot," I hollered. "I think we should turn tail and hang on in Ibiza for the wind to veer around to the east . . . It'll be 'round there tomorrow."

Sissie's face dropped. She frowned at me. She looked as if she were about to burst into tears. Her lips moved, but I couldn't hear her in the wind, with the main and mizzen drumming away like steam engines and the banging and clattering of the seas. I leaned over and put my ear close to her face.

" . . . and I was *so* looking forward to seeing if Miss Pomeroy was all right . . . and now I shall have to simply *fret* for anothah *beastly* night. Oh, *deah!*"

"What the hell are you on about?" I yelled at her, and replaced my ear in front of her laughing-gear again, as another sea crashed onboard and we both ducked to dodge the stinging spray.

"Poor, *deah* Miss Pomeroy," she screeched when we rose again. "She's going to be in the hands of that *monstrous*, drunken *predator!*" I heard no more, as another twenty tons of water collapsed onto *Cresswell's* bow and scattered itself into a thousand splatters of silvery stabs.

Moments later, after the boat had recovered from that one, Sissie hollered, a pained look on her face. *"Dahling!"*

I thought she was in trouble, somehow—perhaps one of her ribs had been stove in when she had been thrown against the cockpit bulwark a minute ago? I hoped. I leaned toward her again and poked my ear in front of her face.

"You *did* promise, you know . . . And I'm so *awf'ly* worried. Ai've a funny feeling . . . Reahlly . . . *deah* Miss Pomeroy!"

I was thrown halfway across the cockpit by the boat's next jolt and didn't hear the rest. Oh Christ, I said to myself. I leaned toward her again. "All right, we'll go on, then, if that's what you want." Then I turned to glare at Nelson, who, wet through on the poop, was squinting at me through his one eye, and now and again swallowing the salt off his tongue. I knew he couldn't hear what I said, but I also knew that he was agreeing with what I was thinking. Bloody women, they can't stand the sight of each other when everything's going well, but when one of them is in trouble with a bloke the others don't fancy, watch out! Nelson nodded as I looked at him. Nelson knew the score, all right.

It took us three hours to get through that strait. Then we had another hour's bash west-northwest, another hour east-southeast, then another WSW, another ESE, and we finally came into the lee of the north coast of Formentera island about an hour before dusk. As I hadn't more than a half-gallon of fuel left (complicated, being poor) I had to work my way into Formentera's tiny port under sail. There was little wind and a lot of sea in the protection of the island, but eventually, after fiddling and fuming for another hour and a half, chastised and silent, *Cresswell* finally crept in between the low moles. Sissie tied the boat up while I drank the tea she had made as soon as the "juicy bits" were over.

By the time we were settled down and shipshape, Sissie had all the gear which had been thrown about below back in place. The only thing onboard which showed any sign of wear and tear was yours truly, but after Sissie had shoved a plate of corned beef and chips, peas and radish in front of me, it didn't take long for the brass lamps to be glowing again down below in *Cresswell*.

Sissie wanted to get her shore-boots on and head for San Francisco, the hamlet where Miss Pomeroy lived, right away. I stopped her. "There's no lights. There's no moon. You'll fall into one of those bloody great holes in the road. Anyway, I can't go with you. When the wind backs around it'll be blowing its head off from the north all night. It'll send in quite a sea. If the anchor drags inside this harbor the boat will be smashed against the wall, just like poor old *Fanny Adams* was . . . I just have to be here and watch her. Anything else, with this weather, would be downright stupidity." I wasn't kidding Sissie. This was the case.

Finally, the sense of my argument settled into Sissie's head, and she settled down in her cubbyhole forward. Soon the chinkling notes of her Booth's London Dry Gin bottle and glass tinkled through the forward bulkhead of the main cabin. A little while after, the hushed rustle of her Bible leaves told me that the English lioness was at peace in her lair.

I turned again to my *Oxford Book of English Verse*, in the glimmering light of my oil lamp, and waited for the wind outside to back around to the north, and to do its worst as it started to send worried, frenetic little seas into the narrow mouth of Formentera harbor.

Sure enough, by two a.m. a heavy swell was beating against the seaward sides of the tiny moles, sending wide streams of angry seawater right over the tops of the walls. Through the entrance, like eager fans crushing their way into some darkened concert hall, alive with energy, over-busy with a dozen competing rhythms, crowded with confusion, sea-swell after sea-swell, one after the other, pushed, shoved, surged, and broke through the entrance, against the excited, angry resistance of everything else in the small harbor, including *Cresswell*.

By that time I had run my heavy storm anchor out, in the madly bobbing rubber dinghy, almost clear across the harbor. Then I had delved for my heaviest storm dragline—an inch-diameter rope almost 600 feet long. Sissie and I hauled that, too, right around the harbor and secured it to a bollard on the seawall. *Cresswell* now had two anchors and a heavy storm-line out to windward, to hold her off the wall downwind.

As the wind gathered strength through the night, often driving slashing rain before it, Sissie and I watched the storm-line and anchor cables take the tremendous strain, and we tautened them up from time to time, until they were finally as tight as violin strings. Still the ever-increasing jerking of the boat threatened to drag the anchors or snap the line.

"Oh, *deah*," yelled Sissie, her oilskins streaming rain and spray, about four a.m. "Ai *do* wish that dretted wind would ease a *teeny* while, so you could get some sleep, dahling. Oh deah, you must be *ebsolutely fagged* out. Oh, you poor thing . . . Just a teeny tick—Sissie'll make you some hot cocoa."

As I waited for the cocoa I crouched against the driving rain in *Cresswell*'s cockpit. I pumped out the bilge betimes (she was not self-draining) and hoped that the storm-line would not give to the incessant jerking of the hull, time after time after time—four or five feet up and down, up and down, in the middle of the harbor. I tried to look around me: Nothing but black night, even to leeward. Nothing but a pale, ghostly beam of light every ten seconds, skittering through the myriad drops of spray and rain, from the tiny lighthouse at the harbor entrance; and the ghostly dim glimmer of the cabin oil-lamp down below in *Cresswell*. With the boat bouncing, straining, jerking, and heaving, and the wind roaring, rushing, and screeching all around the little port, it was like being in some nightmarish mael-strom—until Sissie, her oilskin cap streaming water, handed me a steaming mug of cocoa, covered with a saucer. I felt as if she had handed me a reprieve on Death Row.

All night it went on, until just before dawn. Then the wind, exhausted, slumped and shuffled off to its usual quarter in the east. Another half an hour later, about six a.m., I could finally go below and sleep—but not until I had hauled back onboard again the storm-line and the heavy anchor, so that the Ibiza ferry would not foul them when she arrived.

Even in haven, a mariner's lot is not always easy.

It was noon before Sissie woke me. "Yoo-hoo, Skip-pah, dahling—lunch time! Ai've made us some of your very own favorite . . . Look!"

She passed a pot of steaming burgoo under my nose—porridge and bacon and bits of liver, kidney, heart, chi-tlins—all well-laced with rum. I knew it must be some kind of reward—or enticement—for me. Sissie couldn't abide burgoo. For her to sit with me and eat a whole bowl of the stuff, and pretend it was delicious, there simply had to be something in the wind.

After I finished my lunch I went topsides. The breeze was almost down to light airs by now, and the sky was clear. It had been a typical Mediterranean bitch-night, the storm gone just as quickly as it had arrived. No wonder it's so bitchy, said I to myself. What else can be expected with a sea where the blokes that live around it drink wine all day and wear bloody scent? Then, as I frowned, thinking about the effects of regional weather on human temperament, I almost started out of my tee-shirt.

The whole of *Cresswell*'s topsides—the cockpit, the poop, the side-decks, the coachroof, the foredeck—all had been thoroughly washed with fresh water! The varnish of the masts was polished and shining. Not a grain of salt was to be seen anywhere onboard. Not a sign of salt on the green and red navigation lights hanging on the shrouds. Not one speck of white on the compass glass; and the brass binnacle shone as if it were brand-new instead of sixty years old. The brass plates atop the mooring posts; the bronze metal rail trim around the foredeck and poop whale-backs; the brass ship-shields that decorated the companion-way doors—all sparkled, clean and highly polished. Topsides, *Cresswell* looked like she was headed for a boat-show. Hmm, I said to myself—something *is* in the wind.

I went below again, silently. Trying not to make it obvious to Sissie, I stared around. The brass oil-lamps, the brass clock, the brass ladder trimmings—every bit of brass and bronze down below had been polished. The pictures on the forward bulkhead had been cleaned and the glass polished. The galley gleamed. The biscuit tin lid I used as a navigation table—even that was polished. The cabin sole was freshly scrubbed, and so was the table. The navigation and other books had all been taken down, dusted, and replaced on the cleaned shelves. Something was very definitely in the wind.

I studied Sissie. She had on a pair of jeans now. Some tailor must have got a migraine figuring out that shape, I thought. Above them she wore a frilly blouse, with the sleeves unbuttoned and rolled back to the elbows. Her ginger hair looked as if a lion-tamer had finally discovered how to subdue it. As I sat down and inspected her, unnoticed, I thought, except by Nelson, who curiously watched this little game, she kept her eyes downcast on her bowl of burgoo, which she was doggedly trying to finish.

"Good sleep, lass?" I asked, perkily.

"Spiffing, dahling. Slept like a jolly old top! And you?"

"Like a bottom," said I. "Like an elephant's bottom."

"Good." Laconic this morning, our Sissie.

"Bloody weather last night," I said, stupidly.

"*Ghastly.*"

"We took quite a hammering."

"Mmmm."

"I was worried in case that storm-line parted."

"Yes, lucky, weren't we?" Sissie looked at me, the corners of her eyes smiling—but only the corners.

"Nice bit o' burgoo, that was."

"Ai'm so glad you liked it." Head down again.

"Just right, that was." I peered over at Nelson. "Wasn't it, boy?" Nelson wagged his tail, but kept his eye on Sissie. "Really went down well, that did," I said, trailing off.

"I thought you'd like it, dahling." She looked up. There was a big dollopy tear in each eye. She stood up, picked up the lunch bowls, dumped them in the washing bucket, and headed up the ladder. I heard her feet clumping forward, the forward hatch open, and Sissie climbing down into her little caboose in the forepeak. Then there came the sound of subdued sobbing.

Nelson and I looked at each other for a long minute. "Wonder what's up with the second mate today," I murmured to him. He wagged his tail. His tongue drooped a little further.

Oh hell, I said to myself. Then, aloud, so she could hear me through the bulkhead, "What's the matter, Sissie? Did I do something?"

There was silence.

"You might as well tell me, for Chrissake. If you don't, how the heck do you expect it to be put right?"

The sounds of sniffing came from forward.

"Come on, girl, cut out the crap. No good having wrongs hidden in a sailing boat. Hang out your washing, as they say!"

More sniffing.

"All right, then, if you won't tell me, I'll take Nelson ashore for a walk!"

"(Sniffle) . . . Oh, *dahling* . . . (sob) . . . You did so disappoint me, but I know I'm . . . just silly old me . . . (sob) . . . but I did think you would sort of spring up and go with me to see if *deah* Miss Pomeroy is *quaite* all right . . . (sob) . . . Ai'm so terrific'ly worried about her . . . (sob) . . . Ai couldn't sleep one teeny *wink* . . . Ai've been in an ebsolute *fret* all morning . . . (sob) . . ."

For Chrissake, I said to myself. "But I *am* going with you, as soon as my burgoo's settled down. For God's sake, she's managed without you for a pair of weeks—surely a couple of hours won't make any difference?"

"Oh, *dahling*, I simply knew you would! I knew you were only teasing silly old me . . . " Her voice brightened up like a light switched on.

"Of course. I'll be ready for the off as soon as I've closed the skylights."

There was the sound of sudden movement from forward, then the tinkle of London Dry Gin for a second or two, then a scuffle as Sissie shot up through the forward hatch.

"I simply knew you wouldn't let poor *dahling* Miss Pomeroy down," she said as she waited on deck.

I had to look twice when I turned to her. In one hand she held her umbrella, furled, and in the other her hockey stick. Britannia was armed for the fray.

Under the warm Mediterranean winter-blue sky all was still around us, but as Sissie, her blue jeans making her look even more broad in the beam around her stern, jumped for the jetty and *Cresswell*'s own stern shook, it was as if the *Monarch of the Seas* had just set forth to put the world to rights, and the Lesser Breeds without the Law were trembling the world around.

With trepidation I took up Britannia's rear-guard. Nelson, now on sentry duty, watched us as we fell into line-ahead and steamed off to do battle for our country-woman, Miss Pomeroy.

Chorus: *Way, hey, and up she rises! Patent blocks of different sizes!*
Way, hey, and up she rises, earlye in the morning!
What shall we do with a drunken sailor?
What shall we do with a drunken sailor?
What shall we do with a drunken sailor earlye in the morning?

Verses:
Put him in the long boat 'til he's sober (Repeat three times)
Keep him there and make him bail her!
Trice him up with a running bowline!
Lash him to the taffrail as she's yard-arm under!
Put him in the scuppers with a hose-pipe on him!
Give him a dose of the salt and water!
Take him and shake him, and try and wake him!
Give him a taste of the bosun's rope-end!
Shove him off to sea with Reuben Ranzo!
Stick on his bollocks a mustard plaster!
Shove him in a barrel with a press-gang bastard!
Soak him in oil 'til he sprouts a flipper!
Keep him in the galley 'til his bollocks are toasted!
Scrape the hair off his tits with a hoop iron razor!

—"Drunken Sailor"

This was a "runaway" chantey. It was chanted in very quick time when lines had to be hauled fast. It was the only type of worksong allowed in the Royal Navy. It dates from the early nineteenth century. Sailors always pronounced any 'y' at the end of a word as 'eye'. "*Way, hey*" is about as close that this savage-sounding yell can be described. Other questions posed by the chanteyman included the following: What shall we do with a thieving bastard? What shall we do with a Yankee skipper? And, appropriately for the following story, what shall we do with a drunken painter?

13

What Shall We Do?

I DIDN'T TRY to catch up with Sissie until we had passed through the port-hamlet, because I didn't want the fishermen grinning at me too much. I let *Cresswell's* second mate forge ahead, with her umbrella and hockey stick, frilly blouse, and brogue boots. It wasn't until we were around the bend in the road, and over the hill, that I hollered to her. By now she was steaming along ahead of me at about eight knots.

"Sissie!" No answer was the loud reply. Bloody hell, she deaf or something? Another bellow. *"SISSIE!"*

This time she turned her head and decelerated to a slow walk. Even so, it was a good few minutes before I caught up with her.

Sailors, in general, are not eager walkers. I'm not talking about the yogurt-and-nuts-for-breakfast brigade (there are exceptions in any group of people), but I mean the average deckie. Sure, he can manage to plod around to a local bar near the waterfront, and sometimes even to roll back again, but when it comes to cross-country marathons, and especially when he is trying to keep up with an English games-mistress on her way to tackle a seven-and-a-half-foot giant, he is not exactly an odds-on favorite for the four-minute mile.

"Oh, *deah* Tristan!" she yelled when at last I was fifteen yards astern of her, "I feel so jolly *enthused!* Bally silly, ectually . . . of course a few minutes won't make much

219

difference . . . But Ai'm so awf'ly *eagah* to know that dear,
dahling Miss Pomeroy is awl right . . . Oh my goodness,
she's so dreadfully sweet and innocent, and thet . . . thet
cad! Thet simply *obnoxious* boundah!''

As she exploded the last word a black cloud over on
the far eastern horizon suddenly flickered lightning down
to the black sea below. It seemed to me as if a few tortured
souls in the Inferno had all moved up one space to make
way for big Sven from Copenhagen.

At last I was breathlessly alongside the Dragon of
Devon, limping a little from the unaccustomed marching.
Sissie's face, which a moment before had been glowering as
she had consigned the drunken painter to the nethermost
pit of an English hell, suddenly melted into pity. ''Oh, you
poor *dahling!* Ai'm trotting off *much* too fawst, aren't Ai?
Silly old me . . .''

''It's all right. You go on ahead, if you like. I'll catch up
with you. You can wait for me in the little shop at San
Francisco. Don't go into Fonda Alonzo without me.''

''Whyevah *not*, dahling?''

We were passing goats and kids in a field now, and
although Sissie cooed and glanced at them now and again
(''Oh, my deah—look at thet sweet, gorgeous, cozy, *cuddly*
little *angel*. Oh, I could just simply *hug* it!'') there was no
climbing and slithering over the stone walls as there had
been on our previous pilgrimage to the Fonda Alonzo.

''Because if the dangerous Dane is pissed out of his
skull and you start anything with dear little Miss Pomeroy,
he's going to grab you by the ears, swing you 'round, and
fling you five miles back to *Cresswell* all the way from San
Francisco. That's why.''

Sissie shook her hockey stick. She harrumped. ''Ai
should just bally-well like to see him try!''

There was silence between us for another half-mile, as
Sissie forged ahead and I trotted along just astern of her.
Then I said, ''What are you going to do, then, Sissie?''

''Ai'm going to dashed-well make sure that deah Miss
Pomeroy is awl right.''

"And if she's not? What then?"

"Ai shell give her my address!"

My heart almost stopped. "What, on the boat?"

"No, of course not, dahling! In England, through *deah* Willie!"

"Then what?"

"Well, if thet *dreadful* foreign *beast* bullies her, Ai mean simply herds her to bally *distraction*, she must write. Ai shell tell her to pack her jolly old *kitbag* and simply march out and *fly* to Willie!"

"Mmm . . . that'll be nice." In my mind's eye I could see the bishop and the lady children's author having tea in some leafy bower, a phantasmic black-dressed Miss Benedict hovering in the background with a croquet mallet:

"OhI'msorelievedtobebackinEngland (giggle)."

"England is the only country, my dear Miss Pomeroy, where we understand liberty? And where, consequently, no one cares about justice?"

"OhBishopSaintJohn,soclever (giggle)!"

As I imagined this meeting of minds in some faraway English cathedral town, Sissie went on. "It's the only thing Ai . . . *we* can do, my deah skippah. Thet poor little sweet soul is out heah in this dreadful, *peasanty* place, living in awf'ly *abject* misery in thet *scungy* hovel with thet . . . thet . . ." Sissie's expression was intense as she sought some way to describe what she thought of Sven. Suddenly she turned to me. ". . . thet *white-slavah!*"

As she yelled this, small birds started from their nests in stone walls half a mile away; billy-goats meh-heh-heh'd; and an ancient windmill's sails shook as if they had been awakened. I had a vision of sixty-year-old Miss Pomeroy as the star of the Checkalov whorehouse in Buenos Aires, smothered in paste jewels, black fishnet stockings and all.

"*Nawsty* feller," Sissie said later, a little quieter now. Billy-goats and donkeys panicked and raced away from the sides of the road. "*Awful* chep!"

"I don't think you like him, Sissie," I observed.

"Ai wish we had *deah* Toby with us. He'd know what to jolly-well do! Chased those *awful* Germans all ovah the bally desert. Oh, *deah* Toby. I do hope thet *dreadful* chorus gal hasn't . . . " As the tiny hamlet of San Francisco Javier hove into sight, she left the rest unsaid.

"I wish we had the whole bloody parachute regiment with us," I commented as we traipsed along the deserted street towards the Fonda Alonzo, which awaited us like a whitewashed nemesis. "And the Royal Marines, fully booted and spurred."

Alonzo was sitting behind his otherwise empty bar when Sissie and I walked in. His jowls were still in his hands. He was yet staring into space. He started as I greeted him. He dashed around the corner and hoisted Sissie's hand, hockey stick and all, to his lips. By now Sissie was getting used to this, or perhaps it was because the hand-kisser wasn't Lieutenant Francisco; anyway, she accepted the greeting regally and smiled down at the top of Alonzo's bent head, not batting an eyelid.

"*Señora!*" Alonzo gazed up at her Saxon-blue eyes in adoration as he slobbered. "*Encantado! Mi casa es su casa . . .* " Enchanted! My house is yours.

I ordered wine. "Make it a good one, Alonzo—not that stuff we had last time. I was shitting blue lights for three days after that last little lot," I said in Castilian. A colorful language, Spanish.

Alonzo dashed around the bar again. Hurriedly he gazed over the bottles. "*Lo siento . . .* I'm sorry, *Señor Capitán*, nothing here is good enough for your mercy and the *señora*, but down in the cellar . . . Please take a table." He rushed out from the bar and disappeared through the back door.

Sissie and I sat down at a corner table in the dark bar and gazed at a greasy calendar for 1957. It showed two seamen in French navy uniforms, with red pompoms on their caps, both looking like they came off a 1920 toothpaste advertisement. They were grinning at a bonny lass with her hair in a bun and a red rose in her teeth, all frills and flounces.

Sissie saw me inspecting the calendar. "She's a hostess at a Sailor's Home," she said.

"She's off to dance a bloomin' fandango, only her shoes are too tight, and anyway, she knows them froggies are skint . . . "

Even as I spoke, the sunlight streaming through the front door of the Fonda Alonzo suddenly dimmed, as if God had pulled a switch. Our immense Danish white-slaver had arrived.

The whole floor shook as Sven rolled his shoulders over toward us. Even while he was yards away from us his haunch-like hand was held out in front of him, and his great face—what I could see of it behind his mop of blond hair—was beaming. His little blue piggy eyes shone.

"Hey, what you know! The English seamens!" The giant grabbed Sissie's hand as she went rigid, and smacked it a kiss. With his other hand he reached over and ruffled my head. It was as if I was being buffeted by a swinging main-boom. For a moment my ears rang.

Sven was still dressed exactly the same as he had been the last time we had seen him. He still had five huge toes on each foot and yet another layer of dirt on them. "You come back to Formentera, hey?" he boomed. He looked wildly around him. "Where's that bloody Alonzo? *ALONZO!*" he yelled at the top of his voice. The old calendar on the wall shook with the vibrations.

"He's in the cellar," I started to say.

"Cellar? Fuckin' cellar? I put him in his grave!"

No sooner had the huge painter said this than Alonzo came scooting in, followed by his diminutive wife, who bore a bottle. Breathlessly humble, Alonzo grabbed the bottle from his wife and pulled the cork. "Very good, this one, *señores*. From Zaragossa." He sprang behind the bar, panting, and grabbed three glasses.

As he reached the table again, Sven seized the bottle and, just like the last time, slopped the wine—a fine, golden vintage—over the table and into the glasses. He mauled his glass and turned to Sissie. "To your health and beauty, my dear English lady!" he toasted.

Sissie's voice was small, piercing, and very steady. "I have *not* come here to be *toasted*, Mister Knutsen," said she with a sniff.

Sven jerked his huge head and shoulders back and stared at her. He tossed the glass to his lips and swallowed the lot. He slammed the glass down on the table and hunched toward her. "What do you mean?" he growled. "What do you mean, you don't come here to be toasted? I'll toast you, all right!"

Sissie was sitting at attention now, her hockey stick on the seat beside her. "I have come here," she said, "to jolly-well see *Miss Pomeroy*."

Slowly the giant turned his eyes toward me. They were crafty now. "And you? What you here for, Engelsman-who-don't-go-fuckin'-nowhere?"

"I'm with her," I replied, nodding at Sissie, who now stared directly at the Dane. She looked like Queen Victoria holding an audience with Jack the Ripper.

"You with her, eh?" the monster bawled at me. "You can't go nowhere on your own?"

"I like her company," I replied quietly, as he slopped another glassful of wine straight down his throat.

"I toast you!" Sven shouted at me. "I fuckin' toast you. You toast me, right?"

"Why don't you toast me in Danish," I said, "and I'll toast you in my language. OK?"

"Ja! OK!" He lifted his half-filled glass. *"SKOAL!"* he roared.

I lifted my glass. Out of the corner of my eye I saw Sissie glaring at me as though I had betrayed England. I looked the blond monster straight in his piggy eyes. I smiled at him and spoke very slowly. *"Budreddi drwg ar chwi!"* I toasted him in Welsh. I slugged off my whole glassful of the best Zaragossa wine.

There was a silence for a while as Sven sloshed off two more glasses and emptied the bottle. Then he turned to Sissie. "What for you wanna see Miss bloody Pomeroy?" he slurred.

"Because she's my friend," said Sissie.

"Your friend? *YOUR FRIEND!*" The giant slammed a fist down in front of him. "That little bitch, she nobody's friend!"

I chimed in. "She's not my friend, Sven. What do you say if Sissie goes up and sees Miss Pomeroy, and you and me have a few snorters?"

"Snorters?"

"Glasses of wine. Bloody women can't drink. You know that."

"Ja!" The giant reached over and hit me on the shoulder, almost displacing my collarbone. I still had a deep-blue bruise there a week later. "Only good in bed, hey?"

"Right . . . Alonzo!"

Alonzo stopped studying Sissie's only curve—the one on her nose—and sprang to attention.

"Four bottles of house wine—and make it snappy!"

"*Si, Señor Capitán. Inmediatamente!*"

Sissie started to rise from her seat. I turned right around and winked at her. "Now, Sissie, you go up and see Miss Pomeroy, right? And of course you *simply, awf'ly* realize that I don't want to see you bringing that *dreadful, peasanty, pimply person* down into Alonzo's bar. This is men's business!"

Sissie looked at me, perplexed. I went on. "Now off you trot upstairs and see that *dreadful harridan.* Of course you know we *don't* want to see that *shocking* wretch down *here.*"

As I went on parodying Sissie's speech I could see that she was guessing at my irony, although it was obvious that she was not quite sure.

Still in a small voice she muttered, "Of course, Skippah. Ai shell only be a few teeny minutes." She picked up her hockey stick and umbrella just as Alonzo set the four wine bottles on the table and Sven, completely ignoring Sissie, grabbed a bottle. He slurped the blackish-red, bitter vinegar into his and my glasses, spilling a pint on the table in the process.

"Bloody women . . . " I said to the giant.

He leered a smile at me. "Hey, Engelsman—you good guy, you know that?"

"Oh, we do our best," I said, sipping my wine.

"But you drink like a fuckin' fairy. Like a bloody woman." He slopped more wine into our glasses. "Look, we know how to drink in Copenhagen, I tell you. Watch me."

He raised his glass. "*SKOAL!*" Down it went. It just disappeared. His adam's apple seemed not to move at all. "Now, you do that!" He rested both his elbows on the table in front of him and glared at me.

I lifted my glass. "*Budreddi drwg ar chwi!*" shouted I, and somehow knocked the bitter liquid down past the back of my throat. My stomach shuddered.

Even as the painter raised his glass again, in marched Sissie, dragging behind her, like a wretched wraith, the sniveling Miss Pomeroy. For a moment, as the acidic wine attacked my stomach and my eyes, and against the sunlight shining through the door, I could not see either of them very well—but I had already sensed Sissie's indignation as she had steamed in.

Sven gurgled down his glass and again reached for a bottle.

"Tristan!" Sissie's voice was distrait.

"Wazzup, love?"

"Ai . . . Ai'm . . . Look!"

"Wazzup?" I peered at Sissie. I could hear Miss Pomeroy sniffling.

"Well, don't just sit theah—look at poor Miss *Pomeroy!*"

Sven took no notice as he poured out another wine for himself. I managed to drag myself to my feet. Miss Pomeroy was hiding her face. Her blue-rinsed hair was all astraggle. Sissie gently put a red, blistered finger under the little elderly woman's chin and lifted her face. La Pomeroy looked as if she had been half-butchered. Both her eyes were closed blue bruises, streaked with runny mascara. On her forehead was another bruise, big and round like a purple goose egg. A great plaster was stuck over one side of her chin. Her lips were split and swollen.

I sucked in my breath. Still Sven sat with his back to us. Sissie started to say "Thet great . . . " I laid a hand hard on her arm.

"Walked into a door and fell down the steps, eh love?" I said to La Pomeroy.

Her head fell onto my tee-shirt. She sobbed. I patted her shoulder. "That's all right, Miss P. Accidents happen in the best-regulated families," I said stupidly, trying to keep bloody screaming murder out of my voice. "I'll tell you what—why don't you go with Sissie down to the port. They've got some steaks in the fridge in the hotel down there . . ." I nudged Sissie's arm with my elbow, hard.

"She not go nowhere. She my woman!" came a growl from Sven, who still didn't look around.

"They can be back in a hour. I'll ask Alonzo to run them down in his donkey-trap," I told the Dane.

"She not go nowhere. She stay here!"

I sat down. "Oh, all right," I said, "but let Sissie go upstairs with her for a while at least."

"OK, but if I don't hear them up there . . ." He pointed to the bar ceiling with a massive finger, "then I fuckin' kill her!"

I looked at Sissie. She was trembling with rage and fear at the same time.

"Me and Sven's going to have a drink or two together. You take Miss P. upstairs again, eh? Try and make her comfortable or something, lass."

Sven had his head tossed back, eyes closed. I nodded my head violently in the direction of the port as Sissie stared at me. She turned away from us, leading the half-blinded Miss Pomeroy. As she reached the door I shouted, "Sissie!"

She turned abruptly. "What?"

"I won't be more than an hour . . . It'll take that long."

With thin little Miss P. sobbing desperately against her shoulder, Sissie passed out under the stares of a hundred locals, gathered, sadly curious, at the door of the Fonda Alonzo. I somehow knew that Sissie was heading straight for *Cresswell*. I also knew that if footsteps were not heard overhead very shortly, the great bully across the table would be after them. I hoped against hope that the Dane had not learned any Spanish. I kept my voice as steady as I could.

"Alonzo!"

"*Si, señor?*"

"Four more bottles and send your wife upstairs to walk around."

"*Si, señor, inmediatamente—a sus ordenes!*"

Soon four more bottles were on the table. Then, for the next hour, the giant lady-killer and I matched each other at swigging the foul, tart vintage, glass after bloody glass, measure for flaming measure, and toast for bleeding toast.

"*SKOAL!*"

"*Budreddi drwg ar chi!*"

Again and again and again.

Every few minutes Sven stopped yelling and howling, craftily gazed up at the ceiling, and listened to the footsteps above. Then off again we went, hell-bent to get plastered.

It took a total of six bottles before the giant finally slumped over. How I managed to keep up with him I'll never know. It must have been the thought of Sissie's disgusted tone with me after I had first toasted the Dane; or my imagining him catching up with them on the road; or the anger that was in me at the insults hurled my way by this bullying idiot; or the recollection of the terrible damage done to the tiny lady's face.

Somehow, with the aid of all the sea gods that ever helped a mariner ashore, I did it. I even managed to pay

Alonzo, and then to stagger into the back of his little donkey-trap, and there collapse.

"I sent the *señoras* on ahead," said Alonzo. "We can pick them up on the road, and all get back to the boat together, *Señor Capitán*."

I remember nothing else until I woke up in *Cresswell*, on my berth. My head felt as if it had been stamped on by an enraged ox. Groaning, I lifted myself up and stared around. Through the companionway I could see that both Nelson and Sissie were standing guard on the stern. She was still wielding her hockey stick. The thought struck me, even as I stared at the prone body of La Pomeroy on the spare berth opposite, that I had never seen Sissie and Nelson ever do *anything* together before. I groaned again.

"Just a teeny tick, dahling, Ai'll make you some coffee," Sissie sang out.

That half-sobered me right away. "What?" I moaned.

"Coffee! Your head must be bally-well bursting!"

"Coffee? Don't give me any of that crap—what do you think I am, a bloody Frenchman? For Chrissake, make some tea, and none o' that damned Burma blend, either! I've got to sober up before that bloody great Skywegian oaf does, and get the boat the hell out of here. What's the time?"

"Nine o'clock, dahling. Listen, the lawst ferry's just leaving!"

I nodded toward the slumbering Pomeroy. "Pity she's not on it."

Sissie rattled a teaspoon in protest. She looked at me. "Oh, but where would poor, *dear* Miss Pomeroy *go*? Thet *dreadful* foreign brute has jolly well spent all her allowance!"

"Great." I reached for the tea mug. "Just what I need— a non-paying passenger."

Miss Pomeroy groaned and rolled over a little. Her face was a mess, like a slab of raw beef, only the colors of a dead octopus.

I relented a little. I stretched myself up, trying to raise my raging head and my aching stomach at the same time. It was dark outside. "Oh, well, we can at least get her over to

Ibiza. Maybe something'll turn up. One thing's for sure . . ." I paused for a moment as fifty rusty iron rasps scraped across my brain.

"What's thet, dahling? Oh, poor *deah*—shell Ai put a poultice on your forehead?"

"No, make another cuppa tea, and for Chrissake make it strong."

"What were you going to say, deah?"

"Wha . . . "

"Before you asked for the tea? You said one thing was for sure."

I groaned as I sat down again. "Oh, yeah. One thing's for sure—if she stays here she'll be dead inside a month, with that crazy bastard back there." Another thought occurred to me. "What time did you leave the Fonda, Sissie?"

"About four."

"I must have left around five, then. And it's nine o'clock now. Four hours since that sod keeled over . . . Christ!" I jerked myself onto my feet. "Come on, he'll be charging down here any minute! Let's get the boat out . . . We've no fuel . . . We'll have to work her out under sail . . . And if there's a northerly . . ."

Sissie chimed in. "The wind's in the east, deah, and rawthah *boisterous*." With Sissie that meant anything from a fresh breeze to a hurricane.

"Well, at least we can get out of port, then, before that bloomin' human tractor comes roaring down here."

Even as I said this there was a loud moan from Miss Pomeroy. Sissie laid a hand on her forehead—the bit that wasn't bruised. "Oh, *deah* Miss Pomeroy, nevah you fret— you're safe now. We're bally-well taking you to Ibiza!"

La Pomeroy gurgled through her split lips. But Sissie merely patted the blanket she had thrown over the wounded lady. "Now, now, don't you try to say one *teeny* word. You're in safe, *British* hands now."

"I wish they were safer," I commented, thinking of the Great Dane. "I wish they were in bloody China!"

In aches and pains and agony I made my way topsides to untie the mainsail and the jib. I'd just got the working jib hanked onto the forestay when there was an huge commotion under the electric lamp at the end of the jetty. I stared over. "God Almighty, he's here already! Quick Sissie!"

No reply.

"*SISSIE!*"

Sissie stuck her head up over the top of the companionway ladder. "Yoo hoo?"

"Get your ass up here as fast as Christ will let you, girl—that bloody Skywegian is heading straight down the jetty, and . . . Wait a minute, that's funny—he's got the local coppers with him."

There were three Guardia Civil on the island. Two of them, both big men, were right now trying to hold onto the giant Dane. Sven was shrugging them off as he stumbled along, like a bear tossing terriers.

"Slip the mooring lines, fast!" I shouted, but Sissie was already at them. She threw the untied lines onboard and heaved *Cresswell* away from the jetty before she leaped onboard. I started to haul up the main halyard, but was stopped by a high, piping voice: "*Señor! Señor! Espera!* Wait!"

It was a big police sergeant waving at me. His mate was still arguing with Sven at the root of the mole, clutching now and again at the Dane's poncho, trying to hold him back.

I let go of the halyard. The boat was now about eight feet from the jetty. Too far for anyone to jump onboard, I reckoned quickly. "What's the matter, *señor?*" I hollered against the wind, as innocently as I could.

"This gentleman says you have his wife onboard, but we know him. Alonzo has told us how he treats her. We know, too, that it's not his wife. He has been . . . living in sin!" He removed his black leather hat and wiped his brow.

"She's very badly beaten-up," I shouted, my hands cupped around my lips. "I'm going to get her to a doctor in Ibiza! Anyway, it's true that she wasn't his wife. She was his . . . paramour!"

"That's all very well for a woman, living in sin," shouted the sergeant. "I mean they're easily led, aren't they? But for a man—an artist!"

While the sergeant was giving me his lecture on comparative morality, Sven was howling in the night gale at the top of his voice, waving his arms around violently, and steadily approaching the boat as the sergeant's colleague tried to hold onto his giant frame.

First he was shouting and bawling in Danish, then he broke into English as he neared the spot under the lamp on the jetty opposite to where the boat was floating free. "That's my woman you got there, you English bastard! You stop or I fuckin' *kill* you! I sink your boat! I murder that whore of an English lady!"

"Miss Pomeroy is going to see a doctor!" I hollered back, both at Sven and the policemen.

"I give her a doctor! She need a fuckin' doctor when I finish, OK!"

The huge painter ranted and raved. He tried to jump into the harbor to reach us. Both policemen were upon him. The sergeant stepped back and drew his pistol from its holster. He pointed it at Sven. Sissie and I, horrified, gazed at the scene. We saw Sven stop. We watched as he glared at the sergeant. He started to stagger toward the policeman. The sergeant shouted something. Sven stopped again. The sergeant shouted again.

A group of fishermen who had been crowded on the jetty, watching, all suddenly rushed up behind Sven and jumped on him. With the police private and the fishermen all hanging onto him, Sven went under, but it took another five or six minutes before, still struggling, they had him down on the jetty with handcuffs on his wrists and the police private's Sam Browne belt strapped tight around his ankles. All the while Sven hollered and screamed, until, when he was securely lashed up, a fisherman dumped a fishing net over him. Still he bellowed, moaned, groaned, and tried to lash out with his hands and feet.

The sergeant somehow recovered his leather hat, which had fallen into the harbor water, and laid it down on the stone jetty to drain. As he wiped his brow again in the moonlight he breathed so hard that I could hear it twelve or so yards away. "Despicable! Living in sin!" he shouted again to me. "But this isn't the problem, *señor*!"

"*Que hay, entonces?* What is it, then?"

"*Señora* Puig is . . . in a certain condition! There are complications! Her child is not due for another month! The island doctor is away at a conference in Palma! The ferry is gone! The telephone lines came down in the storm yesterday! We cannot raise anyone on the radio transmitter! We can't hear them, in Ibiza, and we don't know if they can hear us!"

"So, what do you want? Shall I tell them when I get to Ibiza?"

"No, *señor*, we have *Señora* Puig down here now! She's in the hotel! She has . . . much pain! Her husband, Antonio Puig, is here with her now! For the love of God and the blessed Virgin, *señor*, can you take her with you to Ibiza?"

This was a turn for the books. I stared at the sergeant as he stood hatless in the moonlight. I looked at all the other pleading faces in the pale light around him. The fishermen's boats were far too small to risk a passage on a night like this, through the strait with an easterly gale.

"It'll be a rough passage," I sang out. The wind was steadily blowing the boat farther away from the group on the jetty. I think the sergeant's face brightened. "But I'll tell you what, sergeant!"

"*Que?*"

"If you keep that animal locked up for ten days, and make sure he doesn't get on the Ibiza ferry, or find any other way to Ibiza, then I'll do it!"

"*Seguro! No hay problema!* Right, you're on!" he yelled back.

I heaved a line over. The sergeant caught it.

I turned to Sissie, who was staring at me in the dim light. "Any problems?" I asked her.

"No. But I'm still a little bit cross with you, dahling."

"For what? What the *hell* have I done *now*, lass?" I started hauling the boat back to the jetty.

"Exchanging toasts with that *beastly* chep!"

I laughed quietly. "D'ye know what I told him, in Welsh?"

She shook her head. "No, of course not."

"*Bad cess to you!* And I told him at least a dozen times, and the bugger's built like the Tower Bridge!"

Then began a nightmare night passage that I shall never forget as long as my blood can turn cold, nor yet as long as my heart can warm itself on memories.

Sleep, sleep, beauty bright,
Dreaming o'er joys of night;
Sleep, sleep; in thy sleep
Little sorrows sit and weep.

Sweet babe, in thy face
Soft desires I can trace,
Secret joys and secret smiles,
Little pretty infant wiles.

As thy softest limbs I feel,
Smiles as of the morning steal
O'er thy cheek and o'er thy breast
Where thy little heart doth rest.

O the cunning wiles that creep
In thy little heart asleep!
When thy little heart doth wake,
Then the dreadful night shall break.

"Cradle Song"
—William Blake

14

Cradle Song

By THE TIME Sissie and I had hauled *Cresswell* back alongside the jetty, six fishermen, one of whom was the sick woman's husband, Antonio Puig, had arrived with the *señora* lying on a makeshift stretcher made from an old door. The woman appeared to be in a very bad way. With her eyes closed and an expression of intense agony on her face, she thrashed her head around and moaned grievously. At times her moans rose to a loud screech of pain. The rain had begun to hiss down again, and the wind had risen to a howl.

The fishermen were accompanied by a local priest, a young man about thirty, who wore a long black cloak over his cassock. "God will bless you," were his first words to me.

"Let's hope not too soon," said I. "Anyway, can you find out if there's any diesel oil around?" I knew that the small, open fishing boats used kerosene, but I wasn't sure if there might not be diesel fuel stored for the use of a truck or the electrical generating plant. Hurriedly, the priest asked the oilskin-clad fishermen in the local version of Catalan. There were downcast faces and vigorous waggings of regret.

By now we were all wet through. Señora Puig, with Sissie effusing sympathy all over her, was being helped down the companionway ladder. The priest turned to me. "Unfortunately, Spain is not rich in petroleum, you see,

237

Señor Capitán—but we make kerosene from the coal of the Asturias." He started to go onboard.

"*Donde vas?* Where are you going?" I asked him, squinting against the rain.

"Onboard, to have a word with Señora Puig."

"If you set one foot onboard my boat, I don't sail. We've already had one of your gang onboard a few days ago."

"Superstitions. Pagan super . . . "

I didn't let him finish. "Look," I told him, "there's two very sick women onboard *Cresswell*. It's going to be very difficult getting east through the strait between here and Ibiza, with this wind howling dead against us. So far as I know the boat's in good order. I'm not particularly super-stitious—but I'm taking no chances. So kindly stay ashore and do us all a favor, *señor* priest?"

I felt a little sorry for the young man. He seemed a decent type—trying to be helpful in this situation, but not what I needed now. Sadly he made a gesture of resignation and acceptance, and turned away toward the dry hotel at the end of the jetty. As he went he called back to me through the rain, "*Vaya con Dios, y que Dios te bendiga!* Go with God, and may He bless you!"

I watched him disappear into the rain, then turned to Antonio, the father-to-be, and patted his shoulder. "He meant you," I told him. "Of course you're coming with us. How's your sailing? Haven't forgotten it, have you, with those engines you use nowadays?"

Antonio grinned at me. We'd had quite a few jars together in the hotel bar. Of all the Formentera fishermen I had met, I liked Antonio the best. He was about twenty-eight, bigger than the average local man, clean-shaven, but with the very same black hair and eyes. He was clearly worried, naturally. It was to be his wife's second delivery. The first had been a little girl who had miscarried, he told me. "My sailing's good—but God grant a boy this time. It's not much fun . . . The other fishermen have been . . . "

He left the rest unsaid, but I guessed that it would have been " . . . making jokes about me. You're not a man until you have a son." It was a tenet of their lives.

I nodded at the bow. Antonio knew what to do. As the rain slashed down in the black night, he hopped to the jetty, cast off the stern-line, untied the bow-line, and started hauling the boat to the seaward end of the little mole. His black oilskin overcoat gleamed in the pale light of the harbor beacon as it flashed every five seconds. What with the rain pelting down, the wind howling in the shrouds, the squealing of the mainsail parrel rings as I strained at the main halyard, and the agonized screams from *Señora* Puig below, it was like a scene from Purgatory.

At the last second, Antonio handed the bow line to one of his fisher-friends and leaped onboard, even as *Cresswell*, with the jib up and drawing, pregnant with the gale, shot out of the harbor mouth. He grabbed the main halyard from me and I sprang down and took the wheel. As I flashed by the companionway I glanced into the cabin. The scene was chaotic. In the dim, reddish-yellow glow of the oil lamp Sissie was bending over, holding tightly the hand of the flailing, screaming *señora*. On the other berth the prone Miss Pomeroy, her face now cleaned of blood but still bruised and bashed, was on her side, trying to open her cruelly swollen eyes; trying, it seemed to me as I took all this in through a second or two, to speak to Sissie.

I grabbed the wheel and heaved the boat around the leeward mole-end. We were lucky. The priest might have been right. We missed the wall by no more than an inch or two. By now Antonio was back hauling in the mainsheet as we both stared through the lashing rain, stupefied, and prayed our way past the great stones under the harbor beacon. As *Cresswell* shot clear of our first hazard, Antonio visibly heaved with relief. He secured the mainsheet and headed for the cabin. I stopped him. I didn't say anything for a moment; there were far too many things running through my head. On top of all the calculations of wind and currents, hazards and dangers, I was almost frantic with worry that Señora Puig might die. The noise from below did nothing to allay my fears for her. I grabbed Antonio's shoulder as my other hand strained at the wheel. Now we were getting the full blasts of the wind, although the sea, in the shelter of the northern point of Formentera, was still fairly flat. *Cresswell* laid over in the sudden, mighty blasts and put her bow-cheek to the sea.

The Mediterranean wind frequently doesn't blow with a regular force, as it mostly does in other climes. It pulses. It's bitchy. One minute it's down to fifteen knots, the next minute comes a bluster, anything up to thirty or forty knots or more. It needs a lot of attention. You have to have eyes and ears in your elbows. You have to concentrate all the time. It's not easy sailing in the Mediterranean at night with a full gale blowing all the way from Vesuvius. With a badly beaten-up woman below, and another screaming her head off, my own head was too full of concerns for me to say anything much to Antonio for a minute or two. He started to pull away, but I kept a hold on him. "Nice weather for ducks, eh?" I said.

Antonio looked at me, perplexed. I pulled myself together, remembering that his English was nil. I hoped he could understand my Castilian. "There's a bottle of gin up in the forepeak. I don't have any drugs onboard . . . no anesthetic . . . Go up there, get that bottle to your wife, and let her . . . "

Antonio nodded violently as I shouted. Already he was off to the forepeak. Soon he was back, bearing Sissie's precious sanity-saver. He grinned and offered me the bottle.

"No—only fools and passengers drink at sea!" I bawled. "Give it to your *wife!*"

All the while the sea's violence was increasing. *Cresswell* zoomed ahead in the gale. By now she was well heeled over, at hull speed, doing around six and a half knots. Steadily her movement increased. She was rearing and descending, bucking and bashing, as she reached the open water west of the strait.

As Antonio held onto me, his face close to mine, trying to make out what I was howling at him, Sissie appeared on deck. She was still in her blue jeans and frilly shirt, soaked through, with her ginger hair now dark and hanging like rats' tails over her eyes, which frowned with worry, as well they might have. She shouted at me from the companionway. In the roar of the wind I couldn't hear a word she said. I handed over the helm to Antonio, half-conscious at the time that this would tend to steady him up a bit. I grabbed the gin bottle from his hand and scrambled up onto the weatherdeck to shove my ear in front of Sissie's face.

"Oh, *deah*—Ai'm terribly afraid for her, Skippah!"

I rammed the gin bottle into her damp, cold hand. Señora Puig's howls had reached a crescendo, defeating even the blasts of the wind and the crashes of the seas as *Cresswell* smashed into them. "Here," I shouted, "shove this into her! It's all we've got, lass!"

Sissie started to move down the ladder. I reached down and grabbed her shoulder. I was not surprised to see that she was crying. "Listen, girl, I've got to start pumping. We're taking water in badly! Get the *Reed's Nautical Almanac* off the navigation-book shelf. It's an old one, but there's instructions for emergency childbirth in it. Look it up in the index. Have you ever midwifed before?"

Sissie blinked through her tears and half-smiled. She looked like a half-drowned spaniel, but a brave one. "Oh, *deah*, thet's what worries me so, dahling!" she hollered. Then her face brightened a touch. "But I *did* set Toby's ankle thet time he broke it on the slopes of the Matterhorn!" As she said this her lips pressed firmly together. Britannia, I knew, would *cope*. The awful spell of ignorance, fear, and panic was broken.

"Don't you fret, skippah, we shell jolly-well manage somehow!" She started to head for Señora Puig, who had just let rip an excruciating bellow. "Oh, deah, poor *dahling* Señora Puig!" Sissie wagged her dank head. She stared at the other berth for a second. "And poor *deah* Miss Pomeroy!"

I stared at the incredible scene in *Cresswell*'s cabin for a moment. It was truly horrifying. Over *Cresswell*'s smashing, jerking, crashing deck I headed back for the bilge pump and desperately heaved away at the great brass handle until the pump got a suction. From then on it was "Armstrong's Patent"—pump, pump, and more pump. Half the night Antonio and I spelled each other at the heavy pump and the heaving wheel, as the wind rose to full storm force and piled up frenetic seas in their millions over the mile-wide, shallow bank under the strait.

We'd left the harbor at about ten o'clock at night. By eleven we were to the west of the strait. By twelve we were about a mile farther east. By one o'clock *Cresswell*, after zigzagging furiously against the blind eye of the wind, had moved a mere hundred yards or so against the raging blasts. Still we persisted. If we could drag ourselves only one more mile east, to clear the southernmost cape of Ibiza, then we could lay *Cresswell* off the wind and shoot up to Ibiza harbor on a broad reach. That was my intention—to get to Ibiza town direct, and get Señora Puig to a hospital as fast as we could.

After I'd pumped out about a ton of seawater which had sluiced onboard, I checked out the cabin again. The scene topsides was bad enough, but below, in the ghostly light of the oil lamp, purposely kept dim so as to preserve our night vision, it was a view of horror. By now Sissie had managed to get about a quarter of the gin down the heaving, lashing *señora*, so at least her screams were a little less terrifying. It looked as if Sissie had had a slug, too—there was a gleam of determination in her eyes now that brought to mind Karsh's portrait of Churchill glowering.

"Deah Skippah!" she crowed, "what a topping ideah of yours! Ai've managed to give *dahling* Miss Pomeroy a teeny drop, too! The poor deah is in a *frightful fret*. I think Señora Puig is feeling a weeny bit better, now!"

"Good," I shouted back at her, as Nelson gazed damply up from under the table in abject misery. "I'm not letting her husband down here. I don't want any panic. It's obvious he loves her far too much to help her a great deal. You stay with her. Try to get a little bit more gin into her—not too much. And for God's sake, make some cocoa or something! We need cheering up, lass—death's abroad! There's only us and the gin to stove its bloody face in!"

Then I recovered myself and subdued my Welshness. It's not much help when the English are determined. "Did you read that thing about a-borning in *Reed's*?" I asked her.

"Ai'm trying to. It's jolly difficult in this light. Can we turn the lamp up a little?"

"No, take the book over to the stove when you boil the water—and for Chrissake, be careful!" Then I staggered back on deck to relieve Antonio after another fifteen minutes of wild pumping. All heavy work.

By two o'clock we had smashed our way another fifty yards or so to the east against the bitter wind. At two-fifteen Sissie appeared on deck and leaped down into the cockpit beside me. "Oh, *deah*, she's in heavy labor!" The water streamed off Sissie's thin, frilly blouse, and the tears streamed from her eyes.

I was too astounded to say anything for a moment. I stared at Sissie, squinting against the flailing rain and lashing spray, and gritted my teeth. Then I made up my mind. I would have to stop this almost hopeless fray with the storm and head *with* the wind. Our argument with the Fates was far too futile. They would never accede to our powerful demands and our puny strength. We were being too big for our boots.

"I'm wearing her around, Sissie. It'll take all night and tomorrow forenoon to buck this bloody strait!"

I started to move the wheel around to pass *Cresswell's* bow away from the raging wind. Slowly the boat obeyed me. Antonio nodded his head as he eased the mainsheet. He had already figured out my intentions. Sissie stood by the jib sheet, ready to pay it out a touch. Then, as the noise of the wind and sea lessened while *Cresswell* disdainfully turned her back on them, there was a particularly dreadful howl from down below. I half-pushed Sissie toward the cabin, and concentrated on the helm. It's not an easy maneuver, wearing off in a full storm.

"I'm making for the west coast of Ibiza, Antonio. I'm going to seek shelter in the lee, or get her around to San Antonio!" This was a small port and holiday resort on the northwest side of Ibiza island. "We can get her to a doctor there!"

The weather, now that we were running away from it, was far less violent. *Cresswell* retreated to the west into the black nothingness of the night. Antonio leaned his streaming wet head close to me. "Yes, she will be safe if we do that. Saint Anthony is my patron saint!"

I grinned at him, despite the hell we were undergoing. "Mine's Charlie Chaplin," I shouted.

He actually laughed as I handed him the wheel and relieved him at the pump.

From the strait to Es Vedra, on the southwest tip of Ibiza, was about fourteen miles. Off the wind, on a dead run, still with all sail up, *Cresswell* flew, her stern yawing this way and that, more or less on an even keel now, but rearing and pitching like a maddened steer. Antonio and I still fought the stiff pump and struggling helm.

By five o'clock, in the murky light of a rain-ripped gray sky, weary by now, only kept ataut by Sissie's cocoa and the screams of Señora Puig, we sighted, about a quarter of a mile away, the great conical rock of Es Vedra, almost a thousand feet high, huge and ghostly as it reared up to the low black clouds, straight from the seabed. Then we knew there might be hope for us in this insane night.

I managed to get a peep down below again. Sissie and now Miss Pomeroy were both bending over the squirming shape of *Señora* Puig. I called down, "OK, Sissie?"

She turned to me sternly. "Go away!" she shouted abruptly. Then she seemed to gather herself together. She braced herself against the midship sponson in the wildly pitching cabin. "Oh, *deah* Skippah!" she howled, back to normal now, "it reahlly, honestly is not the place for a *chep* down heah! Ai'm sure that Señora Puig will be *dreadfully* embarrassed . . . and with you being British and every-thing!" As she hollered she moved toward the steaming kettle on the stove. Behind her, hanging onto the berth-side for dear life, La Pomeroy, her battered face the color of some ghastly painter's palette, tried to see me through her almost-closed eyes. A glimmer of a smile flitted across the slab of beaten beef.

"Cocoa?" I said hopefully to Sissie. "We'll soon be in the lee of Es Vedra." Another almighty scream of pain broke loose from Señora Puig.

"No more cocoa, dahling Skippah!" shouted Sissie. "This is for us . . . Ai'll make you some as soon as the boat steadies up. Oh, you poor souls—you and Antonio must be simply . . ."

I didn't hear the rest of Sissie's comment. Antonio was now steering directly for a point about ten yards off Es Vedra rock.

"Plenty of depth?" I asked him.

"Sure, the rock drops down, almost vertical, to the . . ."

Even as he said it, *Cresswell*, with an almighty crash, yammered and stammered over *something*. Aghast, I glanced over the side. She was sliding over a rock only two or three feet below the surface!

All hell let itself loose. As we held on, Antonio and I, stupefied, the seas lifted *Cresswell*'s hull and crashed it down on the flat-topped rock. With a roar terrible to a sailor's ear—horrible to *anyone's* ear—*Cresswell* scraped over the rock for twenty yards or so, lift and scrape, lift and scrape, with a noise like a steam train flying in and out of a short, dark tunnel. But the boat took it—right to the very last moment.

Then it happened.

I somehow knew it was going to happen. It wasn't a case of calculating the likelihood. It was more an instant prescience. The stern smashed down on the far edge of the rock just as we were about to clear the danger, miraculously, so we had thought, scot-free. The rudder hit the rock, the shock broke the rudder cable bottle-screws, and the rudder, being removable, jumped off its pintles.

The rudder was secured to the hull by a rope lanyard about six feet long, so we didn't lose it; but we were, in effect, rudderless. It would be extremely hazardous, even foolish, with the boat bouncing around as she was, to try to lean over the whaleback stern and recover the rudder. There were more pressing demands, to say the least.

It isn't often, thank all the gods, that a sailor finds himself out in a raging gale, with a possibly damaged keel, and rudderless, with an agonized, hysterical pregnant woman below, screaming blue murder, another one so badly beaten up that she can hardly see, and another who has never had any midwifery training.

I didn't need to tell Antonio. He pulled me to the wheel, cast off all the sheets, levitated himself somehow to the foot of the wildly swinging mainmast, and let go the jib, the gaff, and the main halyard. The mainsail came down with a clatter as Antonio scrabbled at the terylene and dragged the flailing sail down onto the coachroof. It was a performance which would have made a Chinese acrobat look like an undertaker.

With the boat now almost stopped in the crazily heaving seas, I could now leave the wheel and rescue the rudder. Soon, after panting and moaning for ten minutes, stretched right over the bouncing, narrow whaleback stern, I somehow managed to wangle the gudgeons of the eighty-pound rudder over the pintles on the pounding and lunging sternpost, re-screw the steering cables, and regain command of the boat.

Within minutes of getting underway again, *Cresswell* had zoomed beyond Es Vedra rock. Quite suddenly, as the rock loomed over us, very close, there was no more wind, no more panicky seas. It was as though the storm had never been. *Cresswell* was one minute yawing, pounding, rising, and falling like a started stag; the next minute upright, sedate, and slowing. Now almost the only noises were the loud groans and sobs of Señora Puig below.

I turned to Antonio. He looked exhausted and very glum indeed. "We'll stay in the lee here until we get things straightened up a bit below. It's like a pig-sty down there. You get the bilges pumped out and I'll check the keel. Then we'll high-tail it for San Antonio. We can be there in two hours or so."

We lowered the main and jib again, and left the mizzen up to cock her bow against any stray gust of wind which might find *Cresswell*'s hiding place. Then, both exhausted, Antonio and I collapsed to smoke a dry cigarette for once. A mite of comfort.

The groans now coming from down below were heart-rending, nerve-shattering—almost soul-destroying. It was horrible. I could not think of anything that sounded more terrifying since the 'berg had almost capsized onto *Cresswell* in the Arctic five years before. The screams were truly dreadful to hear. Now Antonio broke down. He bent his head forward and burst out sobbing.

I leaned over and clutched his shoulder. "Come on, Antonio, we'll leave the mess below. Let's get underway again. We can be in San Antonio by eight." It was now dawn. Idleness is no cure for grief.

No sooner had Antonio dragged himself to his feet again, still sobbing, when another sound came from down below. It was not a high-pitched scream now; not a low, agonized moan; not a bellow of pain. It was thin but quite loud—loud enough to echo back from the almost vertical sides of the great rock only a few yards away from the bedraggled *Cresswell*. This voice yelled and gurgled. It screamed protest, it demanded justice, it hollered violent indignation. For a moment Antonio and I stood, quite close to one another, staring in disbelief into each other's eyes.

"*No lo creo!* I don't believe it . . . " murmured Antonio. Then he grabbed the mainsheet horse-rail and swung him-self over it. "*Un chiquito?* A boy?" he shouted.

Sissie's voice sounded as if she were in a transport of delight. Of course she didn't understand Antonio's bellowed question. I translated for him as I came out of my shock. "Is it a lad or a lass, Sissie?"

"Oh, *deah* Skippah! Antonio, dahling," she wheezed, "it's a lovely little *cheppie*—oh, so tiny and cuddly and *eb*solutely *cozy* and warm and *charming* . . . Oh, I could simply ooze oodles and oodles . . . "

By this time Antonio and I were crowding the companionway hatch, both excited. All our bone-weariness was now completely forgotten. I peered down at the mess below. Sissie was standing, still wet through, her breasts heaving under the now dirty and bedraggled frilly blouse. In her arms she held a bundle wrapped in one of my shirts. Her faced beamed.

La Pomeroy somehow squeezed past us, a bucket in hand. Antonio rushed down the ladder and tried to grab the bundle from Sissie, but she wouldn't let go. "Skippah, tell him to be careful!"

I didn't need to. Antonio sensed that he was not in order, and poked one of his calloused fingers into the bundle. Now he was cooing, too. Behind him again now, Miss Pomeroy, all bashed and battered, took the hands of a weakly smiling, silent Señora Puig. Then Antonio looked down at his wife, reached for her, and broke into great, deep sobs.

By this time I had managed to drag myself down the ladder and take a peek at the tiny face. It wasn't very handsome. It looked a bit like a walnut, all creases and little wrinkles—rather like a miniature version of Miss Pomeroy's. The tiny lad's eyes were open. Sissie told me later that he couldn't see yet, but he looked at me and I could swear he winked. Then he stared at me for a few seconds longer, wondering just what kind of a world he had entered. He gazed into my salt-begrimed, sleep-begging, filthy, bearded face, curled his little mouth up, frowned, and let out a bellow which I told Sissie would be heard in Gibraltar.

"He's going to be a big, strong fisherman," cooed Sissie. "Aren't you, oh you *adorable* little cheppie."

"More like a bloody cattle-boat skipper, with a voice like that," said I.

Now Antonio was on his knees, praying. In his hands he held his wife's rosary. As I turned and started up the ladder to get the sails up and head for San Antonio with our new passenger, I noticed Sissie's hands. Both were scalded and blistered by hot water from the fallen kettle.

That's how Antonio Cecilio Tristan Vedra Pomeroy Cresswell Puig of Formentera received his name.

We got into San Antonio at about nine a.m. Señora Puig was collected by a hastily called doctor, who also examined Sissie and Miss Pomeroy before Antonio and I carried the baby's mother ashore. Sissie, despite her bandaged hands, insisted on carrying the baby to the car, clucking and cooing at it all the way down the jetty, with La Pomeroy at her side, holding blindly to Sissie's hem. It was like a refugee arrival.

Sissie paid for Miss Pomeroy's treatment, of course, and in another few days they were both their old selves again, La Pomeroy even down to moaning about the turn her late love affair had taken. "OhpoorpoorSven! Idon'tknowwhathe'lldonowwithnoonetolookafterhim!"

"Serve the bugger right," I told her. "I can't understand you, Miss P. There he's been knocking seven bells out of you, and now you're worrying about him . . . "

Sissie, still bandaged but healing fast, sat at Miss Pomeroy's side. She said nothing, but from her look I knew she thought me hard.

Miss Pomeroy burst into silent tears and bent her gray-rooted, blue-rinsed hair over her twelve strings of pearls and her now-washed blue silk dress. The silver shoes looked very much out of place in *Cresswell*'s cabin.

It had been decided that Miss Pomeroy would stay with Sissie and me until her "guardian" in Leeds (whoever *he* was) sent her the fare home to England in reply to a hastily written letter from Sissie. It is not often that a sailor finds himself trapped with a bishop's sister and a star of the 1919 Follies. I realized that I had been singled out by the Fates for a singular honor. I resigned myself to acceptance. The fare wouldn't be too long arriving; then Miss P. would disappear over the horizon in the general direction of some obscure Yorkshire suburb, and I would again be able to look the small, dark fishermen of Ibiza straight in the eye.

"OhI'msomuchlookingforwardtobeingindearoldEn- glandagainbutIshallsomisspoorSven . . . "

I waited for no more. I asked Sissie for the loan of two dollars and headed with Nelson to a nearby fisherman's bar in the now almost deserted resort of San Antonio. Nelson wagged his tail as he looked up at me striding along, as if he were trying to cheer me up. I looked down at him. "Bloody women! Don't know if they're on their ass or their elbows!" Nelson wheezed.

A week later, with Sissie's hands and Miss Pomeroy's face almost healed, Sissie and I sailed back around to Ibiza town. We sent Miss P. back overland by bus. There would have been no escaping that squealing voice at sea.

Sissie bought some diesel fuel before we sailed, and we had a good, steady passage back.

Going into Ibiza harbor was as near as I'll ever feel to going home. The little general's converted fishing boat wasn't at the outer mole, but there was a brand-new- looking twenty-four-foot converted ship's lifeboat, all gleaming white and sparkling in the sun. I stared at it as we dropped our anchor, then realized, astonished, that it was in fact none other than *Dreadnaught*. The elderly, bronzed, mustachioed Romeo in the new gray suit, standing on deck, was none other than Amyas Cupling, the engineer- poet.

"Amyas! What ho!" I called out to him.

He leaned forward on a brand-new steel guard-rail and hollered back at me. "*Cresswell*, ahoy! Tristan, old man! Miss Saint John! Had a good cruise, as it were?"

"Pretty fair! *Dreadnaught* looks . . . splendid!" I replied. *Cresswell* was almost alongside *Dreadnaught* by now.

"Thanks. Of course the engine is still down, as it were. I'm going to refit it in Venice for the winter!"

We were quite close now, after I'd tied up the stern-line. "Venice? That's a longish run, Amyas—about a thousand miles."

"Oh, that's all right. No hurry. Just sort of bimble from port to port, as it were."

"You've sure been busy," I said.

Amyas watched Sissie, shyly, as she leaped onto the jetty and marched off to the post office. When she was out of hearing he said, in a low voice, "Well, Tristan, did you pop her the question, as it were?"

"Yes. Nothing doing, Amyas. She's too fond of Nelson, and the dog seems to have taken a shine to her now. It would be a pity for Sissie, and of course Nelson would be heartbroken."

Amyas bent his head, downcast. Even his mustache drooped. "Of course . . . wouldn't dream of . . . never do to break up a friendship, would it?"

We were silent for a few moments; then I had a brilliant flash of inspiration. "That dinner you invited us to—is it still on, Amyas?"

"Of course. Tonight, if you like," he replied.

"Good, we'll be there, and I think we can make it very worth your while, my friend."

"Oh? How's that?"

"I've an extra passenger for a few days. She's not onboard yet—she's coming by bus from San Antonio. You know that takes forever while they drop the chickens off at every bloomin' farm en route . . . But she'll be here in a while. She's a real corker, Amyas."

Amyas' eyebrows shot up. His mustache cocked its ends.

"Yes. Friend of Sissie's, actually. Fell out with some bloke in Formentera, so she's a bit cut up right now, but she's not too bad, normally, if you don't look too carefully. Steady, like—a children's writer."

Amyas listened and thought intently for a moment. Then he said, "Sounds ideal, as it were."

"Yes, suit old *Dreadnaught* down to the ground, she will."

"Do you think she likes steel boats, Tristan?"

"Loves 'em," I lied. "At least that's what she told me."

"Looks nice now, eh, the old *Dreadnaught*?"

"Smashing, Amyas. You painted her inside, too?"

"Oh, no, not yet. I'm saving that for when the refit's finished, in Venice." His eyes took on a dreamy, poetical look.

"Doesn't matter too much anyway, Amyas. Miss P. isn't all that particular. All she needs really is a goodish bloke . . . "

"Miss P?"

"Oh, sorry. Actually her name's Pomeroy."

"Oh? What's her first name?"

"I'm not sure. I think it's Miss."

"Oh . . . " Amyas thought hard for another minute, then looked up at me again. "Yes, as you were saying the other day, funny people, women."

"Oh, this one's all right. You'll always know where you are with her."

Amyas smiled. "Good. Just the ticket, as it were, eh?" Then he followed my gaze along the jetty and stared as Miss Pomeroy made her grand entrance—blue-rinsed hair, mascara, rouge, face powder, strings of pearls, 1920s Alice-blue dress, beige silk stockings, silver slippers, three-inch heels—the works. She looked like Mistinguette heading for the Moulin Rouge.

Amyas' face at first squinted; then, slowly, as La Pomeroy swung and sashayed and jerked her way toward us, it softly subsided into an idiotic grin of desperate welcome.

Never seek to tell thy love,
Love that never told can be;
For the gentle wind doth move
Silently, invisibly.

I told my love, I told my love,
I told her all my heart;
Trembling, cold, in ghastly fears.
Ah! she did depart!

Soon as she was gone from me,
A traveller came by,
Silently, invisibly:
He took her with a sigh.

"Love's Secret"
—William Blake

15

Love's Secret

IT WAS quite a job, assisting La Pomeroy to navigate her way in her tight blue dress and three-inch heels over *Cresswell*'s stern and down into the cabin. Amyas Cupling had, of course, sprung to help, with his mustache bristling in the direction of Miss P's eyes. Her hair was even shorter and bluer now. I guessed that she had been to a hairdresser on the way back from San Antonio.

"Ohthankyousomuchsojollykindofyou," she gushed at Amyas, who blushed.

"Have to make sure the little ladies are all right, as it were," he said, after I had introduced them to each other.

I was curious about Miss P's new hair-do. "You're looking more chipper," I said, wondering where the money had come from.

"YesmyguardiansentthemoneyandIcanleavetomorrow . . . I'msogratefultoyoubutIstillthinkIoughttogobackandmakesurepoorSvenisallright," she screeched from over her drooping dozens of tiny pearls.

"Well, you can't go over to Formentera tonight. Amyas has invited us all to dinner. He'll be very cut up if you don't go. He's a great admirer of children's writers—Enid Blyton . . . Dorothy Parker . . . Agatha Christie . . . the lot. Amyas laps 'em up. Terribly literary, he is."

Even as I lied to Miss P., Sissie clattered back onboard. "Yoo-hoo! Dahling skippah! Deah Miss Pomeroy! And

Nelson, oh you perfectly *sweet* old things . . . I've brought us some *supah* fresh mullet for suppah!"

I started to make for the hatch. "You'd better go to that French gin palace moored along the jetty. Get a bit of ice. Stick the mullet in a bucket. We're off ashore to eat tonight. Amyas next door has invited us . . . "

Sissie's Saxon-blue eyes gleamed like a hearse's wheel-spokes. Her eyebrows shot up. Her frizzy ginger hair seemed to crackle. "Oh, jolly-dee! A dinnah-party! How *supah!* I do so simply *adore* a meal ashore!" She pecked my beard.

"Don't thank me—thank Amyas," I muttered as I climbed the ladder. Nelson hobbled up after me. He knew when it was time for the males to adjourn. It was bad enough when Sissie alone had been onboard and getting dolled up to go ashore in the tiny, poky forepeak—but with La Pomeroy already delving into her sequined purse for paper towels and face powder, it was time for us two to be conspicuous by our absences. We left the Dragon of Devon and the children's author to work their mysteries, and clambered over onto *Dreadnaught* after courteously calling out to Amyas, who was below.

I observed, as I passed over the brand-new yellow paint on her deck, that Amyas had completely transformed *Dreadnaught*, at least topsides. There were now at least three coats of white gloss paint all over her hull and superstructure, and the masts had been replaced by shiny, new oak spars. She had no filthy sail rigged. I called down the hatch into the gloom below. "Very nice job up here, Amyas!"

Amyas was shaving his chin. "Sort of have to spruce up a bit, if the little ladies are going to be interested, as it were, eh?" His mustache, half-surrounded by soap lather, bristled at me. "Think she'll like it? I mean Miss Pomeroy?"

"She's already told me how good *Dreadnaught* looks," I fibbed.

"Come on down. I'll soon be finished sprucing up."

I clambered down the still-rusty cabin ladder. The scene below was almost as rustily chaotic as it had been a week or more ago, before the boat had been sunk. The only difference that I could see was that now all the engine bits were sacked up in potato bags lying in the bilge, and that Amyas was now using a blow-torch for cooking.

As Amyas scraped away, staring into a tiny mirror hung over the blow-torch cooker, there was silence between us until he said, "Nice little thing. Sort of delicate, as it were?"

"Oh, Miss P's one of the best."

"From the North?"

"Yorkshire. Same as Emily Brontë."

"Fine country. Sturdy folk, as it were."

"Not too profligate."

"Good engineers, too."

"George Stevenson."

"Where it all started. Sheffield steel."

"Not bad looking, either."

Amyas grinned. "No spring chicken," said he, "but I've never been much of a one for flighty young things. The lads used to go ashore and get into all kinds of scrapes with them. You know how it is—boys will be boys, I suppose."

"Feel their oats."

"But I was never much of a one for that, as it were. Spent my time studying for my certificates. Only met one who was a bit interested in slide-valves and things like that. My missus. But she sort of turned off it after we were wed."

Amyas donned his new suit jacket and straightened out his tie. I studied him in the rusty gloom. Apart from his shirt collar, which was awry and a mite grubby, he looked quite presentable now.

"Look all right, old chap?" His mustache ends met his ears.

"Splendiferous." I turned and preceded the captain of the good ship *Dreadnaught* up the bent, rusty ladder.

We waited in the gloaming for an hour or so while our ladies made themselves shipshape and Bristol-fashion. Conscientiously, both Amyas and I kept our eyes and his mustache turned away from *Cresswell*'s companionway as we waited and waited, and Amyas discussed propeller pitches and compression ratios in a mute voice, so as not to disturb the ladies' toilette.

It was quite dark by the time Sissie and La Pomeroy emerged from the cabin. In the dim light of the jetty lamps, Sissie's ginger hair shone like a new pan-scourer. She had it lashed taut over her ears with a blue ribbon. She wore her white dress cluttered up with more roses than they ever saw at one time in the Scilly Isles. La Pomeroy was thinly resplendent in her newly cleaned, low-waisted blue dress, and had brightened it up even more with a great red silk sash, almost as big as she was, tied in a bow on her quarter. Her blue Eton crop shone wanly in the lamplight over the mascara and rouge. I watched Amyas' face as he helped La Pomeroy over *Cresswell*'s stern-rail. He was beaming. "My, we do look elegant this evening," he stammered, as he gently took Miss P's scrawny hand into his stubby engineer's mitts.

Miss Pomeroy's make-up cracked as she smiled at Amyas. Sissie screeched, "Oh, deah Mistah Cupling, it's so jolly *supah* of you . . . "

Then the four of us forged ahead along the jetty, toward the lower Ibiza town. Amyas still clutched Miss Pomeroy's elbow; Sissie marched along at Miss P's other side; and I hung back a bit to the rear until we had passed away from the waterfront and the grinning fishermen outside the bodega Antonio.

Amyas proudly led us into the little whitewashed restaurant, "Es Quinques," which means "The Lamps" in Catalan. It was owned and run by a fat, merry-looking man called Enrique, together with his family. All around the crowded restaurant, which was open to the street like a garage, great black wrought-iron lamps provided the only decoration, except for a picture of Jesus gazing upward and sideways and holding a heart, which glowed and dripped blood, in his hands.

Several of the waterfront habitués were in Es Quinques. The Dutch lady who said she had been Gurdjieff's lover (and looked it); the exiled American writer, Steel, not yet waving his arms but obviously, as he glared at his wine bottle, girding his muscles; the Finnish poet, half-slumped over toward Alf the London horse-punter; and, at the side of the Hope of Erin, Rory O'Boggarty, holding forth on love and death, a beautiful young woman who stared glazily at Sissie and La Pomeroy as they squeezed past her table. It was like some villainous Valhalla.

Obsequiously, Enrique fanned us to a corner table. There, after a flurry of finding places for purses and ribbons and other feminine whatnot, we all settled down to a romantic dinner by candlelight.

Sissie kicked off as we waited for the wine and food. "Oh, deah Mistah Cupling, Ai haven't really met any engineeahs before. Ai'm sure it must be jolly-well interesting?"

Amyas gazed into Miss Pomeroy's eyes. They were almost completely healed now, though some puffiness still lingered under the eighth-of-an-inch mascara. La Pomeroy sighed and smiled at Amyas.

"Have you been dreadfully far yet, Mistah Cupling?" Sissie beseeched.

Amyas tore his eyes away from the tiny children's author. "Oh, sort of bimbled a bit here and there, as it were. I'm not in any hurry, actually, Miss Saint John. Have you come very far with *Cresswell*?"

"Ectually from Frawnce. It was all jolly int'resting and supah . . . " Sissie paused for a moment as Amyas poured wine, first for Miss P., then for Sissie, then for me. Then she went on. "But I did so want to go to the south of Spain, and to Morocco—so dashed int'resting . . . " Sissie sighed as Enrique clattered plates onto the table. " . . . but poor deah Tristan has so many jolly awful difficulties, and does all sorts of exciting boat deliveries. It looks as if we're sort of stuck around the bally Balearic Islands for at least a few weeks, yet."

Miss Pomeroy piped up. "Ohthankgoodnessyou-wereheretorescuemefromthatawfulman!"

"Now, now, Miss P., " I said, "we really shouldn't discuss that here. Let bygones be bygones. Enjoy yourself, lass."

Miss P. slurped her wine. She smiled at Amyas. "OfcourseImustn'tspoilMisterCupling'seveningmustI?"

"No," I told her.

After soup Amyas beamed up at Sissie. "I've been down that way in *Dreadnaught*—I mean the south of Spain.

"How jolly exciting for you, Mistah Cupling!"

"Not really," said Amyas. "I did mean to refit my engine in Málaga, as it were, only I found a dead body in the sea off Torremolinos . . . "

We all looked at Amyas. Our steamed cod and chips had just been served. "A what?" I asked.

Amyas' mustache grinned from ear to ear. "Yes," he said, "it was a biggish chap. I was making my way up the coast and there he was, just sort of floating along, as it were. As I said, a biggish chap. Of course, by that time he must have been to the bottom and come up again. All gray and bloated, as it were. No hair left, of course. Fish had been at him. I say 'him', though I never knew if it was a man or a woman."

"So what did you do, Amyas?" I asked.

Sissie dropped her fork on her plate, half-horrified, half-fascinated. Miss P. gazed into the engineer-poet's eyes.

"Well, I tied a line around his ankle. I had to make it a longish line. He was a bit ripe by then, as it were, and I had to retie it after a few hours. The sea was a mite roughish, you see, and his foot came off. So I retied it around his chest, under his arms, as it were."

"What was your idea?" This was a new one on me. I was intrigued.

"Oh, I was going to tow him into port, get him a decent burial, as it were, but when I got to Málaga the next day the harbor police turned me away. Said that the sight of a dead body would make the tourists unhappy. Upset them, as it were."

By now Sissie seemed to have completely forgotten her steamed cod.

Miss P. gazed in adoration at Amyas as he went on. "So I towed him back down the coast to the beach at Torremolinos. There was hardly any wind at the time, and I was still refitting the engine, of course. Took a day and a half to sail *Dreadnaught* down there." Amyas swallowed a great forkful of steamed cod, sipped his wine, and continued. "But it was the same story in Torremolinos. In fact the harbormaster even threatened to arrest *Dreadnaught* if I didn't leave immediately. There was still no wind and I had to push her out with my sculling oar."

"How dreadfully ghastly, Mistah Cupling!" Sissie exclaimed. "But of course theah are so many sort of delaightful, *supah* places in the Mediterranean, aren't there?" she supplicated.

"Almeria's not bad. The old castle on the hill and everything, as it were," replied Amyas, smiling at Sissie. "But even there it was no good. By that time, of course, I'd had the body tied up astern for almost a week. It was practically bright green by the time I got to Aguilas. The police there were very polite, but they were having none of it. There was no identification on the body. There could hardly have been any way of telling how the poor chap had died."

A big tear sprang to Sissie's eye. She desperately tried not to look down at the now rapidly cooling steamed cod on her plate. Miss P., in between finicky nibbles at her fish, still gazed at Amyas and his mustache, as it increasingly bristled in her direction.

"I know, Miss Saint John," said Amyas, as a tear slid down her rose-bedecked chest, "I felt the same, as it were. Of course I couldn't let the poor chap just float around, as it were."

"So what did you do with him?" I asked *Dreadnaught's* skipper.

"Well, he was sinking again by now, of course. I'd been towing him around for over a week by the time we sailed into Cartagena. I had to lash a few of my plastic fenders around him to keep the poor devil afloat."

"Why didn't you just let him sink? You could have said a prayer," I said.

"Oh, I couldn't do that. I thought he ought to have a decent Christian burial. But they wouldn't accept the body anywhere, and I towed it around for three weeks. It wasn't easy . . . "

Amyas dug again into his cod and lifted a great mound of dead-white fish flesh into his mouth. I gazed at the bleeding-heart picture behind Miss P. Sissie softly pushed her plate away from her. "Dahling," she addressed me, "Ai simply cawn't imagine why, but I just don't have one teeny weeny bit of appetite tonight. Oh, deah Mistah Cupling, do, please, forgive me!" she begged.

"Of course, dear lady," said Amyas. "As I was saying, it wasn't easy, because he had been a heavy man. Bits and pieces started coming off when the weather got a bit uppity—his intestines and everything. Finally I lost him in a gale off Valencia. I'd been taking him there, you see? Thought there might be a chance they'd accept him, as it were, in Valencia—not as touristy as it is farther south, is it? *Dreadnaught* got quite a bit of buffeting that night, and of course I couldn't just sit there in the wind and rain watching a corpse floating around, could I? Anyway, by that time the line had been paid out almost three hundred feet. Almost impossible, as it were, to see the body in the high seas rising up and down, and in the rain and dark . . ."

Sissie stood up. She winced apologetically down at me as I finished my steamed cod. Miss Pomeroy forced her eyes away from Amyas and gazed, startled, up at Sissie, who held her breath and patted her tummy. "Ai cawn't imagine why. I've suddenly come over *dreadfully* dizzy! Oh,

Mistah Cupling, forgive me! Ai think Ai'm going to have one of my dreadful turns!" Sissie's voice was faint.

La Pomeroy jumped up and put her scrawny arm around Sissie's games-mistress shoulders. "OhyoupoordearIshalltakeyoubacktotheboatrightaway!"

"Oh, dahling skippah," Sissie sniffled, her head down, her face white, "do forgive silly old me. Ai shell go back onboard!"

I said nothing as I stared at Sissie, surprised.

"Dear Miss Saint John . . . " Amyas started to rise.

"Oh, no, Mistah Cupling; no, deah skippah, please don't bothah yourselves," moaned Sissie as La Pomeroy half-pulled, half-led her away from the table and out of the now half-empty restaurant.

"One of those female things, as it were, eh?" Amyas suggested, when the two Englishwomen had left us.

"Might be the wine," I said. "She usually drinks Booth's gin."

Amyas poured himself another measure of wine and bent to attack a rubbery yellow *flan* pudding. "Funny creatures, as you say."

"Delicate," said I, chewing away at my *flan*.

"Think Miss Pomeroy's taken a liking to me, old man?"

"Oh, absolutely, Amyas. She's completely forgotten that foreign bloke in Formentera."

"Always better to be among your own, as it were?"

"Of course. Can't mix oil and water."

Amyas' ears picked up at that. For another hour and a half, over one more bottle of wine, he treated me to the story of how *Dreadnaught*'s fuel tanks were rusted right through and how he was going to replace them with copper tanks. "Only thing you can't trust steel plate for, as it were . . . "

The next day when Sissie woke me, she was short with me. I stared, bleary-eyed, at her for a minute or two. As Nelson slapped my leg under the table with his tail I glanced over at La Pomeroy's berth. She was nowhere in

sight. No Alice-blue dress, no mascara, no silver slippers—
nothing. Only an abandoned blanket.

"Hello, where's Miss P?" I slurred.

Sissie slammed my steaming tea mug in front of me on
the tabletop and harrumphed. "Hmmm . . . you might
jolly-well awsk," she muttered.

"She's gone back home, then?"

"No."

"Formentera?"

"No."

"Where the heck is she, then, Sissie?"

She rammed a teaspoon into her cup and viciously
stirred away.

"Sissie?" I sat up now.

She glowered at me silently.

"No! She's not . . . "

Sissie almost screamed at me. "She most certainly is!"

"On *Dreadnaught*?" I took a sip of tea. "Already?
When?"

"Thet *dreadful* hussy! Surely . . . Oh, deah skippah,
didn't you notice lawst night, when you came onboard, thet
Miss Pomeroy wasn't heah? At her age, too . . . Why,
she's . . ."

"Of course, not. Amyas and I were ashore until about
two, knocked back a few in the George and Dragon. Didn't
notice a thing. Why, what did she do, for Chrissake?"

Sissie huffed. "Miss Pomeroy brought me back
onboard, saw me safely out of the way, in my cabin, and
then, as I was just . . . " Sissie almost said "taking my
nightcap," but she remembered I was not supposed to
know about it. " . . . as I was reading the twenty-first
psalm, I heard her simply scrabble her things into that
dreadful handbag of hers and climb ovah onto that bally old
Dreadnaught!"

"So? What's wrong with that? She brought you home
OK, didn't she? I think that was good of her, considering
that Amyas had invited her along specially so he could get
to know her."

"But throwing herself at him like that, deah skippah! Ai mean it's not as if she were a terribly *young* gal, is it?"

"All the more reason she should be eager," I observed.

"But what will all these . . . these foreigners in the othah boats think of us? Oh poor, *dahling* Tristan—of course you just don't jolly-well *see* things the way we women see them, do you, you poor deah? More tea? Oh, you poor, poor men, and deah Mistah Cupling in the hends of thet *dreadful* woman!" Sissie wagged her head from side to side and clucked her tongue.

"Amyas was *trying* to get her onboard," I said calmly.

"Well, of course . . . thet *Salome* had designs on him right from the very start. But to creep onboard his boat in the middle of the night, like a . . . " Sissie almost burst into tears, " . . . a *fallen woman!* Ai simply won't know where to bally-well look when Ai pass those *awful* foreigners . . . And thet dreadful *harridan* on thet Andorran motor yacht—what will she think of us in thet awful, *devious* head of hers?"

I looked at Sissie. She was violently stirring porridge in a pan on the galley stove. "But what about you?" I asked her. "I mean you've been living alone with me onboard *Cresswell*. Don't you think they imagine we're . . . having . . . " I searched for a phrase Sissie would understand, " . . . living in sin?"

Sissie stared at me imperiously. "Of course not! How would they bally-well dare? They know perfectly well . . . I always tell them. Ai have my own private cabin heah!" She spoke as if the poky den in *Cresswell*'s bows was the Queen of Spain's own stateroom.

"Well then, why should they imagine that Miss P. is having her end away with Mister Cupling?"

"Because they don't have separate bally *cabins*, thet's why!"

"Well, Amyas can soon fix that. Get a sheet of steel plate, weld it across *Dreadnaught*'s cabin, cut a bloody door in it, no problem. He's a handy enough bloke!"

"Thet's not the point!" Sissie slapped a plate of porridge in front of me. "The point is thet Miss Pomeroy slept onboard thet poor man's crawft lawst night!"

"But blimey, Sissie, she's been sleeping in my cabin for the past week. She snores, too!"

"Thet's different. Miss Pomeroy was a *guest* onboard *Cresswell*!"

"Well, now she's a guest onboard *Dreadnaught*."

"She didn't sneak onboard *Cresswell* in the middle of the night like . . . like a *woman of the streets*!"

"Keep your voice down, Sissie. She'll hear you."

"I just bally-well hope she *does!*"

I sent Sissie ashore to shop and simmer down for the rest of the morning, while I cleaned out *Cresswell*'s bilges. It was almost noon when I heard Amyas calling for me from *Dreadnaught*. I clambered up on deck. He was back in his oily coveralls. His feet were again bare. His mustache ends were cocked up at angles of forty-five degrees from the horizontal. His eyes glowed.

"Morning, Amyas!"

"Hullo, old chap. Lovely day, as it were?"

"Not bad," I replied, "but Sissie's still a bit upset."

"Still tummy trouble, as it were?"

"I reckon so."

"Well, you can expect that sort of thing in these foreign places, eh?"

"Of course, that's what I told her. Sent her shopping. Keep 'em busy . . . "

"That's the ticket!"

"Where's Miss P? She shopping, too?"

"Yes, just gone off to bring some flowers." Amyas gazed down at his feet for a few moments, then shyly looked up again. "They like that sort of thing, you know. Of course it's a bit awkward at sea, obviously—no flowers, I mean—but I told her I could get some eighth-inch plate and cut and weld some up. Slap a bit of paint on 'em. Never know the difference, as it were."

"When you leaving for Venice, Amyas?"

"Oh, we're heading for Palma first. We can get . . . I popped the question to Bernice last night."

I looked at Amyas, a puzzled expression on my face.

"Oh, that's her first name. Nice, eh? Of course she's accepted, so we're going to Palma first. It's not a bad place for doing a spot of refitting . . . and they've got an English church there."

I still stared at Amyas in silence.

"Of course you and Miss Saint John are invited to the wedding, old chap. Might be a British cruise ship in . . . I'll get the engineers along—hold up the swords, as it were, eh?"

I finally recovered my composure. "Well, delighted, Amyas. When did all this happen?"

"Last night. She came over and made me a cup of *Bovril* . . . " Amyas turned and stared along the jetty as he spoke. "Nice little party, she is. Just the ticket, as it were."

"If I were you," I said, "I'd take off for Palma right away. That painter bloke in Formentera is due out of jail tomorrow. He's built like the bloody *Q.E. 2*, and when he gets a few noggins inside him he makes a battlewagon look like a bloomin' ice-cream cart."

Amyas grinned. "Oh, yes, Bernice and I have discussed our fine-feathered friend in detail. We're sailing as soon as she gets back. I don't have my new mainsail yet. I've written home to have it sent on to Venice. We can manage with the old one, though, until the new one comes. Shouldn't take more than a few months . . . "

"How does Miss P . . . sorry, Bernice, like the boat, Amyas?"

"Oh, she thinks it's home away from home, as it were. Of course, as I told her, it needs a little woman's touch. She wanted to start painting this morning, but I told her no sense in it until we get the engine refit finished."

It was "we" now. I knew Miss Pomeroy had made a hit. Momentarily, a vision of her, still in her Alice-blue dress, her pearls dangling, wielding a huge spanner in the gloomy, dank confines of *Dreadnaught*'s bilges, passed through my mind. "She seems to be a handy soul," I said.

"Yes, she's sending for her sewing machine from Palma. Says if the new mainsail doesn't arrive in a few months she'll sort of make me a new one, as it were." As Amyas said this he fidgeted nervously. Then he said in a low voice, rapidly, "Ah, here she comes now."

I turned to peer down the length of the jetty. I stared. La Pomeroy's walk was unmistakable—a sort of jerky jiggle, but at first I wasn't sure that the approaching figure was, in fact, Miss P. The great bunch of flowers she carried were bursts of color held close against the front buttons of a brand-new pair of black-blue overalls, much too big for her tiny frame. On her head she wore Amyas' best white-covered yachting cap, and on her feet were a pair of new deck slippers.

"Looks good, eh?" Amyas murmured as La Pomeroy, now, for the first time since I had clapped eyes on her, smiled at me shyly from behind the flower—mascaraless, rougeless, and powderless.

"Can't really sail a boat in dresses and things, eh?" Amyas said quietly. "Bought 'em for her this morning. I've already showed her through the tool-kit, of course."

"Morning, Miss P. Congratulations!" I hollered, as Amyas helped his bride-to-be over the brand-new stern-rail of the sparkling *Dreadnaught*.

"OhdearTristanI'msoveryhappytodayandofcourseSis-sieandyouarecomingtoourwedding? (giggle)" The first giggle since Formentera.

"Of course. When's the big day?"

Amyas aimed his mustache at me, as his tiny fiancée almost lost her balance trying to reach his cheek and peck it. "Oh, not until after Christmas," he said. "I wanted it right away, but Bernice . . . " he hugged Miss P's arm so hard that she seemed to wince, " . . . insists on waiting a while longer. A bit more respectable, as it were."

"Yes. Wouldn't do to look as if you were rushing things, Amyas."

"No. Not among these foreigners, anyway. They're always jumping to conclusions, aren't they? Funny chaps, but then, what can you expect?"

"I know. It's all that spicy food."

"Well, of course Bernice and I are going in for good old plain English cooking."

"That's the ticket, Amyas—roast beef, Yorkshire pud and gravy, eh? None of that damned immoral Continental nonsense."

"DearAmyaslovesYorkshirepuddingdon'tyoudear?"

"Of course. Never know where all that other stuff might lead you."

Amyas then half-carried Miss Pomeroy to the rusty gloom of her new home. As they reached the hatchway, Miss P., nervously excited, dropped the flowers through the hatch. They scattered in the oily bilge below.

"Ohdearwhatapity! (giggle) Wellneverminddearyou-canmakesomeinPalmaasyousaid."

"Of course; gives me something to do in between refitting the engine," replied the engineer-poet to his bride-to-be. "Can't stay idle . . . " Amyas grinned hugely over at me as he gently lowered Miss P. with one arm into *Dread-naught*'s corroded insides. "The devil has work for idle hands, as it were."

Sissie was back onboard shortly after. It took another few minutes of argument and reasoning before she came to see that love in any form, anywhere, between any souls, is good. Eventually, after some shy resistance to my persuasion, she accompanied me on deck to call farewell to Amyas and Miss Pomeroy.

Captain Cupling, as I let go his mooring lines for him, shoved away at a great sweep oar. Silently, little *Dread-naught* slid away from the Ibiza mole. Miss P., her face wildly happy, her new overalls already streaked here and there with black oil, her black glistening footsteps trailing over the brand-new yellow paint on deck, was excitedly trying to fit the tattered, black, ancient mainsail to the shining new masts.

"Oh, *deah* Miss Pomeroy, oh my deah, I shell so much bally-well look *forward* to the ceremony! It will be *splendidly spiffing!*" yelled Sissie as *Dreadnaught* crept away.

Amyas, straining at the long oar, looked up at me suddenly, puffing. "Not a lot of wind, as it were, eh?"

"You'll get a bit outside, when you clear the point, Amyas!" I hollered.

"OhgoodbyecheerioawfflythanksforeverythingdearSissie-andTristan!"

"Bye bye, Miss P!"

Sissie and I went to the wedding at the Palma Evangelical Church, just after Christmas. In early 1966 *Dreadnaught* sailed for Venice. She called at Bonifacio in Corsica, Cagliari in Sardinia, Palermo and Siracusa in Sicily. She sailed from Siracusa in May of 'sixty-six.

Nothing was ever heard from *Dreadnaught* again. When I called at Venice in 'sixty-nine, no one had seen her. I know that Amyas Cupling and Miss Pomeroy are in a quiet haven onboard *Dreadnaught*, still oily and rusty, with Amyas' painted, eighth-inch welded-steel flowers down below, and the engine still being "refitted."

Let me not to the marriage of true minds
Admit impediments. Love is not love,
Which alters when it alteration finds,
Or bends with the remover to remove:
O, no! it is an ever-fixèd mark,
That looks on tempests and is never shaken;
It is a star to every wand'ring bark,
Whose worth's unknown, although his height be taken.
Love's not Time's fool, though rosy lips and cheeks
Within his bending sickle's compass come;
Love alters not with his brief hours and weeks,
But bears it out even to the edge of doom.
If this be error and upon me proved,
I never writ, nor no man ever loved.

Sonnet 116
—William Shakespeare

16

The Bending Sickle's Compass

A WHILE AFTER Amyas and Miss Pomeroy were married, I lost Nelson and sold *Cresswell*. Sissie left to meet Willie in Morocco and then go back to Southchester.

I returned to Ibiza in late 1967. Between then and late 1968 was a remarkable time for me, but these are not the pages in which to set down those tales.

In late 1968, after the sale of *Cresswell* and the loss of *Banjo*, my twenty-six-foot Folkboat sloop (the loss courtesy of an American film producer, as described in my book, *Saga of a Wayward Sailor*), I hung around with the father of my crew-man, Steve Llewellyn, for a few days while I searched the waterfronts of the Balearic Islands for a delivery job. Much water had passed under the hulls of a couple of dozen sailing craft I had skippered, including the unfortunate *Two Brothers*, which had foundered *en voyage* to South America.

In the two and three-quarter years since *Dreadnaught* had bid Sissie and me goodbye, there had been a hundred adventures and almost as many misadventures, but some-how I had managed to stay afloat with a boat under my feet and a rocking berth to lay my head on. Now, at long last, after sixteen years of impecunious, miraculous survival afloat, I found myself boatless. But I wasn't friendless, and that's what really matters.

The ways of destiny are sometimes very strange. Later, when I looked back on that time in my life, 1966 to 1969, I could only come to the conclusion that most of us really never know what is actually happening when it happens. If we did, we'd either be saints or insufferable prigs. Being neither (we hope) we can only be thankful that our destinies, the paths of our lives, are, in the making, obscure to us. Whether our future is to be tragic or comic, rich or poor, the obscurity of Fate's intentions is a kindness in any case. For that kindness we should be grateful.

No matter what we live through, or how many hazards and dangers we have somehow passed, or how rough and imperfect, how torn and bedraggled, how seemingly irreparably wounded our lives might appear, it is futile for us to try to imagine how it would have been otherwise. If we look back objectively at our lives, no matter how messy and jagged and illogical it all has been, and despite all the mistakes, the further we get in time from the events, the more they line up in an orderly array to join a pattern of eternal fitness, and even, perhaps, at times, of heroic grandeur and poetical beauty.

In nature nothing follows a straight line, and so it usually is with a person's life. If it isn't so, then God help him or her. Normally, it is only after a time, sometimes a very long time, that all the ragged threads of our lives appear to fall into place. But they never really have done. The course of a person's life, with all its myriad twists and turns, is a maze. Some events happen at one time which we would never, until much later, dream of relating to other events which occurred at another time. This view of life is one of the saving graces of late middle age; one of the consolations for not being young. The lack of this view of life is one of youth's tragedies. This lack of perspective is one of the root's of youth's arrogance. My advice to anyone under the age of forty is to try to understand an older person's view of destiny. The sooner you do, the kinder you'll be. It's got nothing to do with hassocks and cassocks and little green things that go bump in the night. It's got to do with learning to treat other people with the same understanding that you treat yourself when you look back and see what a fool, at times, you've been. It's got to do with being able to laugh at yourself. As Voltaire put it, "God is a

comedian playing to an audience who's afraid to laugh."
Well, we must laugh.

Now that I've got that little lot on the ship's manifest,
I'll tell you why.

Losing *Two Brothers* 600 miles west of the Azores led to
my seeing some of the strangest sights I ever saw. Now, if
anyone had been around that drifting rubber raft, with me
in it, foodless and dying of thirst, and had told me that I
should cheer up; that it was all a part of destiny, of course I
should have told him to take a running jump at himself.
But there was no one around, and so it was left for time to
work its wonders and put events into perspective.

I'd bought *Banjo* from Willie the German, and it was he
who took me in his fast motorboat to Ensenada Hondo, where
my boat had been lost while I was ashore. There we searched
for wreckage, and found the ensign staff and flag. That's all.

Willie landed me on the rocks of the high cliff. He had to
carry on around Ibiza island to the holiday camp where he
was manager. Alone now, I kept a straight face while he
roared off into the blue. Then I stared down into the water
below the rocks, at the iron keel of my boat lying on the sea-
bottom. I could plainly see it through the clear, calm water of
the deep bay. There wasn't one shred of timber left on the
keel. *Banjo* had been beaten to death on the jagged fangs of
one of the worst anchorages in the western Mediterranean.

I gazed on the watery grave for quite a while. All I now
had was what I stood in—my Breton sailing jerkin, a pair of
paint-spattered corduroy pants, and a beaten-up pair of
deck slippers. And about four dollars in Spanish pesetas.

I turned and clambered up the high cliff without once
looking back down at *Banjo*'s resting place. It wasn't difficult to do; the cliff was almost all overgrown with dense
brambles, high grass, and stubby little trees hanging on to
narrow ledges overlooking the abyss. The sun, even in late
September, beat down. I knew that even when I got to the
top of the cliff I would have a good five-mile walk along the
clifftops until I reached the road. Then I would have at least

an hour's wait for a bus to take me back to Ibiza town. What would happen then was up to the gods.

Cliff-climbing isn't the usual sailor's idea of exercise. Some of them do it for fun, of course, but for the majority of yachties it is usually an exercise reserved for howling nights with the boat pounding the rocks at the base of the cliff. Somehow I made the 600 feet or so to the top.

There was a little old man, in black peasant's garb, watching me as I pulled myself over the topmost clump of thick, high grass. Breathless now, I stood and panted, about twenty yards away from the peasant. Slowly, but at a steady pace, he approached me. I saw that he was very old. His nut-brown face was lined and creased with at least eighty years of laboring on thin soil under a relentless sun. He was no more than five feet, three inches or so, and bent. He wore the typical black felt hat, black jacket, black trousers, and woolen shirt, collarless, of the Ibizan countryman. I stared at him as he reached up and made to doff his hat. By this time I could reasonably understand the Ibizan version of Castilian.

"Good day, *señor*." He greeted me with as much courtesy as if I had been in an immaculate suit at a Sunday parade in Ibiza. There was no sign that I was damp with perspiration and breathing heavily; dirty and bedraggled after losing my footing half a dozen times on the way up the steep cliff. No sign that we were at least three miles from the nearest habitation.

"Good day, *señor*," I panted.

"Tourist?" said the little old man. His eyes were slits against the bright sun. He carried a hoe.

"Sailor. My boat's down there," I told him.

"That is not a good place to leave a boat, *señor*." His voice was high-pitched, but clear.

"I know. My boat's sunk."

"*Hundido?* Sunk?"

"Yes. It happened last night. I wasn't onboard her. I've just been down to see if I could salvage anything. There's nothing left."

"It is God's will, *señor*."

We were silent for a few moments while the old man tried to lean over and peer down the cliff. As I stood there the full import of my disastrous loss struck home. I felt utterly wretched.

"I've lost everything I have, *señor*! Everything!"

The little old man looked me straight in the eye. His eyes were like a hawk's, dark and piercing. "Any life lost?" he asked, quietly.

"No, no lives. But they were lucky."

"And you are still alive?" The little old man asked the obvious question in the penetrating Spanish way.

"Yes . . . But I've lost . . . "

"Then thank God, *señor*. You have lost little. With no lives lost . . . and even if there had been . . . it is God's will. He has other intentions for you, for the others. Now, take a cigarette. Here."

He handed me an ancient tin. Inside were tobacco and papers. As I rolled a cigarette he said again, "No lives lost . . . "

I thanked him, and wished him many more years.

"Go with God, *señor*." He lifted his hoe onto his shoulder.

I walked away from him strong and free and even a little happy.

Willie the German's friend, Christian, who was a Frenchman and kept a scuba-gear store outside Ibiza, arranged that I should sleep onboard the tiny sloop *Coquette*, which was moored for the winter in Ibiza harbor, until I could find a delivery job or in some other way earn my keep until I had my fare home.

Coquette was only eighteen feet long; more like a closed-deck dinghy than anything else. There were only two berths in her, and her galley was tiny and primitive, but it was better than nothing.

By the time I had been sleeping onboard *Coquette* for a couple of weeks, and helping Willie and Christian out a bit in return for their help, I had written letters to a dozen maritime contacts from Scotland to Malta, but no boats were moving. It was too late in the year for westward-bound trans-Atlantic deliveries, and only a madman or novice sails very far in the Mediterranean after the equinoctials—but bit by bit I was getting my fare home.

I built a bird-coop for a children's primary school. I helped some fishermen caulk their keels. I painted a couple of boats, and slowly the money came in. I never went short of a meal, of course—Antonio at the bodega and Josélito the fisherman saw to that.

It must have been mid-October when Jonnie the Swiss showed up. His boat was an old French sail-fishing smack. She was about thirty-five feet long and rigged as a ketch, the same as *Cresswell* had been. As soon as I saw her come sweeping around the harbor entrance, all weather-beaten and odd, with her rig somehow not seeming to belong to her hull, I reckoned it might be worthwhile to get to know her owner. I would have done it in any case, but I hopped from *Coquette* onto the outer mole to help him moor up.

As *Sans Culotte* dropped her anchor her owner shouted, "No motor!"

I sang out, "That's all right! Throw me a line!"

I climbed onboard a deserted motor yacht, ran to her bows, and waited for him to heave me a line. *Sans Culotte*'s deck was littered with fishing gear. There were lines and nets and lobster pots all scattered about. She had a Swiss ensign drooping from her stern.

As her owner got a line ready, I noticed that he handled it clumsily, slowly. "You Spanish?" I called out to him.

His English was guttural. "Swiss!"

"You won't be very welcome here, with all that fishing gear lying around!"

I caught his line and secured it. He looked at me quizzically as his boat's stern swung toward me.

"The local fishermen aren't doing too well here," I continued. "If they see that little lot . . . " I gestured at the dozen lobster pots lying on his deck, " . . . well, the least they'll do is report it to the harbormaster, and the most they'll do . . . You'll be lucky if they don't burn your boat!"

"What shall I do?" he shouted.

"Stow it all below! Hide it! Get rid of it as fast as you can!"

As soon as *Sans Culotte* was tied up, Jonnie (he had introduced himself by then) collected all the fishing tackle and somehow rammed it below into the cabin. He was no more than about twenty-three or -four, no taller than about five feet, six inches; mousy, straggly haired, lean, wiry— and he had a perfectly insane look in his dark blue eyes. When I looked at his face it was like looking at a benevolent fanatic. He was sunburned, of course, and looked strong and healthy. His hands were calloused and scarred. He was dressed in shorts and a light jersey.

"Nice boat," said I. By this time I was below in *Sans Culotte*.

"Ja. Found her on the beach at Fréjus."

"Never been there—somewhere near Nice, isn't it?" I asked.

"I never been to sea before. Never worked on a boat. I fix this one up in two months!" The boat was tidy and well-painted below.

"Where are you going?" I asked.

"I stay around here until spring, then Gibraltar and the West Indies. I do some fishing here, some fishing there, ja?"

"You'll have to be careful with the local fishermen, Jonnie."

"Oh, I make friends with them, quick. See, I know . . . how you say . . . magic. You know, all that kind of thing."

"Conjuring?"

"Ja. Go to parties, make the kids laugh."

Jonnie handed me a strong cup of coffee. I don't usually drink it, but I was too intrigued by the idea of a sailing conjuror to refuse it. As he handed the cup to me he stared from below his brows. It amazed me to see that devilish look in such a young face.

He turned to his galley and took a bottle from the shelf. Then he reached into a cupboard and brought out two deflated party balloons. As I watched in astonishment he blew up the balloons, his eyes still gleaming brightly. "Watch," he whispered. "Magic for der kids, ja?"

He tied the balloons, now inflated so much as to have almost lost their colors, to a hook overhead. Then he grabbed the small, dark bottle with one hand and delved into his pocket with the other. He brought out a box of matches, gasped in, took a swig from the bottle, turned loose those mad, staring eyes toward the balloons, struck a match, lifted it in front of his mouth, closed his lips, threw his arms in the air, and blew a six-foot flame at the balloons, which exploded.

"Yow!" he roared, as little traces of flame ran around the beams above.

I flinched, expecting the whole boat to burn down to the waterline around our scorched ears.

Jonnie turned to me, his eyes now wide open, shining like a child's, innocent and happy. "You like? Look, I do it again, ja?"

"No, that's all right. I'm convinced, Jonnie. But isn't it a bit dangerous, I mean in a wooden boat?"

"I practice every day. I even do it over the side. Attracts the fish at night! The kids in Fréjus, they love it so much!"

I supped onboard *Sans Culotte* with Jonnie that evening. He had some freshly caught mullet and a couple of small squid. As I ate I stared around the cabin. There was no sign of any navigation books or instruments. Casually I brought the matter up. "You use the British tables or the French, Jonnie?"

"The table—I make it good, ja?" He slapped the cabin table, a wooden job, rough but well-made and sturdy.

I grinned. "No, I mean navigation tables."

"Yow!" Again the Swiss flung his arms out. "I don't have the time to learn yet. I use . . . " He scrambled up and reached under the mattress of his berth. He slapped a large book in front of me. It was a French school atlas. Quickly he turned over the pages. On a map of the Atlantic ocean he had scrawled an unsteady line right across the pages from Gibraltar to Barbados . . .

Next day, when I returned from the post office, Jonnie and *Sans Culotte* were gone. He had confided in me the night before, over supper, that he knew a good fishing place off the southeast tip of Formentera. I guessed that was where he had headed, to catch his next few days' food. He had told me he was out of money.

The storm rose about nine o'clock that evening. The local fishing boats were already in harbor, in the safest place from the howling easterly, right in front of the bodega Antonio. I had made sure that tiny *Coquette* was secured up, but her movement in the sea which the wind was sending into the harbor was far too sickeningly violent for me to remain onboard in any kind of comfort. It was bad enough that she had a mere three feet of headroom, but added to that, a foot's continual bouncing up and down sent me ashore in the wind and rain. I stuck my head into the bodega as I passed by. It was crowded with about twenty fishermen.

"Anyone seen the Swiss ketch that left this morning?" I asked. There was a sudden quenching of talk. Most heads shook. Fishermen are not the best of company ashore when the catches are lean and the weather is unsettled. I headed out into the rain again.

I had walked for half a minute on the otherwise deserted waterfront when Josélito caught up with me. Ever since my Halloween visit to the graveyard with Rory O'Boggarty, Josélito had been more of a confidant of mine than any other Ibizan.

"I saw the Swiss this morning, *Señor Capitán.*"

I turned into the rain and wind to face Josélito. "Where?"

"He was fishing off Punta de Cala Calador." José's eyes looked hurt.

"Christ, he's got no engine and he's on a lee shore. With a rig like he's got he'll never beat his way offshore! The wind'll have his boat on the rocks! We've got to do something, José!"

"It's God's will. He was stealing our fish. He had some lobster pots down, too. We're not stupid. We watch every boat, *señor*. We have to—our families' lives depend on it!"

"Then you won't help me, José? I have no boat now . . ."

"No fisherman will help you to go out for the one who steals our living. Anything else, *señor*, you know we would help, but this . . . *nunca*! Never! Only God can help him now, if he's still out there. We can pray for him, of course, but no help for a poacher!"

"Then I shall have to give God a hand."

"Goodnight, *Señor Capitán*. Go with God!" The rain poured off his peaked cap.

"Good night, Josélito."

I headed for the hangouts of the foreign exiles wintering in Ibiza.

The Isleno was a tiny restaurant owned by young Americans who served excellent chili-con-carne. There was no one but the owner and a dumpy figure in a fur coat, hunched in one corner. As I stood at the open door, with the rain sluicing down outside, the figure turned to look at me. It was Elmyr the art-collector. He looked wretched. I nodded to him. He bowed, slightly, back at me. The young American owner grinned at me. No help there. "Nice weather for ducks," I muttered, and turned away again into the night.

On a night like this there was only one other chance. Only the steady boozers would be out in this weather. They would be in the George and Dragon. I ran around the corner into the Calle Mayor and flung myself down the steps of the English pub. All I could see in the lights behind the bar was the dark, curly-haired young bartender, grinning eagerly at me as he fished around for a glass. Otherwise it was too dark to see who was in front of the bar.

"Bass, Tristan?"

"Yeah, put it on the slate, Tim. Pay you tomorrow."

I slugged at the Bass ale and peered around me. The only other customer was Alf, the London horse-punter. It was the first time I'd ever seen him unaccompanied by a beautiful woman.

Alf nodded at me. He was obviously half-crocked but . . . any port in a storm, and beggars can't be choosers.

"How're you doin', Alf?" I didn't wait for a reply. "Here, you were in the navy, weren't you? I think you told me . . ."

Alf nodded, his eyes half-closed as he tried to see me.

"I need a hand, Alf. There's a bloke out in this little lot. He was fishing off Formentera."

"Like a bit o' fishin'," said Alf. "Me and my mates used to go out regular off Brighton pier . . . " Alf's gold tie-pin gleamed in the gloom.

"I want to go look for the bugger."

"Need a 'and, then, Tris?"

I calmed down a bit. "Well, you know how these bloomin' foreigners are . . . "

"Don't know a puddin' from a pisspot, most of 'em," slurred Alf.

"Right, well, this bloke's Swiss, and he's a decent sort, only he was at the back of the line when they dished out brains. He left the harbor this morning. I can't get the locals interested . . . "

"Khyfer, that's all they're int'rested in," Alf observed.

"Yeah. Anyway, Alf, I've got a little three-horse out-board engine onboard this here French boat. She's a lively little sod, and she can claw off from the shore all right. We can pass Jonnie—that's the Swiss bloke—the outboard, and that'll help him off. If not, we might be able to tow him off. It's a fart in a colander's chance, but you never know. I mean we can't leave the poor blighter out there, can we? And you're the only ex-navy bloke I know here, except for Gordon, and he's away."

Alf slammed his drink on the counter. Unsteadily he grabbed my arm. "Lead on, MacDuff!" he said, and we climbed the steps, me still dripping rainwater and Alf in his gray business suit, gold tie-pin, and shiny brown shoes.

I've heard it said that you can never truly gain experience from reading about it. It may be so; it may not be so—but no one who has *not* ever been in a storm at sea in an eighteen-foot, covered-in dinghy will ever be able to know what it means. If you haven't slammed up and down for fourteen hours, and been thrown yards every two seconds, unable to see anything in the driving rain, unable to drink or eat anything, unable to smoke, hardly able to breathe; numb, cold, wet through, and tired—then thank your lucky stars and rest content, for you know not the depths of utter misery.

We didn't find Jonnie. The chances of doing so in that visibility were nil. It was almost impossible for me to even guess at our position most of the night. Jonnie's boat was never found, nor any wreckage.

It was early afternoon the next day when *Coquette*, with her mainsail almost ripped to shreds and her jib a tattered joke, finally crept into Ibiza harbor again. By the time we had reached the calm water behind the mole, Alf had made me a cup of tea. How he did it, with the boat still jerking around, is yet a complete mystery to me. Neither of us had slept, of course. We had merely relieved each other at the tiller an hour on, an hour off, all night. Off the helm we had crouched, wet through, in the tiny cabin as it bounced around like an elevator gone stark, raving mad.

Now, as I wearily kicked *Coquette*'s anchor over her bow, I thanked him. "Ta, Alf."

His face was haggard. It was bad enough, having a hang-over, but that night . . . "Cor, mate, that was somethin', eh?" he said.

"We'll soon know if he's safe somewhere, Alf. And if not—well, we did our best."

"Can't do mor'n 'at," Alf said. His suit was a soggy shambles. His gold tie-pin was gone. His shoes were ruined.

"You did very well, Alf. Thanks a lot," I said, as the tiny stern fetched up near the mole. "In the navy long, were you?" It had been almost impossible to converse during the wretched night, with the wind howling and the boat smashing around.

"Nah. Only did National Service. You know, the old two-year bit. I tried to get on a ship, but they kept me ashore at Portsmouth Barracks."

"Portsmouth Barracks?"

"Yeah, di'n' I tell you? I was an Officer's Steward."

I didn't meet Alf again for several days after that. When I did, it was in the George and Dragon. He was again half-crocked.

"'At was somethin', eh, Tris?" he said.

Of course I knew what he meant, but I wanted to talk of other things. My fare was fixed up and I was leaving for England shortly. "You're looking well, Alf," was all I said. "Nice new suit."

"Yeah," he said. "I'm off up to the local nick in a few minutes." He meant the island jail.

"Oh, what're you going there for?" I asked idly.

"'Aven't you heard? Old Bill—the Spanish police—'ave nicked Elmyr the art-collector. They reckon 'e's screwed 'alf the nobs in Europe an' the States out of bloomin' millions!"

"How'd he do that, Alf?"

"Forgin'."

"Forging? What, money?"

"Nah, for Chrissake, Tristan—where' you been all your laife? *Pictures!* Forgin' bloomin' Picassos and Whatsisnames. You know, all them Froggie painters. Ol' Elmyr's been doin' the lot!"

I saw in my mind's eye again Elmyr sitting miserably in the tiny, chilly bar on that rainy night a few days back. "So that was it," I said.

Alf looked at me. "You wanna come up with me? I'm goin' to take 'im some grub. I mean Oi've been to about a dozen of 'is bloomin' parties. Wouldn't want 'im to think I ain't grateful, would I?"

Sing Ho! for a brave and gallant ship, and a fair and fav'ring
    breeze,
With a bully crew and captain too, to carry me over the seas.
To carry me over the seas, my boys, to my true love far away.
I'm taking a trip on a government ship, ten thousand miles away!

Chorus: Then blow you winds and blow! A-roving I will go.
I'll stay no more on England's shore to hear sweet music play,
For I'm on the move to my own true love, ten thousand miles
    away!

Oh it was a summer morning when I last saw my Meg;
She'd a government band around each hand, and another one
    'round her leg,
And another one 'round her leg, my boys, as the big ship left the
    bay.
Goodbye, she said, remember me, when I'm in Botany Bay.

Oh the sun may shine through the London fog, or the river run
    quite clear,
Or the ocean brine turn into wine, or I forget my beer,
Or I forget my beer, my boys, or the landlord's quarter-day,
But I'll never forget my own true love, ten thousand miles away!

This was sometimes a capstan chantey, but mostly it was a
"forebitter," sung in the rare off-duty moments of ease in
sailing ships. Botany Bay was, of course, the penal settle-
ment in Australia to which Britons were exiled in thou-
sands, often for crimes as petty as stealing a loaf of bread.

17

Ten Thousand
Miles Away

I SUPPOSE that the only valid way to gauge people is by their standards of morality. I don't mean by their own moral standards—many have never had any. They've never had the bishop of Southchester to show them what morality was all about. But all the people I've ever met—and they've ranged from angels almost too good for heaven to monsters almost too diabolical for hell—all have at least acknowledged some standard of morality outside themselves. I've known debt-collectors who thought nothing of nailing a debtor's hands to his own kitchen table, yet could not pass an old lady in the street without pressing a pound-note into her hand.

Alf the London betting man, the hyena of the beach gigolos' stupefied nymphomaniac leavings; the vulture of all the well-off exiles who made up the Nescafé Society of Ibiza; the gremlin of the turbo-prop set, had, by the bishop's standards, absolutely no morals at all. This didn't bother Alf, of course. He was happy and generous—and that, to Alf and his like, was all that ever mattered. In other words, he had his own standards, and he stuck to them. He was consistent. So I accompanied him to Ibiza jail.

We slowly climbed the steep hill up to the walls of the Old Town. Around us peasants pushed heavy bicycles loaded with crates of clucking white hens; one with a small pig lashed, squealing, over the saddle; one with a turtle towed astern by a short rope, upside-down with its shell scraping the pavement. Little old ladies, all in black, hauled crates of cabbages and lettuce up the hill. Younger women carried bundles of clean laundry.

Down the hill came troops of gaily dressed office-workers, headed for the tourist agencies in the lower town; well-suited businessmen going to their real estate offices; bell-bottomed lads with frilly shirts and Beatle haircuts on their way to wait on tables at the hotels along the beach at Figueretas. The Old Town hill at eleven a.m. was a microcosm of the tourist industry and its effects on a community which, until a few years before, had been content and self-supporting. Now it was anxious and becoming avid for that nebulous thing known in the places where many of the tourists hailed from as "the good life." The faces of the recently emerged businessmen were drawn and worried, as if they were wondering where they would go to spend *their* holidays.

"What did they collar Elmyr for, then, Alf?" I asked him as I huffed and he puffed up the hill.

"Well, it seems 'e didn't break any law in Spain—like none of the forged pictures were sold in this country, and they couldn't just nick 'im for painting a few pictures—so the Franco boys got their heads together when the report came out in *Look* magazine in Yankeeland, and they clobbered 'im for a law they calls . . . " Alf frowned deeply as he tried to remember, " . . . Vagrants and Mal . . . "

"*Vagos y Maleantes*? Vagrants and Undesirables?" I prompted.

"Yeah, tha's it. It seems they can stick anyone in the nick they want to, anytime, under that law. It's a bit laike our 'Loitering with Intent to Commit a Felony' law—the old "suss" bit. Bloody cheek, if you ask me."

"He could hardly be a vagrant, Alf. When I went up to his villa with Sissie and the bishop he looked like he had cash growing out of his ears."

"'E did. 'E was down in the cellar 'alf the time, turnin' out the old Mateuses."

"Matisses."

"Well, whatever that Frog bloke's name is."

Alf stopped for a moment. He was not exactly in Olympic sprinting condition. Neither was I. He went on. "They reckon old Elmyr was knocking out a grands' worth of paintin' before 'e got 'is dressin' gown belt on in the morning. An' by the time the cat was out of the bag 'e 'ad about six of 'is young boyfriends—all paintin' students, see—slappin' on the easy bits. They reckon it was laike Ford's factory down there."

"Nothing like private enterprise when it shows its good side—getting quality stuff out to the most people at the right price," I observed. "As for the undesirable bit, hell, he seems to have been keeping half the younger lads on the island going, one way and the other."

"'Ad more blokes living with 'im than Dorofy Paget 'ad 'orses at Aintree stables," said Alf as we ducked our heads and passed into a low, whitewashed bar to slake our thirst. Dry work for sailors, walking up hills.

"Belgians, Spanish, Germans; even 'ad one of our blokes—a renter from the Dilly—for a bodyguard," Alf continued. "'E was a regular bloody young man's employment agency and stud stable combined. 'E never just threw anyone out, neither. Always passed 'em on, old Elmyr did." Alf raised his beer and slurped it. "'E must 'ave supplied every girl and poufter in the islands wif boyfriends of one sort or another, and they always left Elmyr wif a few bob. Old Elmyr was a good bloke."

Alf thought deeply for a moment, then continued. "You see that bloke what was livin' with him—English, real toff-looking? Came on a boat from Monaco with some old French bird? What was 'is . . . Nigel, that was it. Nigel?"

"He had a Yank up there, and three others when I was there. What did this Nigel look like, Alf?"

"Bloody film star. Burly bloke. Looked like James Bond."

"What about him?"

"Well, last time I was in London one of my girlfriends got in a spot of bother. She drew six months in Holloway Prison. So I goes up to see her, don't I? And what do you think I saw there, in the bloomin' visitors' room in Holloway?"

"Not Nigel . . . he wasn't . . . "

"Nah, nothin' like that, but what they had was just one picture on the wall—an advertisement from the Gas Board—and there was Nigel. 'E was modeling on it, see, lying on a bloomin' beach with a girl. Lovely piece of stuff, too. I thought that was funny, the only bloke they had on a picture in a woman's prison bein' Elmyr's boyfriend! I didn't say nothin' to Elsie, though—I mean if it takes Nigel to cheer 'em up, well, bloomin' good luck to 'em, eh?"

"Poor buggers," I said. "Must be much worse for women."

Ibiza jail was not anything like Alcatraz or Sing Sing. It hardly looked like a jailhouse at all from the outside, and not much more like one from the inside, either. It occupied part of a building next to the handsome old town hall. Alf and I entered the cool, whitewashed hallway after knocking on a massive wooden door for five minutes, to no avail. At the end of the hallway was a flight of stone steps, at the top of which lounged a collarless, jacketless, carpet-slippered prison guard. He looked as if he was on his way to the bathroom for his weekly shave.

"*Buenos días, señores?* he greeted us politely.

"Mornin'. Elmyr, please?" called Alf, puffing up the steps ahead of me, clutching his package of corned beef sandwiches and six bottles of San Miguel beer.

"*El señor artista!*" the guard shouted.

Alf looked around at me. "Excitable, ain't they?" he said.

"Yes, the *señor* artist, please," I confirmed to the guard.

"*Si, señores, inmediatamente! Sargento!*" the guard bellowed for the sergeant.

There was silence, except for a low murmur from somewhere within the building. The guard placed his shaving mug on an ancient table which looked like the Moors had forgotten it when they left the island five centuries before. Suddenly the guard started, as if he'd remembered something. "Ah, yes, *señores*, you will wait please a minute. The sergeant has gone to the mayor's office. He won't be long . . ."

No sooner had the guard said this than the massive wooden doors at the jail entrance slowly creaked partly open, and the sergeant, a small, fat man with a red face and a cloth-covered tray appeared. He made his way carefully up the steps. Speed was not a virtue in Spain; not then, not in prisons, anyway.

"*Buenos días, señores?*" The sergeant put the tray down on the table.

"These gentlemen wish to visit the *señor* artist!" said the guard, importantly.

The sergeant almost sprang to attention. "*Si, señores! Sigueme!* Follow me!" He picked up the tray again, carefully. His minion unlocked another massive wooden door. We found ourselves on one side of an iron-railed balcony surrounding three sides of a flower-bedecked courtyard below. Alf and I realized that the sounds we had heard earlier had been rising from the courtyard. We waited and watched as the sergeant carefully laid down his tray again. He selected a large wicker basket from a pile on the balcony, and, as Alf and I stared in wonder, he uncovered the tray and delicately placed its contents in the basket. As he did so he quietly muttered off to himself a list: "*Pâté de foie gras*, eight ounces; asparagus soup, two bowls; duck *à l'orange* with peas and potatoes. Ice for the . . . ah!" He lovingly lifted a large green bottle from the tray and read the label: "Champagne Mouton Rothschild . . . " Another bottle: "Maison Lafitte . . . " And another, smaller bottle: "Perrier water."

Then he picked up a small box and gazed at its label. Puzzled, he passed it over to Alf. "What's this, *señor*?"

Alf looked at the label. "Looks like bloomin' Chinese to me," he said, and handed it to me.

I inspected it. The label was finely engraved, like an old English five-pound note. The printing was Cyrillic. "Russian. Probably caviar," I announced.

The sergeant looked at me quizzically.

"Fish eggs," I said. "Russian." I didn't know the Spanish word for caviar.

The sergeant thrust the tiny box into the basket. "*Rusos*, eh?" He shrugged his shoulders. "Strange people, no? Fishes' eggs?" Then he leaned over the balcony and shouted, "Hey, Rubio! Rubito!"

An American voice replied from below. "Yeah! Yagotit?"

Alf and I stared over the balcony at the figure below, as it waited for the sergeant to slowly, carefully lower the basket on a rope.

The man below was, from our foreshortened view, tall; his body, naked from the waist up, was sunbronzed, lithe, and sinewy. His long blond hair was tied in a ponytail at the back. His features were far too classical ever to have gazed on anything as mundane as hard work. His eyes shone a wide grin at us. "Hi, fellas!" he called.

"'Ow're you doin'?" called Alf.

"It's a bum bend in here, but we're doin' OK. You comin' down?" Below the waist he wore a standard pair of faded blue jeans, as favored by the Legion of the Lost Ones; a wide leather belt (which surprised me, given the surroundings); and a pair of locally made canvas-and-rope slippers. He was cleaner than the sergeant, the guard, and me.

As the basket finally reached the ground at the blond youth's feet, Alf called, "We come up to see Elmyr!"

Blondie picked up the basket. "OK, fellas, I'll tell him!" He then disappeared.

The sergeant hauled up the rope and stood again almost at attention. I looked at him quizzically.

"Wait, *señores*," he said. "The *señor* artist's servant has gone to inform him that you are here."

Alf's Spanish was not very good. I translated for him.

"Blimey, they do all right in 'ere, eh?" he said. "Nothin' like bloody Holloway!"

The blond lad was back below us shortly. "OK, you guys come on down! OK, *sargento!*"

The sergeant sprang into action and led us along the balcony to a barred gate at the top of a flight of worn stone steps. He unlocked the gate, and Alf and I passed through and down the steps. At the bottom we emerged into the courtyard, bright in sunlight in the center, shady under the balcony, surrounded on three sides by whitewashed, flower-bedecked walls, all splashes of red and gold and purple. On the other side of the courtyard was a line of wide doors, giving into large, cool cells, each with a small, barred window in its wall. In the shade was a group of about twenty-five long-haired males. We knew they were males by the scraggy beards that many of them sported, and the half-naked dirtiness of the others.

The tall blond was at the bottom of the steps to greet us. I guessed he was no more than nineteen or so. "Peace, brothers," he said. "Step right this way."

He turned abruptly as for a long moment I stared at the contrast between his spotless cleanliness and the scruffiness of the other inmates lounging on the ground all around. As he led us along, he spoke over his shoulder. "British, huh?"

"London," muttered Alf. "'Ow long you been here, mate?"

"Arr, they busted me for sleepin' on a goddamn bench. I was freaked out with a chick over on Figueretas two weeks ago, and they found my stash. But I'm OK, Elmyr's cool. I guess I'm doin' better in this joint than I was outside."

I tried not to be too obvious as we passed the group of pale, bearded hippies lounging in the shade. It would have been difficult not to observe more closely, as we passed them, their air of absolute resignation and yet a sort of sniffing disdain as Alf, in his suit, passed by. I was all right, it seemed. They looked right through me. It's not easy, or very rewarding, to despise a pink Breton sailing jacket, all torn and salt-stained. But to an observer it's a distinct advantage to know that he himself is not being observed. Then he can be as objective as it is possible for him to be. I took in their studied lack of involvement; these essences of individuality, and in a flash saw just how alike they were, like peas in a pod. None of them appeared to be over twenty-five or so, and a few were probably much younger.

. As we passed out of the shade of the guards' balcony, through a low arch, and into a smaller sunlit courtyard, I saw Elmyr.

From the time I had last seen him, hunched miserably in his fur coat in the scruffy little chili bar on that rainy night a week or so before, this was an unbelievable transformation. He was bareheaded, the sun gleaming on his false black hair, his real hair graying over his ears. He wore dark horizontal glasses, a huge horizontal smile of welcome, a sleeveless orange silk sports shirt, white shorts, beautifully polished leather sandals, and his Cartier wristwatch. Only the gold monocle was missing.

He was reclining in a deck chair, with a small, wrought-iron, white-painted table at his side, a huge "Cinzano" sunshade over it. On the table were laid out the contents of the tray which the sergeant of the guard had brought from the town hall next door.

Elmyr swept a gold-ringed hand in front of him. "Ah, Mister . . . "

"Alf," said Alf. "An' this is Tristan."

"Ah, yes, Mister Alf. Please do make yourself at home." Elmyr gazed from behind his dark glasses at me for a moment. "Yes, we've met before, of course. You were with the beautiful Miss Saint John, were you not, Mister Tristan?"

"That's it," said I, as the blond American placed two folding chairs for us. "And her brother, the bishop."

"Charming people," observed Elmyr. "Champagne? Ice?"

"We brought you some San Miguel and some corned beef," Alf said, his chubby face reddening as he gazed at the luscious repast on the table.

"Oh, you dear man!" Elmyr seemed to shudder. "Thank you so much, but actually I never drink beer. I have more than enough for my small needs, and for Roger, here . . . " He flapped his hand in the direction of the tall blond, who was now sitting on a little blanket on the concrete floor, to one side and slightly behind the *señor* artist.

Roger flickered a grin at us as Elmyr passed him a soup bowl and a spoon. Elmyr inspected the spoon before he passed it to the lad. "We must take care with the cleaning of our cutlery in these places, gentlemen," he said gravely.

He removed his glasses. His toad's eyes were more mournful now than when I had first seen them two years and more before. There was now, despite his sporty rig and outer gaiety, an air of sadness about him. He looked like he'd been to a funeral.

" 'Ow long have you been in 'ere?" asked Alf. "I only 'eard about it yesterday, 'ow they'd collar . . . imprisoned you."

"Oh, I do not consider myself *imprisoned* at all, Alf," said Elmyr. "*Interned*, that is what I consider I am." He handed Alf and me a glass each of champagne. "May I invite you to join me for a bite? Roger will fetch some plates, will you not, Roger dear?"

The lanky American rose languidly. "Sure thing."

"You 'aven't got enough for yourself, there, Elmyr," said Alf. "I'll tell you what—Tris and I will yaffle the corned dog and we can share the beer with the other blokes back there." Alf pointed a thumb over his shoulder at the lounging hippies astern of us.

"Yes, that's good, as long as you tell them it's from you," said Elmyr. He saw me watching Roger as he headed for the plates. "Roger's from California, are you not, Roger?" he called.

"Uh, huh," the Californian grunted over his shoulder.

"A student, are you not, Roger?"

"Yeah. Marine biology," came Roger's voice from the shade of Elmyr's cell.

My eyes could now penetrate the shade to see that Elmyr's cell was tastefully furnished with a large double bed and monogrammed sheets—pink, with a great black

"EDB" on them. Around the cell was much of the furniture I had seen in Elmyr's villa. As I gazed, classical music came from the cell.

"I persuaded our friends here," said Elmyr, looking fondly at the first guard, now shaven, who leaned down from the window overhead, "to bring me my stereo. And of course they did bring all my record collection, and they did let me have all my pottery and some of my pictures . . . " His face clouded momentarily. " . . . the ones that swine Legros would let them take. Awful man. He did ruin the art market, you know . . . But of course you do not, eh?"

"Well, we 'eard 'e'd been sellin' sort of phony paintings 'ere and there," murmured Alf, all ears.

Elmyr put down his champagne glass and waved his Cartier-bound wrist. "Oh, I do not wish to talk about that now, Alf. I am, after all, here for a holiday from business . . . and art!" He spooned a little caviar on a minute piece of toasted bread. "Let's talk about London, eh? I know everybody there, especially to do with the arts, and I did dine with the Aga Khan and Sir Anthony Blunt, you know. He collects for your beautiful queen . . . And my first patroness was your Lady Malcolm Campbell. Beautiful lady! Of course none of this would have happened if she had not mistook one of my drawings for a Pic . . . " Elmyr suddenly stopped, and in a louder voice said, "More champagne, gentlemen?"

It was the only time in my life that I've walked out of a prison half-crocked.

"Funny bloke," said Alf as we tramped back down the hill. "Gotta 'and it to 'im, though—'e's got 'is head screwed on. No fault of 'is 'e's in there. 'is mate Legros got clever and sold some phony pictures to this Yank in Texas. 'E was giving a party, and this art-dealer from London was invited. 'Course the Yank shows the dealer 'is collection, and one of the paintings—the dealer 'ad the exact same one in 'is gallery back in the Smoke. That blew the gaff. They reckon there's about sixty million dollars involved. This toff, 'e's a Lord, but 'e's a reporter for the *Daily Courier*—'e told me that Elmyr didn't really copy many pictures. What 'e did was sort of copy the style of all these famous painters, see? All except for a couple. Now they got Elmyr's phonies all over the place, and they can't tell which are the genuine ones and which are Elmyr's, and the thing is, they never will be able to . . ."

I turned to Alf. "You coming to the airport with me? I'm off to London this evening. Haven't got any more money left. Got to find a job."

"I can't, Tristan. There's this Swedish judy over at Santa Eulalia. This local bloke's ditched her . . . 'e owns a hotel . . . But 'ere, mate . . . " Alf slipped a couple of hundred pesetas into my hand. "That's for the boat-ride the other week. Gave me a yarn to spin to every bit of stuff I come across."

"Thanks, Alf. I'll remember that. Pay you back someday."

I did, too, less than half a year later, when I passed through Ibiza in the yawl *Barbara*, on the way from Connecticut to the Dead Sea and South America (as I described in *The Incredible Voyage*).

I much later learned that the value of Elmyr's paintings, which had been passed off as the works of modern masters, was, at 1981 rates, more than $100 million dollars, and that many of them are still displayed in art galleries and collections the world over.

I left Ibiza, after I'd bought Willie the German and George Llewellyn a drink at the airport, with the exact equivalent of one dollar, ten cents.

Elmyr committed suicide in Switzerland several years later.

Epilogue

In memory of my two lost boats, *Two Brothers* and *Banjo*

My life closed twice before its close;
It yet remains to see
If Immortality unveil
A third event to me

So huge, so hopeless to conceive,
As these that twice befell.
Parting is all we know of heaven,
And all we need of hell.

"Parting"
—Emily Dickinson